Centenary Subjects

Race, Reason, and
Rupture in the Americas

SHAWN MCDANIEL

Vanderbilt University Press
Nashville, Tennessee

Library of Congress Cataloging-in-Publication Data on file

978-0-8265-0229-2 (paperback)
978-0-8265-0230-8 (hardcover)
978-0-8265-0231-5 (epub)
978-0-8265-0232-2 (PDF)

CONTENTS

ACKNOWLEDGMENTS

MY INITIAL INCURSIONS into what became this book began in the Department of Latin American, Iberian, and Latino Cultures at The Graduate Center, CUNY, where I found unwavering support from Oscar Montero, José del Valle, Araceli Tinajero, Sharina Maillo-Pozo, and Marcos Wasem.

My thanks to the entire team at Vanderbilt University Press, especially Zack Gresham, Gianna Mosser, and Joell Smith-Borne, for their enthusiasm and professionalism. I am deeply grateful to the two anonymous reviewers of the manuscript for their invaluable comments and suggestions. Two chapters of this book are informed by much earlier publications which I have revised. A portion of Chapter 1 draws from "*Votre América*: Blackness and Pan-Latinism in *Les démocraties latines de l'Amérique*," which appeared in *Revista Hispánica Moderna* 68, no. 2 (2015): 127–45, and part of Chapter 2 builds on "*Arielista* Elitism and Geopolitical Exigencies in Post-War Colombia, 1902–1910," which was published in *Ciberletras* 29 (2012).

This book has been shaped in so many ways by Gerard Aching's unparalleled mentorship. I would like to thank him, as well as Ron Briggs and Mariano Siskind, for the astute insights they generously offered in a book workshop that was funded by the Department of Romance Studies and the College of Arts and Sciences at Cornell University. My thanks to Andy Alfonso, who provided pivotal research assistance, and to Sam Carter, whose adept proofreading was instrumental in putting the finishing touches on this book. Colleagues and students in the Department of Romance Studies, the Latina/o Studies Program, and the Latin American Studies Program at Cornell University supported this project in numerous ways. Thank you to Debra Castillo, Julia Chang, Ananda Cohen-Aponte, Ray Craib, María Cristina García, Patty Keller, Tom McEnaney, and Ken Roberts. I also drew inspiration from all of my wonderful colleagues in the Department of American Studies and Ethnicity at the University of Southern California. Thank you to Natalia Molina, John Carlos Rowe, George Sánchez, and Nayan Shah for their steadfast support of my work.

For the crucial assistance they provided as I conducted research for this book, I would like to extend my sincere gratitude to colleagues at the Biblioteca Nacional José Martí, the Instituto de Literatura y Lingüística, the Biblioteca Histórica Cubana y Americana Francisco González del Valle, the Biblioteca Nacional de Uruguay, the Biblioteca Nacional de la República Argentina, the Biblioteca Nacional de España, the Ibero-Amerikanisches Institut, the Benson Latin American Collection at the University of Texas at Austin, the New York Public Library, and the libraries at The Graduate Center, CUNY, Columbia University, New York University, Harvard University, Cornell University, and the University of Southern California.

Despite long distances, the love and support of my friends and family have sustained me and given me joy. Chris Kneifl, Marka Seale Kyle, and Jaime Symonds kept me both afloat and grounded. Rae, Dag, and the Pointer Sisters kept it automatic. Dad, Sandy, and the Tulsa crew kept the party going. Sorry this book doesn't have more pictures. Johnny Loflin provided an eclectic and generative soundtrack for this book. Oscar Montero's brilliance and generosity informed this project in countless ways from inception to completion, and I am grateful for his guidance and friendship. Evenings with Oscar, Johnny, and Peggy Gómez in Upper Manhattan inspired many of the book's developments. Randy Kliewer made so many light bulbs go off. The boundless love of my mother, Betty Kliewer, has sustained me my entire life. I am so lucky to be her son. My dog, Bagel, my copilot of many years, knew just when it was time to stop typing and go for a walk. It made all the difference. Oneka LaBennett's immeasurable love, support, and encouragement made this book, and everything else, possible. Every step of the way, and in every conceivable way, she has been a source of optimism, acuity, comfort, and delight. I cherish above all else the life and laughs we create together. 'S mór mo ghaol ort, fad na h-ùineadh, cho fad 's a bhios mi beò, agus anns an ath-bheatha cuideachd.

Introduction

Arielismo, or, The Efficacy of Ambiguity

"Remembrance restores possibility to the past, making
what happened incomplete and completing what never
was. Remembrance is neither what happened nor what
did not happen but, rather, their potentialization, their
becoming possible once again."

GIORGIO AGAMBEN, *Potentialities: Collected Essays in Philosophy*

THIS BOOK ANALYZES how overlooked racial anxieties, epistemological and spiritual fissures, and iconoclastic agendas structure,
and at times smother the ambiguous contours of *arielismo*, one of
Latin America's most influential cultural paradigms—backbone of
idealistic pedagogies and anti-imperialist movements—derived from
Uruguayan modernist writer José Enrique Rodó's foundational essay,
Ariel (1900). It argues that Rodó's canonical clout has eclipsed the
distinctive features of the work of the so-called *arielistas*—a generation of writers, radicals, politicians, and pedagogues of diverse
stripes who wrote essays on Americanist themes during the centenary era of Latin American independence (the 1910s)—which

accounts for over a century of assumptions, effacements, conflations, and neglect of the *arielista* archive.[1] *Centenary Subjects*, therefore, recovers a series of important but understudied essays from throughout Latin America during an era of rampant US imperialism in the hemisphere. It provides a fresh reading of the *arielista* archive that explores the ways in which *arielista* intellectuals imagined and interpellated what I call the *centenary subject*—a new kind of heroic young agent invested with unprecedented cultural capital, increasing political power, and an urgent mandate to break with the past, stave off US intrusion and allure, and forge a more assured course for Latin America's future. The political and pedagogical inscriptions of the centenary subject in the *arielista* archive that I examine in this book are not merely derivative of Rodó's work, nor are they abstract ideals or utopian longings. Instead, I highlight consequential strains and cleavages that indicate that *arielismo* is not the archive of unbridled optimism and transcendence that it is perceived to be, but rather one of crisis and containment.

This book revises that fundamental premise of *arielismo*'s prestige as a primary archetype of exceptionalism by making four primary claims, which are elucidated in the following chapters. The first contests the purported racelessness attributed to *arielismo* and shows the manifold ways in which anti-blackness and other forms of assigning alterity are cornerstones of the *arielistas'* white supremacist racial imaginary. The second challenges the long-standing thesis that *arielismo* was first and foremost a spiritual movement and argues that even though the *arielistas* attempted to implement a modernized epistemological model of heroism founded on introspective self-development, secular enlightenment, and disinterested truth, they in fact reinscribed the authority of the very hegemonies they sought to abolish, which reveals the prescriptive underbelly of their seemingly emancipatory projects. The third maintains that the *arielista* archive metabolizes individual anarchism, which skews and often effaces dissident counter proposals that encourage young people to reject the normative aspects of the *arielista* interpellation. The fourth contends that despite persistent accusations of Rodó's obsolescence and the exhaustion of *arielista* motifs, *neoarielista* formulations have surfaced as ample schemas of contestation in contemporary debates of the twenty-first century.

Taken together, the chapters that follow bring to light previously obfuscated problematics ingrained in the *arielista* archive, the centenary era, and the essay genre in Latin America. I make the concept of centenary subjects the cynosure of my analysis because doing so prompts us to discern how the ambiguity of the term *arielismo* masks the complexity of the ideological polemics of the centenary era. Not only that, it brings the dynamics of youth subjectivation—which desultory historicist treatments of Latin American student activism and university reform movements tend to discount—into sharp relief, thereby complementing a diverse body of literary and cultural criticism and intellectual history that investigates discourses on modernity, racial formation, epistemology, religion, and radicalism in the Americas. In this way, the idea of centenary subjects emerges as a generative prism that gives us a renewed understanding of the obscured nuances and stark limitations of one of the most prevalent, malleable, and murky paradigms of Latin American empowerment.

Written in the aftermath of the appropriation by the United States of Cuba's War of Independence in 1898, Rodó's *Ariel* was a visionary treatise whose hopeful message of transcendence as an antidote to the incursions of American empire resonated with Latin Americans.[2] Through his veiled narrative voice as Prospero, an old professor who delivers the last lecture of the term to a group of young students (who remain silent throughout his monologue), Rodó preached humanist values of introspection, self-development, and disinterestedness and incited a cultural awakening that countered the crass materialism and utilitarianism of the United States with the spiritual agency of the "Latin" peoples of the south. Prospero's "sacred oratory" sent vitalist shockwaves throughout the Americas.[3] Readers on both sides of the Atlantic venerated its inspirational outlook and took to the pages of prominent newspapers and magazines to exalt the spirit, when not the exact tenets of Rodó's "American gospel."[4] "For many years," Pedro Henríquez Ureña writes, "from Mexico and the Antilles to Argentina and Chile, everyone read and discussed *Ariel*, and '*Arielismo*' replaced a fascination with US culture (*nordomanía*), especially among many of the young people."[5] As the "first modern essay in Latin America," *Ariel* was a slim volume that packed a big punch.[6] It elaborately tackled yet efficiently condensed countless vital topics and concerns, which is why it has been read in many ways over the years, including as a "spiritual breviary," or "anti-utilitarian manifesto," and, more broadly, as a "civic-pedagogical program" and "aesthetic-political project" that permeated Latin American literature, culture, politics, philosophy, and education for decades, including in the current century.[7]

My treatment, however, does not focus on Rodó or *Ariel*, but rather on the so-called *arielistas*, those essayists and student activists who responded to Rodó's call to action after the tipping point of US imperialism in the region. The *arielista* platform was one of invigoration, obligation, and futurity, which is why it is frequently credited as an originary force for university student activism in Latin America. I consider both youth, as an object of pedagogy, and the pedagogues themselves as centenary subjects, and I seek to better understand the power relations between them, rather than simply reinforce the customary Ariel/Caliban polarities that tend to flatten the intricacies of those dynamics.

Unlike *Ariel*, whose centrality in Latin American culture is well documented, *arielismo* has been a far more slippery, not to mention disregarded, phenomenon in literary and intellectual histories. In fact, my initial incursions into *arielismo* were animated by the ubiquity of that label as well as the deceptive coherency attributed to it. It remains a designator without clear referents, which makes the traits that connect its practitioners both pervasive and elusive. To simply assume, for instance, that *arielismo* is nothing more than Rodó's influence, or that of his seminal work, on Latin American culture and politics is rather nebulous. Does *arielismo*, then, connote a movement, an epoch, an aesthetic, or an ideology? What does *arielismo* really signify? Indeed, we would be hard-pressed to think of another movement, particularly one of such magnitude, that has not been studied at length and in great detail. What other "ism" has been granted such ontological and ideological leeway? Situating texts within movements is customary and useful in differentiating tendencies within certain time periods and places. Although labels like romanticism and surrealism—to name but two among many— cannot capture the discrepancies contained within those aesthetics, they do provide an intelligible starting point or shorthand, which, of course is inherently susceptible to generalizations and exclusions. But why have we not asked the same kinds of questions about *arie- lismo* that have been, and continue to be asked about, say, natural- ism or modernism?

Although critics frequently reference an *arielista* movement in Latin America, there is little consensus as to its content, forms, practitioners, and timeline.[8] The term *arielismo* was first coined in Mexico in 1908, even though it was not widely used at the time, and ultimately described a tendency that came to fruition around 1910.[9] Some scholars equate *arielismo* with what Rodó asserts in *Ariel*.[10] Others, in contrast, think more broadly in terms of the "echo of his *ariélico* message," or the "process of reception, diffusion, and influence of *Ariel*."[11] And while there are those who readily consider *arielismo* a "full-blown social and intellectual movement," others approach it on a smaller scale, conceiving of an *arielista* network or circuit culminating around 1910 in which "a series of authors, ideas, works, that in one way or another . . . were brought together by Rodó's essay."[12] Such imprecise criteria ("in one way or another") signal the constitutive ambiguity of *arielismo*, which is why some scholars view it as a "repertoire of attitudes."[13] Its persistence, not to mention popularity as a roaming pronoun, owes as much to the vagueness of the many concepts outlined in *Ariel* (such as spirit, will, personality, beauty, good) as it does to its functionality as a poly- semic "catch-all."[14]

Mexican intellectual Enrique Krauze, for example, summarizes *arielismo*'s capacious coordinates in the following way:

> Young people in Latin America awoke to the twentieth century reading *Ariel*. Editions appeared throughout the entire continent, to such a degree that in Peru, like many other places, young intel- lectuals formed *"arielista"* groups. Part of José Vasconcelos's work

in the 1920s—*The Cosmic Race*, a prophecy of Latin America as a melting pot of races and cultures—can be seen as a variation on Rodó's topic. The Bolivarian echo of *"arielismo"* was not lost on those writers, that is, the ideal of a nation of nations united by, in Rodó's words, "the lofty values of the spirit." The *"arielismo"* that they preached was, in short, the first alternative ideology generated in our countries, against classical liberalism and its direct descendants like positivism and evolutionism. As time passed, *arielismo* constituted an antecedent or a complement—whether close or remote, unspoken or explicit—to the most looming and impassioned -isms in twentieth-century Latin America: anarchism, socialism, indigenism, nationalism, Hispanism, populism, fascism, and communism.[15]

Krauze's brief overview of *arielismo*'s reach attests to both its omnipresence and elusiveness. While this pliability in part accounts for *arielismo*'s prevalence as a popular cultural template, its indeterminacy also shapes the *arielista* archive around a series of unresolved equivocations and misreadings. For instance, literary history—the principal venue that registers, albeit succinctly, *arielismo* as an essayistic movement—is rife with expectations that the *arielistas*, as that label implies, are the Uruguayan's disciples, with their respective bodies of work only resembling or replicating his formula. One result of this commonplace presumption is that the work of the *arielistas* tends to get summarily overlooked, since their reputations within the panorama of Latin American literature and intellectual history are firmly situated as *arielistas*. *Centenary Subjects* responds to this bypass by recentering the neglected work of those essayists that constitute the *arielista* archive.

As even a cursory survey of literary history evidences, the cast of *arielismo* is already defined, yet at the same time it is also distensible. Included in the line-up of usual suspects we find essayists—pivotal in their heyday, today seldom read (with notable exceptions)—like Francisco García Calderón (Peru), Carlos Arturo Torres (Colombia), Pedro Henríquez Ureña (Dominican Republic), Antonio Caso and José Vasconcelos (Mexico), Jesús Castellanos (Cuba), and Rufino Blanco-Fombona (Venezuela), to name only the most often-cited proponents.[16] Literary history also frequently categorizes many other essayists from every Latin American country as *arielistas*, including anti-imperialist stalwarts like Manuel Ugarte (Argentina) and humanist intellectuals like Alfonso Reyes (Mexico). The same was true of pedagogues and politicians—both eminent and 'minor'—from Montevideo, Lima, Havana, Quito, not to mention university student groups who adopted the banner of Rodó's essay in Buenos Aires, San José, Santiago, Tegucigalpa, Asunción, Rio de Janeiro, among other places, a trend that would continue sporadically through the 1960s.[17]

In fact, one cannot help but notice that, during the period in which centennial celebrations of Latin American independence coincided with the height of US interventionism in the region, the essay genre in Latin America was virtuously synonymous with *arielismo*, and vice versa. As a label of convenience, and certainly esteem, *arielismo* is meant to designate a multitude of writers, philosophers, politicians, educators, and critics—conservatives, radicals, Christians, and atheists alike—whose work addressed, in a wide variety of ways, Americanist themes, cultural identity, politics, aesthetics, and philosophy. Even if they by and large echoed Rodó's prophetic tone, pedagogical purpose, and expectant take on Latin America's future, rarely did the *arielistas* come close to reproducing the exquisite *modernista* prose style of the Uruguayan's spiritualist treatise.[18] Furthermore, they straddled the temporal boundaries of *modernismo* and the avant-garde, without subscribing to either aesthetic, which perhaps accounts for their rather tepid critical reception when compared with other genres of the era. In short, the *arielistas* have fallen through the cracks and out of fashion, which is, in my view, symptomatic of the presuppositions of tedium that get attributed to the essay genre writ large.

Although much has been written about its fragmentary, protean nature, the essay genre continues to be susceptible to uniform postulates, inflexible parameters, and static readings. The essay's relative insipidness stems in part from the fact that its story, in the context of early twentieth century Latin America, has been tantamount in many ways to that of Rodó. The Uruguayan's luminosity—embodied in enlightening young minds and irradiating the path for Americanist ideals—was undeniably inspirational, but, in another sense, it clouded the way we read a generation of essayists. For that reason, this book unveils the shrouded effulgence of the work of the so-called *arielistas.* Looking beyond the eclipse impelled by Rodó's "almost miraculous and enigmatic character," instead of gazing directly at it, brings into view the inherent indefiniteness of the genre. Important theorists of the essay have emphasized its inconclusive and invisible qualities, as if there were always something more to be unearthed aside from what is readily perceptible.[19] For example, in "On the Nature and Form of the Essay" (1910), Georg Lukács opines that "were one to compare the forms of literature with sunlight refracted in a prism, the writings of the essayists would be the ultra-violet rays."[20] For his part, Theodor Adorno begins his meditation on the essay with an epigraph from Goethe that reads, "Destined to see what is illuminated, not the light."[21] Sensing that the *arielista* archive has not been read deeply enough, I position the essay genre in early twentieth century Latin America both with and against its requisite *arielista* affiliation. This overdue re-reading takes into account Lukács's and Adorno's respective exhortations to unfetter the genre from origins and recognize its incapability of resolution or totality, and focuses on the unattended particularities of Latin American essays that give us a new way to reconfigure and reconceptualize how centenary subjectivations of youth operate in the *arielista* archive.

The reasons for *Ariel*'s success are easy to comprehend, as it was a widely read, enthusiastically marketed, succinct, and, above all, confident vision of Latin America, whose brighter days were predicted to be on the horizon. In turn, *arielismo* preserved this unyielding faith in the future as a core principle. In fact, the apogee of *arielismo* coincided with the 1910 centennial celebrations of Latin American independence, and its energizing exhortation paired nicely with the retrospective glances and futuristic calls for a unified front, which took on more exigent tones with the aggressive expanse of US imperialism.[22] As part of a five-member special delegation that Uruguayan president Claudio Williman sent to Chile in honor of their independence festivities, Rodó made a speech in which he affirmed the principles of a consolidated American conscience: "Above the centenary of Chile, or that of Argentina, or Mexico, I feel and sense the centenary of Spanish America. In the spirit and truth of history, there is only one Hispanic American centenary."[23] Rather than a lone event, however, the centenary spanned many years, even as it sought to foster a singular spirit of consonance. Since Latin American countries do not share the same dates of formal political independence—which range from 1810 to 1825, with the exception of Cuba, Puerto Rico, and Panama, whose fraught experiences with US meddling begot disagreements about the *real* dates of independence—the centenary can be understood as its own epoch and ethos that predated, culminated around, and continued after 1910.[24]

Rather than attempt to insulate or compartmentalize the centenary and *arielismo*—two phenomena with indeterminate chronologies—in terms of historicist or temporal demarcations, I employ Alain Badiou's model of epochal thinking to unveil the epistemic constructs and currents of knowledge production that shaped and sustained them.[25] Much like Michel Foucault's assessment of the archive in *The Archeology of Knowledge*, which rummages through the traces left behind in a certain era in order to ascertain the episteme that drove and structured it, Badiou detects the epochal profiles of the past not in terms of "what took place," but rather "what was thought in it."[26] Given that *arielismo* is arguably the most important intellectual movement in Latin American thought, the epistemic is imperative not only as an esoteric object of analysis, but especially as a methodology capable of elucidating the complex ideological landscape of the centenary era beyond its nationalist affects and public spectacles. By and large, *arielista* intellectuals were alarmed by new social subjectivities and enfranchisements (immigrants, racialized others, industrial workers, women) and pursued ways to control those emerging constituencies. In fact, communists, anarchists, and proto-fascists were all considering how to rally, bridle, and direct the youth and the masses. The work of the *arielistas* was a primary conduit through which those contested formations were devised and manipulated under the anxious tutelage of traditional intellectuals and a range of political leaders. The centenary subject was, as I illustrate through-out this investigation, the product of a host of geopolitical, social, and cultural anxieties that *Ariel's* buoyant influence caused many readers to gloss over. Therefore, *arielismo*—from theory to pedagogical and political practice—constitutes key top-down strategies for assigning select Latin American youth the charge of carrying out their concerns about originality, order, and self-determination.

Centenary Subjects, then, draws from Foucault's thoughts on sub-jectivity to elucidate those power schemes as they appear in the *arielista* archive. In Foucault's formulation, the exertion and main-tenance of power reside in manufacturing individuals into subjects—the latter has a dual significance, in the sense of to "subject to some-one else by control and dependence; and tied to his own identity by a conscience or self-knowledge. Both meanings intimate a form of power which subjugates and makes subject to."[27] One paradox that emerges in this process of subjectivation is an imposed and regulated sense of individualization, which also figures prominently in *arielis-mo's* call to action. However, since Foucault's writings on the subject are not immutable throughout his body of work, he leaves the door open for scenarios of dissent even within techniques of discipline.[28] Teasing out the details of this predicament of restriction under the guise of idiosyncratic subjective fashioning helps put the ploys and pitfalls of didactic *arielista* agendas concerning self-realization and collective obligation on full display, in order to see what brand of youth agency was concocted, and stymied, in the *arielista* laboratory.

Rodó was widely considered the spiritual guide for generations of young people and *arielismo* was first and foremost the youth ethos of an era. Pedagogues and pupils alike embraced *Ariel* as a mystical, sacred text.[29] In 1920, as Rodó's remains were returned to Uruguay from Palermo, where he died in 1917 while on assignment for the Buenos Aires magazine *Caras y Caretas*, Rodolfo Mezzera, the Uru-guayan secretary of public education, credited Rodó with achieving the "true spiritual communion of America":

> That call to the youth of America, which had the virtue of shak-ing it, waking it up, is an eternal monument [. . .] because it is

the first gesture made in favor of the solidarity of America, it is the first manifestation, completed and amplified, that seems to have materialized in our longings, in our thoughts, in our definitive orientations of international politics and even in the intimate enjoyments of our emotional nature and our feelings.

Who would dare deny that the immortal pages of *Ariel* have been, in fact, the verses to a true hymn of America? Who does not know that for twenty years each one of its paragraphs has been repeated like a gospel and taught, from generation to generation, as the highest ideal to which Americanism can aspire, the moral elevation of the continent?[30]

Students also frequently praised Rodó as a "kind conductor of young spirits."[31] For instance, in 1920 the Centro de Estudiantes Ariel in Montevideo published a special issue of their journal, also named *Ariel*, which included a transcribed speech by the president of the Delegation of Paraguayan Students, Juan Vicente Ramírez. In the midst of an apocalyptic aftermath of a devastating war that claimed incalculable casualties, Ramírez writes, "suddenly Rodó's potent and harmonious voice rang out throughout America, that miracle worker of the mind, that rare wizard of ill souls, and his eloquent discourses about the superior energies of the spirit started to spread. Since then, the younger generations of my country have not stopped listening."[32] Such sentiments were widespread, becoming a creed of an era, which attests to the vigor of Rodó's doctrine.

Ariel was undeniably an impetus of youth activism in Latin America. Its cathartic and inspiring message of faith, unity, and reform mobilized students in numerous countries to organize and chart new directions in civic and university life. Representatives at the Congresos Internacionales de Estudiantes Americanos, which took place in Montevideo (1908), Buenos Aires (1910), and Lima (1912), and drew over one hundred student delegates from seven South American countries, clearly integrated *arielista* language, rhetoric, and axioms into their platforms.[33] At the request of those who attended the first Congreso in Montevideo, Rodó made a few improvised remarks at the conference's closing banquet, but, curiously, they were not transcribed. Those gatherings, in conjunction with a flurry of student clubs and movements throughout the region, paved the way for the most significant achievement of youth of the era, the Reforma de Córdoba (1918).[34] Even that movement's manifesto, drafted by student leader Deodoro Roca, is filled with *arielista* precepts, especially the idea that youth are courageous agents of democratic reform in the Americas who synthesize positivism and spiritual ideals.[35]

As we can see, Rodó's uplifting "lay sermon" provided a burst of energy and optimism wrapped in an aura of serenity and transcendence.[36] Without discounting the very real reverberations of the *arielista* directive, this book examines the angst underlying the aspirational interpellations of Latin American youth crafted by *arielista* intellectuals whom Ángel Rama termed, in recognition of their imprints in multiple spheres, "filósofos-educadores-politólogos" (philosophers-educators-political scientists).[37] It lays bare the extent to which the centenary subject had to negotiate conflicting signals with respect to race and place, truth and belief, as well as individuality and sacrifice. Spotlighting such internal tensions tells a different narrative of *arielismo*. Rather than take its professed placidity and ascendancy for granted, I pay close attention to the inter-American and transatlantic racializations, epistemological provisions, spiritual mediations, and recusant reformulations that compel us to question the uniformly optimistic essence of Latin American exceptionalism fabricated in the *arielista* archive.

The first three chapters delve into competing ontological designs that configure the book's trajectory: simulation, Not-Yet Being, and Non-Being. Chapter 1, "Eurontologies: Racial Simulations in the *Arielista* Archive" challenges the idea that since *arielismo* circumvents what was commonly framed as the "problem of race," it is then what today we would term a colorblind vision, inclusive of and accessible to all. I make the case that such an assertion universalizes white consciousness in the *arielista* imaginary and is part and parcel of a series of race-making strategies where appraisals of Europeanness, paired with virulent anti-black rhetoric centered on Haiti, Africa, and Sicily, aimed to bolster tenuous white identities on both sides of the Atlantic. Targeting such normalized readings of race in *arielista* discourses, I register the stakes and circumscriptions of white racial formations in and in-between Cuba and Spain, Peru and France, and Argentina and Italy, and aver that in the work of Rufino Blanco-Fombona, Emilio Gaspar Rodríguez, Francisco García Calderón, and José Ingenieros, whiteness is not a presumed absence, but rather the nucleus of categorical, albeit pliant, transatlantic projects of white superiority in the wake of 1898. Construing the personal investments and rhetorical maneuvers of *arielista* racial cartographies divulges the ethnic aspirations, geopolitical alliances, and social phobias at play in centenary imaginaries. In this way, I bring *arielismo* into the fold of comparative studies of racialization in the Americas, and advance Lorgia García-Peña's disruptive methodology of exposing archival silences regarding anti-blackness to substantiate my claim that *blanqueamiento* was the axis for *arielista* triangulations of race hemispherically and globally. Moreover, in conversation with Anke Birkenmaier's examination of race thinking by Latin American and European intellectuals, I elucidate the transatlantic and transpacific coordinates of alterity and primacy that the *arielista* archive traverses in order to consolidate Europe as an idealized wellspring of racial agency (what I call *eurontologies*, or the desire by *arielista* intellectuals to be or seem European).

Chapter 2, "Tethered Transcendence: Juvenescence, Introspection, Illumination" disputes the routine reading of *Ariel*, and by default *arielista* essays, as harmonizing forums in which hazy ideals of rational introspection and spiritual illumination seamlessly merge to shape the epistemological and ethical contours of young people. It exposes the precarious constructions of transcendent discourses aimed at youth by demystifying the stipulations of reason, religiosity, instinct, and intuition—the routes through which young people were instructed to attain enlightenment—and claims that although *arielista* essayists staunchly advocated secular emancipation, they grappled with effecting it and, furthermore, actually capitulated to the compromise and consent they declared to resist. As this chapter demonstrates, that mixed messaging with respect to epistemological integrity and the power of the spirit that the centenary subject had to navigate spanned hyperpartisan political climates in postwar Bogotá, anti-imperialist campaigns from Buenos Aires to New York, and university classrooms in Montevideo and Mexico City. My analysis combines political theory (Wendy Brown), continental philosophy (Friedrich Nietzsche), and the sociology of religion (Jürgen Habermas and Herbert Marcuse) to identify salient aporias that subvert conventional readings of democratization in Colombian diplomat Carlos Arturo Torres's project of national reconciliation, the consummation of Argentine crusader Manuel Ugarte's radicalism, and the audacity of free-thinking pedagogies of philosophers Carlos Vaz Ferreira (Uruguay) and Antonio Caso (Mexico). Instead of confirming the spirit—one of *arielismo*'s notoriously abstract and slippery features—as paragon, I stress its fissures and fragility in the *arielista* political and pedagogical landscape. Amending this intrinsic supposition of *arielismo* evinces that the spirit was not the linchpin of Latin American exemplarity during the centenary era, but rather a byproduct of frustrated attempts to effectuate a secular enlightenment rooted in modern epistemologies.

In "Pedagogies of Dissent: Anarchist Eclipses and the Suicidal Subject" (chapter 3), I analyze misanthropic diatribes in Colombia and Cuba that have been subsumed in literary history under *Ariel*'s monopolizing presence, even though their tactics are overtly contrary to *arielismo*'s affirming propaganda and motives of indoctrinating youth. With the goal of unmasking the norms of personal sacrifice and moral obligation imposed on young people, insolent philosophers José María Vargas Vila and Fernando Lles y Berdayes deploy belligerent proposals that actively corrupt the centenary subject as a way of freeing its mind, unfettering its conscience, and unleashing its true potential. Building on Gerard Aching's work on the *reino interior* (inner/interior realm), I argue that those exercises in subject deformation, which find extreme forms of sovereignty in solitude, not solidarity, desecrate the sanctity of *modernismo*'s predilect figurative space of introspection and subjectivity. Moreover, I examine how both offer notable rewrites of Rodó's use of *The Tempest* by refashioning Shakespeare's plays *Hamlet* and *Timon of Athens* in order to debase the serene designs of *arielismo* with scandalous metaphors of eco-toxicity and suicide. In revisiting those vituperative subjective negations, which have passed largely unnoticed in literary history, I suggest that nationalist causes, canonical logics, and revolutionary exigencies have either dismissed their viability as counterproductive, or even metabolized their aggressive noncompliance into familiar, antithetical forms. In other words, I salvage Vargas Vila and Lles's work to expose how *arielismo* cannibalizes its own archive when confronted with menacing forms of youth individualisms. In doing so, I reveal the distortive capacity of *Ariel*'s influence, which augments Carlos A. Jáuregui's investigation of sinister adaptations of *arielismo* in *Canibalia: canibalismo, calibanismo, antropofagia cultural y consumo en América Latina*. Ultimately, this chapter calls into question the visibility of anarchism in the *arielista* archive, in particular, and, more broadly, in Latin American literature and thought from its circumscribed, marginal place in what Juan Carlos González Espitia terms the "dark side of the archive."[38]

More than a recuperation of texts (as important as that is), the book's principal chapters offer unique, real-time glimpses into the hemispheric, transatlantic, and global brunt of US imperialism in the early twentieth century from Latin American perspectives. Rather than reify lopsided narratives of US interference as an unstoppable geopolitical phenomenon that Latin Americans could do little to counter, I read *arielismo* as a cultural formation and pedagogical current that responded to infiltrations from the North—and the misleading Pan-American promises that accompanied them—with sweeping (and for that reason ill-defined) diagnostics and plans of action eager to raise youth consciousness, as well as compel their conscience toward consent.

Far from derivative or uniform takes, the *arielista* essays I bring together in this book attest to the urgency and experimentalism of their respective and collective initiatives. Their propositions stem from an experience of crisis—confronting imperialist intrusions from the north, revising the racial politics of *latinidad*, and untangling the impasse between epistemological veracity and spiritual potency—and struggle with reviving, reassessing, and reassembling the components of Latin American empowerment that those young men—*arielismo* was, after all, a masculinist project, designed by and destined for men—who were poised to assume leadership positions could carry out.[39] Crisis, as Carlos Alonso confirms, has been an intrinsic feature of cultural discourse throughout Latin American history. In his study of modernity and autochthony, Alonso conveys how intellectuals responding to exigent dilemmas ultimately recreate that crisis in the "rhetorical structure" of their texts.[40] Alonso's insights into what Julio Ramos terms a "rhetoric of crisis" inform my analysis of the vicissitudes of *arielista* implorations of youth to be or become modern.[41] I frame crisis as a default, indelible mode of articulation in the *arielista* archive that precipitates numerous textual hesitancies, contradictions, and failures. However, rather than chalk those internal frictions up as botched attempts at addressing and overcoming the crises that provoke them, I emphasize how they shed unprecedented light on the discursive space clearing that the *arielistas* undertook in order to rethink education, self-reliance, duty, and futurity in compelling and convoluted ways capable of configuring what Nicola Miller calls an "alternative imaginary of modernity."[42] My reading of both the potentiality and volatility of that enterprise to create new ways of knowing and being draws from and complements recent scholarship that recasts deep-seeded hypotheses of identity and difference, deciphers strategies of subjectivation and self-fashioning, and illuminates neglected transnational ebbs and flows of Latin Americanist projects in intellectual history and literature in the pivotal early decades of the twentieth century.[43]

Although *Centenary Subjects* delineates race, reason, and rupture in the *arielista* archive, it does not provide a rigid, point-by-point redefinition of *arielismo*. Attempts to define *arielismo* often yield a multi-part checklist that becomes its own looking glass through which all *arielista* essayists are read. For example, Nancy Ochoa Antich points out the following essential ingredients of *arielismo*: an appreciation for the history, culture, and language of Latin America (while also admiring ancient Greece as a model of identity), an educational endeavor that strives for mental emancipation, a desire to unify the region, a rejection of US utilitarianism, and a belief in ideals and disinterestedness.[44] While such inventories gesture to some of the primary tenets of Rodó's essay, they are not necessarily representative of the work of the so-called *arielistas*. Rather than reproduce customary enumerations (as useful as those are), I am more concerned with how *arielismo* works from the inside, not the top-down. Therefore, I do not read Latin American essays in strict correlation to *Ariel*, nor do I completely discard the latter's significance. At the same time, I do not refashion essayists into well-worn *arielista* molds, nor gauge their *arielista* affiliations based on their fidelity to Rodó's intentions.

As with any canonical figure, one encounters a vast bibliography when researching Rodó. Of course, it is beyond the scope of this study to review and engage all of them. One notable thread of scholarship on Rodó takes shape around polemics about defending or defaming the character and legacy of Montevideo's renowned "Maestro de la Juventud," a controversy into which I elect not to intervene. Although Rodó plays a crucial role in the following pages, he does not get top billing. This is why the book is titled *Centenary Subjects* and not *Arielismo*, since the former suggests that there is more at play than just mimicry of *Ariel*. It is for these reasons that this introduction does not review the many issues surrounding Rodó and his work, as doing so would repeat the very eclipse that I challenge.

While this book does not purport to offer a thorough history of *arielismo*, chapter 4, "Rodó Revered, Reviled, and Revamped: *Neoarielismo* in the Twenty-First Century*" reviews its legacy in the previous century and the enduring impact of *neoarielista* precepts in the current one. It traces the multifarious routes of the *arielista* trajectory in Latin American life, including its origins, adoptions, and eminence, as well as the reworkings and rebukes it has incurred since the turn of the twentieth century. Contrary to allegations about the anachronistic quality of Rodó's body of work, the fatigue of the representative emblems of Ariel and Caliban, and the limitations of *arielismo*'s stature and longevity, the final chapter maintains that *arielismo* remains a liberating yet normative paradigm that continues to be marshaled for various purposes throughout the region. Of particular note is the irony that even though leftist actors have long denounced Rodó as a representative of reactionary class animosities, his work has been an essential source for radical agendas, including those of the Cuban Communist Party, the American Popular Revolutionary Alliance (APRA), the Cuban Revolution, the Revolutionary Armed Forces of Colombia (FARC), the Zapatistas in Chiapas, the Bolivarian Revolution in Venezuela, and the so-called Pink Tide of the 2000s. I conclude with a final reflection on *neoarielista* formulations that have appeared in the Chilean Student Movement (2011), as a way to address issues relating to access and affordability of education, but also disagreements between Latin Americanist scholars in Chile and their counterparts in the United States regarding the authority of representation. These recent iterations of *arielismo* play central roles in contemporary debates in the hemisphere concerning neoliberalism, subalternity, development, and decoloniality.

Centenary Subjects does not repudiate or reify the extent of *Ariel*'s sway, which has been notoriously difficult to pin down.[45] It expounds instead what gets overshadowed by the reverential glow of its reputed progenitor. The purpose of this book, then, is not to simply exaggerate or negate *arielismo*'s relevance at a chronologically germane moment—the wake of the centennial of Rodó's death (2017). Furthermore, arguing that *arielismo*'s pertinence is taken for granted should not be interpreted as rejecting its impact. *Arielismo*'s power—as a critical construct, a political and pedagogical project, and a varied repertoire of activism and attitudes—lies precisely in its vagueness, founded on omissions and erasures, that demands a critical evaluation. Today, there is immense value in reclaiming the *arielista* archive and reading it through a different lens that discloses the considerable cracks in its edifying ambitions, since the ideals and obligations that Rodó popularized a century ago continue to be sourced—whether deliberately or inadvertently—to compel young people to solve pressing problems facing Latin American societies.

Consequently, *Centenary Subjects* makes the idiosyncrasies of *arielismo* legible in a new way that corroborates, rather than skirts the centrality of the somatic stipulations, rifts between free-thinking exigencies and deference to spiritual ideals, and the inconspicuous emergence of individual anarchism in the *arielista* archive. Far from a static corpus of predictable texts, the *arielista* archive crystalizes here as a fraught discursive terrain that manifests the real-time splinters and contested power dynamics at play as young people were tasked with commemorating a significant milestone of the region's sovereignty while also defying US attempts to undermine it. As an axis for an array of transcendent objectives, as well as the anxieties that trouble their actualization, the analytic of centenary subjects serves to extricate the reimaginings of race, the strained compromises of the mind and the spirit, and the iconoclastic schisms that have long been concealed by Rodó's radiant aura that has reverberated throughout Latin American life in so many ways.

CHAPTER 1

Eurontologies

Racial Simulations in the Arielista Archive

It is a sin against humanity to foment and propagate opposition and hate among races.

JOSÉ MARTÍ, "Nuestra América"

IN THE EPILOGUE of her 1995 edition of *Ariel*, Belén Castro Morales writes, "Indeed, the *arielista* model does not analyze realities like *indigenismo* or *mestizaje*, since its worldview is encompassed within an ample '*latinidad*.' But the reasons and opportunity of that message do not need other justifications than those offered by Rodó's work."[1] In contrast, José Buscaglia-Salgado opines that "The most pernicious legacy of *arielismo* is its unqualified support of the racial standard in the Iberian ("white" criollo) ideal that has remained central to both the elite *hispanista* or hispanophile discourse, and most of the populist versions of the Pan-Latin Americanist political ideologies to this day."[2] To be sure, one does not have to peel back too many layers of *La raza cósmica* (1925), for instance, which drew from *Ariel*'s spirit of synthesis and futurity, to perceive the fraught logic of white superiority that undergirds José Vasconce-los's purportedly utopic premise of *mestizaje*.[3] As a racially imbued meditation, or race-making fantasy disguised in thinly veiled eugen-ics garb, *La raza cósmica* seems antithetical to the racelessness that frequently gets attributed to Rodó's *Ariel*.

Even though *Ariel* is one of the foundational visions of Latin American identity, it certainly skirts addressing racial diversity, opting instead to situate Latin Americans as part of an illustrious genealogy that stretches back to the classical world. Rodó's apolo-gists generally cite three reasons for the elision of race in *Ariel*. The first holds that *Ariel* is a transcendental and ultimately universal text, which is why he opts not to distinguish, or even acknowledge, racial difference. The second reason, prominently repeated and confirmed during research stints in Montevideo, argues that Uruguay is a white country and therefore that issue was extraneous to its racial land-scape. As Gustavo Verdesio's work has shown, such investment in racial unison in the "Switzerland of South America" persists, espe-cially in the face of Charrúa reemergent movements.[4] The third rea-son maintains that the dozen or so times that race does appear in *Ariel*—including allusions to "razas superiores"—refer not to race as we understand it today, but rather as synonyms for civilization. All three reasons, which hold that, respectively, white is universal, Uru-guay is a white country, or that race had a different connotation at the turn of twentieth century, bolster an ideology of whiteness as a normalized and unmarked racial designator. Matthew Frye Jacobson responds to those kinds of exculpatory arguments, writing:

> historians have most often cast the history of nineteenth-century immigration in the logic of twentieth-century "ethnic" groups— "race" did not really *mean* "race" back then, in other words. This blithe disbelief not only distorts the historical record but also car-ries with it some troubling baggage. Tacitly assuming that "race" did not mean "race"—that Hebrews, Celts, Mediterraneans, Iber-ics, or Teutons were *really* Caucasians—is worse than merely underestimating the ideological power of racialism: it is surren-dering to that power. To miss the fluidity of race itself in this pro-

cess of becoming Caucasian is to reify a monolithic whiteness, and, further, to cordon that whiteness off from other racial groupings along lines that are silently presumed to be more genuine.[5]

Justifying racial absences—especially in what purports to be an inclusive vision for Latin American identity—signals the implicit or strategic normalization of whiteness. Rodó's exclusionary maneuver of erasing autochthonous or Afro-diasporic presences in order to mediate an imagined community through a Latin lens compels the reader of *Ariel* to interpret implications, insinuations, and omissions.

Of course, looking for race where it seemingly does not exist, and doing so through the concept of whiteness, risks provoking charges that the Anglophone academy wrongly imposes its own racial paradigms on Latin American contexts. While the reasons for such allegations are not always without merit, the problem with such critiques is that they can bolster the invisibility, and thus the supremacy, of whiteness. Moreover, the default setting of downplaying also disguises explicit formulations of whiteness in Latin America, which I would like to recenter in this chapter. Yet, examining white supremacy in *arielista* texts garners its own naysayers. What, some may inquire, does such an approach accomplish beyond identifying the existence of racism? In my opinion, the question is short-sighted as it overlooks (perhaps willingly) the myriad of ways in which white racial formations are constructed, contested, and reformulated. It appears as if racism, as a static phenomenon, were so thoroughly documented that no further scrutiny is in order. More egregiously, it suggests that racism is a thing of the past or has not changed (perhaps other than to disappear), thereby rendering racialism obsolete.

In contrast to these disavowals, studying whiteness in Latin America requires a willingness to see race and racism not solely as historical relics, nor as monolithic processes, but rather as variegated strategies, investments, and procedures of (dis)association. "Whiteness," as Ruth Frankenberg reminds us, "is always constructed, always in the process of being made and unmade. Indeed, its characterization as unmarked marker is itself an 'ideological' effect that seeks to cover the tracks of its constructedness, specificity, and localness, even as they appear."[6] This chapter scrutinizes the rhetorical and relational ways in which whiteness works hemispherically and globally from within the *arielista* archive. The post-1898 era, especially at the centenary of Latin American independence, compelled the need for re-thinking the distinguishing characteristics of race in the Americas, and the *arielistas* were primary players in that enterprise. My close and contextualized reading of their understudied essays draws from the work of racial formation scholars like Michael Omi and Howard Winant, who propose the idea of a racial project as "an interpretation, representation, or explanation of racial dynamics, and an effort to reorganize and redistribute resources along particular racial lines. Racial projects connect what race *means* in a particular discursive practice and the ways in which both social structures and everyday experiences are racially *organized*, based upon that meaning."[7]

In the following pages, I shed light on the *projections* at play in *arielista* racial projects. To *project* in this sense implies several meanings that help me unpack the personal investments, sociocultural anxieties, and geopolitical insecurities that structure race ideologically and discursively in the *arielista* archive. First, the term connotes geographical imaginings that span the Americas, Europe, Africa, and Asia and move through the past, present, and future. In addition, it refers to the display, promotion, and extrapolation of emotional and psychological desires regarding autonomy and otherness. Lastly, there is a textual element that makes visible those affective imprints through the act of writing in the genre of the essay.

I should clarify that my emphasis on the aforementioned aspects of projection does not aim to illuminate a "specter of races," to borrow Anke Birkenmaier's phrase, lurking deep within the *arielista* archive.[8] Rather, the issue of race is one of the most conspicuous features of *arielista* essays, yet its centrality rarely figures into definitions and conceptualizations of *arielismo*. In my view, two reasons account for this oversight: the aforementioned rationalizations of white superiority and superficial repetitions of established narratives. In her analysis of *dominicanidad*, Lorgia García-Peña disrupts routine modes of reading the archive by showing how repetition is a form of silencing that is complicit with racialized violence against black bodies.[9] In other words, the archive is neither objective nor innocent; it regulates, restrains, and rarely rectifies. I follow García-Peña's transnational methodology and disruptive mode of reading in order to highlight the racial triangulations that explicitly structure and sustain the *arielista* archive. Rather than accept or overlook *arielismo*'s enactments of whiteness, which have been bolstered by readings that discount or rationalize white supremacist ideas and ideals, I trace the regional, transatlantic, and global routes through which the *arielistas* survey, measure up, map out, and determine racial consonances and contrasts.[10]

With the United States looming over, and often times into, Latin American affairs, the need to imagine a different future and re-evaluate sources of cultural identity and collective empowerment grew more urgent in the early twentieth century. As this chapter demonstrates, *arielista* racializations did not conform to a rigid dialectical (South/North or Latin/Anglo) arrangement. In fact, parsing the hemispheric features of race in the Americas at this crucial juncture of self-discovery and definition reveals that certain features of Europeanness were retained while others were renegotiated. Dissecting those eurontologies—by which I mean the strategies at play to seem or (re-)imagine oneself as European—unveils the conditions and restrictions of constructing Latin American whiteness through varying coordinates. Each of the following three sections of this chapter surveys how *arielista* essayists envision, position, and market ideologies of whiteness in relation to blackness, indigeneity, and Asianness, and underscores the precarious and provisional nature of this production of white racial consciousness through three keywords: plagiarism, simulation, and conflation.

The first section investigates how Cuban writers Fernando Ortiz and Emilio Gaspar Rodríguez turned away from Spain as a cultural source of empowerment in the aftermath of the Spanish-American War, yet at the same time looked to one of its most problematic figures of the past—the conquistador—as a symbol of (their own) white superiority in the present. The second part of this chapter deconstructs the racial simulations at play in the work of José Ingenieros, an Argentine intellectual whose racist treatises, especially when paired with his background as a Sicilian immigrant, put on display the shifting connotations of blackness among Cape Verde, Sicily, and Buenos Aires, while also calling into question the supposed universality of his synchronous ethical writings aimed at Latin American youth. The final section focuses on the racial scapegoats and culpable geographies (blackness in Haiti) that Peruvian *arielista* Francisco García Calderón creates in *Les démocraties latines de l'Amérique* in order to convince the French State to view Latin America's whiteness as the saving grace of a Pan-Latin culture under siege by US imperialism and other nations vying for power in the region. Overall, this chapter argues that race in the *arielista* archive is not absent, nor a transcendent affair, but rather in constant formation through a complex discursive network of aspirations, alliances, and antagonisms that spans the globe.

Peninsular Pasts, Plagiarized Presents: Conquistadores and Cubanidad in the Age of American Imperialism

Rather than the dialectic reverberation that it produced elsewhere in Latin America, US intervention in Cuba in 1898 sparked an affective ambivalence in Uruguay. As Víctor Pérez Petit writes in *Rodó: su vida, su obra* (published a year after Rodó's death):

> That hard battle threw our spirits, mine and Rodó's, into profound tribulation. We wanted and longed for Cuba's freedom, the last American country that remained under Spain's subjugation despite its virile struggles for independence and the glorious action by the Martís and the Maceos. But, at the same time, we wished that that freedom was won (*conquistada*), just as the freedom of all of South America had been won, by the sons of the conquered nation and, at most, with the help of its kindred countries. A new Bolívar would have filled our hearts with pride. But, what we could in no way accept was intervention by the United States. It is true that it gave rise to Cuba's independence; but we did not appreciate the service. What did that foreign nation have to do with the battles in another race's countries? In that fight we were for Spain.

A free Cuba, yes; but not with the help or for the benefit of the United States.[11]

Denunciations of Spain's last vestiges of empire in the Americas were not unison. Uruguayans, Pérez Petit states, "defend" Spain, which calls into question just how genuine their concern for Cuba's independence was as the United States made the island's war their own: "And just as much as we loved Spain, we disliked the United States."[12] Such ingrained, exculpatory deference to Spain may stem from the constitutive anxieties in *Ariel* concerning the need to confront the "moral conquest [that] [t]he powerful federation is carrying out among us."[13] One of the ways Prospero discourages his pupils from succumbing to impulses of imitating the United States is repeatedly emphasizing notions of triumph and victory, which coalesce around rhetoric and imagery of conquest.[14]

Rodó's Hispanist sympathies take various shapes in *Ariel*, such as when Prospero recommends that his students step up to their vital and continentalist obligations with the "lofty gaze of the conquistador," which reads as a contradictory source of agency for what purports to be a modernizing Americanist project.[15] Early peninsular reviewers of *Ariel* ran with such Hispanist hints. According to Leopoldo "Clarín" Alas in his famous review of the Uruguayan's essay, "what Rodó asks of Latin Americans is that they always be . . . what they are; that is, *Spaniards*, children of classic and Christian life."[16] It would be ironic, to say the least, for Cubans to revert to an identity that was associated with the provenance of their country's coloniality.[17] Furthermore, Clarín's beguiled comments, when paired with Pérez Petit's downplaying of Cuba's wars with Spain as a "complicated family affair" that would have presumably worked itself out without US interference, show how incongruous the perception and resonance of Spanishness were, as a vehicle to both endorse old world despotism *and* resist an emerging American empire.[18] Of course, it would be up to Cubans themselves to parse how real or imagined their connections to Spain would continue to be as they grappled with their burgeoning national consolidation.

In the following section, I examine the fluctuating ideologies and optics of Spanishness in Cuba, as seen through American cameras and negotiated in transatlantic debates involving Fernando Ortiz, Emilio Gaspar Rodríguez, and Rufino Blanco-Fombona. I pay particular attention to how *arielismo* on the island and overseas provided essayistic forums of altercation through which Americanist hostilities toward Spain following 1898 gave way to venerating its conquistadors of yore as sources of idealism, strength, and white supremacy.

INTERVENTIONIST OPTICS

After years of exile in Tampa during the Cuban War of Independence, Bonifacio Byrne returned to the island only to confront the glaring optics of the US colonial occupation of Cuba (1899–1902) in a well-known poem, "Mi bandera" (1899):

> Al volver de distante ribera,
> con el alma enlutada, y sombría
> afanoso busqué mi bandera
> ¡y otra he visto además de la mía!
>   ¿Dónde está mi bandera cubana,
> la bandera más bella que existe?
> ¡Desde el buque la vi esta mañana,
> y no he visto una cosa más triste!
>   Con la fe de las almas austeras
> hoy sostengo con honda energía
> que no deben flotar dos banderas
> donde basta con una: ¡la mía!¹⁹

> *[Upon returning from a distant shore,*
> *Weary of heart and somber,*
> *I searched anxiously for my flag*
> *And saw another flying beside her.*
>   *This morning I looked for my flag,*
> *The most beautiful flag in the world;*

From the ship's deck, I surveyed the skies
And have never seen anything sadder.
With the faith of an austere soul,
In this conviction I have grown
That two flags should not be flown
When one is enough: my own!][20]

Byrne's patriotic verses are rightly a customary touchstone for expressing the incredulity of an intercepted nationalist process decades in the making. For Byrne, the US flag overshadows its Cuban counterpart to the point of imperceptibility. In fact, at another point in the poem, Byrne invites the reader (and by extension all Cubans) to visualize the Cuban flag—"Don't you see it?" (¿No la veis?).[21] Byrne's invocation suggests an absence where previously there were simultaneous standards, which, as Rachel Price points out, evidences a "jagged temporality" that permeated the early years of the Republic, including Byrne's later work.[22] The feeling of illusory (in)dependence would linger for decades.

No entity played with the sense of historical (ir)reality of the transition from Spanish colony to American neo-colony more than Thomas Edison's films of the Spanish-American War.[23] As an "ideological reinforcement through entertainment" for US viewers in vaudeville theaters, Edison's wartime films blurred the lines between real-time footage and staged reenactments, from mundane activities ("Pack Mules with Ammunition on the Santiago Trail, Cuba") to action-based ones (such as Cubans facing a Spanish firing squad in "Shooting Captured Insurgents," which was recreated in New Jersey).[24] Given the complicity of Edison's films with yellow journalist agendas, it should come as no surprise that the stars and stripes figured prominently in their depictions, such as "Raising Old Glory over Morro Castle" (January 1899), which features a close-up shot of the lowering of the Spanish standard, and the unfurling of its replacement, against a rudimentarily sketched backdrop of the Morro. The Edison catalogue reads, "Down goes the Spanish flag, and up floats the Stars and Stripes. Down falls the symbol of tyranny and oppression that has ruled in the new world for four hundred years, and up goes the Banner of Freedom. In the distance are the turrets and battlements of Morro, the last foothold of Spain in America."[25] The facile transition between flags, which bypasses the Cuban one, is representative of a narrative that renders Cuba and its struggles for autonomy invisible in the Spanish-American War.

Byrne's protest comes to particular light in one of Edison's 'authentic' films, "Troops at Evacuation of Havana" (January 1, 1899), which consists of footage of the official start of US occupation when Spanish troops were evacuated from the island.[26] The film features continuous shots of the First Texas troops parading down the Prado, a symbolic dividing line between colonial Havana and the city's more modern expanses. Onlookers—neither jubilant nor downtrodden—line the route as a large American flag waves prominently in the right corner of the shot. A shift in the scene affords a closer view of the military procession, as well as two small flags in the background—the American and the Cuban, of equal size—perched from a small barred window. The large American flag, however, continues to dominate the frame before a wobbly Cuban flag suddenly appears in the crowd, painstakingly vying for space in the frame until, finally, the American flag disappears and the film abruptly ends. Whereas still photographs captured Spanish forces marching in an orderly fashion to their return across the ocean, Edison's film poses the United States as a modern, dynamic force, vivid when compared to the static representations, and commonplace historical narrative, of the Spanish precipitously exiting the Americas.

These visual orchestrations of the disappearing Spaniard are bolstered by the Edison film catalogue's description of "Troops at Evacuation of Havana," which reads, in part: "Many typical Cubans are seen lounging in the foreground, with here and there a Spaniard, if one may judge by sour looks and solemn demeanor."[27] It is curious that such a conclusion could be drawn, especially from subjective criteria, given that we rarely see the crowd's faces since their backs are turned toward the camera. When a select few do direct their gazes at or beyond the camera, they appear to do so out of curiosity for what was at the time a burgeoning technology. Telling the Spaniard apart from the Cuban—not in terms of racial or ethnic difference, but rather affective projection—is hardly discernible through an American lens. In this way, as Dylon Robbins notes, the catalogue descriptions of Edison's films play a pivotal role in nudging the spectator to see the ideological message, even when it is not readily apparent.[28]

Edison's film manipulates what is real and what is simulated at a crucial moment of transition and transformation. One assumes that Spanishness (in a capacious sense) as a wellspring of a collective identity formation would not stand a chance against the nationalist values of the island's homegrown heroes. Yet, as I examine in this chapter, the palimpsestic—to follow José Quiroga—qualities of constructs and formulations of *cubanidad* do not exclude Spanishness. Rather, the latter is written into, and at times over, the former in unexpected ways.[29] The following pages examine which traits of Spanishness that Cubans, as well as other Latin Americans, rejected, retained, repeated, or reimagined on the heels of 1898.

EL GALLEGO EN EL ESPEJO/SPANISH SELF-REFLECTIONS

Historian Louis Pérez notes the dwindling economic and cultural centrality of Spain for Cubans throughout the nineteenth century, and argues, "Cubans defined themselves through denial. They distanced themselves from Spain, differentiated themselves from Spaniards, and otherwise discarded those forms that identified them as Spanish."[30] Repudiating Spanishness induced a predicament of the past, which meant that Cubans "invoked few symbols from which to claim continuity and derive legitimacy."[31] Therefore, Pérez contends, "Cubans proceeded to invent a usable past," and searched for autonomous rather than annexationist sources of empowerment, which they located in The Ten Years' War (1868–1878) and the Little War (1879–1880), the two precursory conflicts of 1895–1898.[32] The bittersweet outcome of the final Cuban War of Independence, after which time the United States disbanded the Cuban Revolutionary Army, interrupted and devitalized the nationalist genealogy and narrative that Cubans had fought to establish.

While other countries in the hemisphere were looking forward to commemorating the centenary of Latin American independence

with grandiose festivities, Cuba contended with the complex aftermath of 1898, which set in motion an era of confusion and chaos
marked by repeated and sustained military occupations, politically
driven violence, voter fraud, rampant corruption, divisive race relations, labor strife, and dizzying cycles of excess and loss. As Lillian
Guerra highlights in *The Myth of José Martí: Conflicting Nationalisms in Early Twentieth Century Cuba*, competing internal factions on the island during that time used Martí to legitimize their
platforms and slander those of their opponents.[33] Staking claims to
Martí is but one facet of what Rafael Rojas terms the "war of discourses" in the early Republic, which was comprised of a wide array
of investments in ethnology, eugenics, and sociological approaches
to formulating and validating the constitutive components of Cuba's
cultural psyche.[34] This multifarious phenomenon was further fragmented by the presence of the United States, the "conquerors of
the century."[35]

In fact, the rhetoric of conquest was pervasive in the decades
following Cuba's provisional independence in 1899. US newspapers
frequently featured Uncle Sam (or Theodore Roosevelt) as a giant
extending its vast reach over Cuba, or giving a stern lesson to the last
of the Spanish colonies—Cuba, Puerto Rico, and the Philippines—
which were portrayed as ignorant and unruly infants, almost always
represented as primitive and racialized as black. With each US intervention in Cuba, those popular representations of the child-island
literally whitened, in the image of its well-behaved "sibling" Puerto
Rico, who was nicely dressed in modern threads, holding Uncle
Sam's hand. The infantilization of the island was also prevalent in
political policy. US senator Orville H. Platt, whose eponymous Platt
Amendment codified US control of Cuba for decades, remarked in
a 1901 article entitled, tellingly, "The Pacification of Cuba," that, "In
many respects, [Cubans] are like children."[36]

Such representations of Cubans as disorderly, underdeveloped,
helpless, and ultimately, vacuous, were only bolstered by the biological and psychological diagnostics that were gaining traction during
that time. Perhaps this in part explains why Manuel Márquez Sterling, one of the most trusted Cuban diplomats of the early Republic—

who even stepped in as president of Cuba for six hours during a turbulent transition on January 18, 1934—dedicated so much attention to the Cuban mind and character in books like *Psicología profana* (1905) and *Alrededor de nuestra psicología* (1906). Covering a range of aspects of civil life, including electoral politics, education, imperialism, literature, crime, and the role of the press, Márquez Sterling's capacious approach to psychology signals a stark reality: "We live a fictitious existence in terms of intellectual matters, a decadent one with respect to morals, and a disastrous one politically."[37] "The danger for Cuba," he continues, "does not consist of the fact that it can be conquered; the fundamental danger resides in the fact that Cubans, since they have not constituted a block, and are far from constituting one, are conquerable."[38] Yet for Afro-Cubans who were sidelined from participation and representation in the Cuban political scene, conquest was not a fear, but rather a remedy. Echoing Antonio Maceo's words during the war, Evaristo Estenoz, founding member of the Partido Independiente de Color, wrote in the first issue of *Previsión* (August 30, 1908): "One does not ask for freedom, nor beg for it, it must be conquered."[39] Appeals to conquest—as a way to either decry foreign imposition or contest internal marginalization—underscore that unity and empowerment were in short supply, which left the door open for Cubans to fill the void with negotiations of competing Pan-Americanist, Pan-Hispanist, and Pan-Latinist frameworks.

Rodó's work was decisive in injecting into the Cuban intellectual scene a sense of idealism that was most readily apparent in the activities of the Sociedad de Conferencias, a group of *arielista* writers led by Jesús Castellanos and the Henríquez Ureña brothers.[40] Rodó provided a breath of fresh air and his influence helped temper the tensions that Cubans felt with respect to identifications with Hispanism. Frustrated efforts to self-define and self-determine made Rodó's conciliatory spirit an attractive option for Cubans to consider. As it had in other Latin American countries, *arielismo* in Cuba became a coalescing prism, as productive as it was knotty, through which to locate collective agency, even if in the very distant past. But while Rodó traced that genealogy of authority to Ancient Greece, Cubans instead looked to the Spanish conquistador as a heroic symbol that they could reconjure in the present. Emilio Gaspar Rodríguez, the "Rodó of Cuba," proved more willing to reconnect the fraternal ties with the *madre patria*, but Fernando Ortiz, for example, was understandably reticent at such maneuvers.[41]

In addition to adding nuance to a transatlantic relationship that, especially after 1898, was subject to oversimplistic dialectic lenses, a careful reading of debates between writers in Cuba and Spain suggests that the ethnic and racial connotations of Pan-Hispanist conveniences and convictions were not restricted to merely retaining a past affiliation. For example, in 1925, the very same year that he would publish *La raza cósmica*, Mexican philosopher José Vasconcelos proudly announces that Cubans have won the "ethnic competition."[42] In contrast to the *mestizaje* frenzy that his foundational essay suggested would one day eradicate racialized differences, Vasconcelos avers in an article dedicated to Cuban youth and penned in the Havana periodical *El Fígaro*, that Cuba has only grown more Spanish in the new century:

> Besides maintaining the inheritance conquered by your heroes, you all have achieved a social triumph, an ethnic triumph the likes of which are not seen in many Latin American countries. You have doubled, tripled the number of inhabitants, while other countries of our race lose their populations due to bad governments, and that increase of your population has been achieved without substitution, without displacement of native blood and with an increase in similar blood. And in these moments you are perhaps more Ibero-American than in the days of Independence. Your multiplied population continues to be Spanish, continues to be Cuban and is now richer and has a superior culture than that of the heroic epoch of Independence. After twenty years of independent life, Cuba is more Cuban. Few American countries could say the same thing. Who cares that your businesses are run from Wall Street.[43]

Such logic—that Cuba is more Cuban because it is more Spanish—exposes the fault lines of a recurring rhetoric on both sides of the

Atlantic that fortifies Spain's centrality in the Americas in the wake of its defeat. The so-called Desastre of 1898 prompted Spanish writers from Emilia Pardo Bazán to Ramiro de Maeztú to take a deep, and at times desperate dive into the idiosyncrasies and collective psyche of Spain, fledging to find a regenerative essence at a moment of crisis. A paradigmatic example of those efforts can be found in Rafael Altamira's *Psicología del pueblo español* (1902), which was followed by his *Mi viaje a América* (1911). The latter details his trip to Argentina, Uruguay, Chile, Peru, Mexico, and Cuba and insinuates that part of Spain's resurgence resides in the Americas—that is, that Spanish academics across the Atlantic have much to offer Latin American universities. The fact that Altamira would offer such tone-deaf thoughts near America's centenary moment was read by Fernando Ortiz in Cuba as trying to compensate for an extinct empire.

SITES AND SLIPPAGES OF RECONQUISTA

In *La reconquista de América: reflexiones sobre el panhispanismo* (1911), Fernando Ortiz—an avid reader of Spanish books and newspapers published abroad and on the island—categorically refutes Altamira's assertions. In an unrelenting verbal thrashing that extends through various chapters of the book, Ortiz issues a corrective to Altamira's conclusions that Cuba nostalgically yearns for their Spanish past and that the "*reespañolización*" of the island has already happened.[44] Taking on other Spaniards like Adolfo Posada and Salvador Rueda, Ortiz rejects the "resurrección de quijotismos," what he sees as a neo-imperialist return of sorts to the Americas fueled by delusions of grandeur in the wake of 1898.[45] To be sure, Spanish intellectuals and writers saw in Cervantes's masterpiece a parallel of their own disillusioned decadence, and looked to it as an animating wellspring of their nation's redemptive trajectory. In *La vida de Don Quijote y Sancho* (1905), Miguel de Unamuno blurs fiction and reality and treats Don Quijote as a real person who embodies the messianic idealism sorely needed in Spain. However, Azorín takes a different approach and goes to La Mancha searching for clues, but finds a monotonous place he describes as frozen in time in *La ruta de Don Quijote* (1905). In his first book, *Meditaciones del Quijote* (1914), José Ortega y Gasset takes issue with the uncritical mythologizations of Cervantes's protagonist as a default source of blind idealism that Spaniards inevitably tap to quell or remedy their country's spiritual and sociopolitical problems. Instead of reviving, reapplying, or conflating the knight-errant, Ortega finds in Cervantes's novel a way to critically engage Spanish identity. Spanish intellectuals, as Germán Labrador Méndez highlights, would continue to use the *Quijote* to interrogate Spain's collective memory of its colonial enterprise overseas, as well as criticize the heavy-handed tactics of the Spanish Restoration (1915–1921).[46]

In the Spanish-speaking world *Don Quijote* was fresh on people's minds in the early twentieth century since the period between 1905 and 1915 marked the tricentenary of Cervantes's novel, which became one of the most widely published and commented texts in Cuba during that time.[47] Interestingly, José Martí's work was being edited during those same years. Yet even despite this stiff competition, the affective connection to the *Quijote* occasionally outweighed those to the island's own national heroes. For example, Cuban intellectual Esteban Borrero Echeverría alludes to the "sensations" that link Cubans, and by extension all Latin Americans, to Cervantes's masterpiece.[48] In contrast, Ortiz argues that "in Cuba we do not dream of quixotic Iberianisms even when they are disinterested; if we do not want to see our modest personality absorbed by the Americans, neither do we wish to be mentally nor politically Spanish; [. . .] *we want to be Cuban, totally Cuban.*"[49] Put more bluntly, the *"Cubanization* of Cuba," he stipulates, "means *de-Hispanizing (deshispanización)."*[50] Others followed Ortiz, such as Cuban *arielista* Jesús Castellanos who opined in an article written from New York, "The Spanish spirit has to say goodbye to America just as the English spirit took its leave of the thirteen colonies a century ago. May the healthy torrent of Spanish workers come to Cuba, to Americanize, Cubanize themselves, but not to become Spaniards."[51] For Ortiz, de-Hispanizing is an important step for replacing what he

considered Cuba's "españolizada psicología" with the "demopsi-
cología cubana," that is, in Castellanos's words, "an original personality and not living by reflection" (*vivir de reflejo*).[52]

Whereas Ortiz unequivocally ridicules and rejects the imperialist aspects of what he terms "neoquijotismo español," he significantly softens his position in his follow-up book, *Entre cubanos . . .*
(psicología tropical) (1913).[53] Aimed at Cuban youth, *Entre cubanos*
encourages the island's own regeneration even as it engages in an
epistolary dialogue with Miguel de Unamuno. Drawing a parallel between the *abulia* that Unamuno studies in *La vida de Don
Quijote y Sancho* and Cuba's situation, Ortiz writes, "We need to,
like you all, resuscitate Don Quijote, our ideal."[54] While previously
Ortiz did not seem too concerned about US influence on the island,
he now laments its nefarious role in exacerbating corruption and
resignation. In other words, he shifts the blame from Spaniards to
Cubans and their American interveners. In his examination of Cuba's
"psycho-social constitution"—which also features meditations on
Afro-Cuban *ñañiguismo* and "Los negros curros," a speech he delivered at the Ateneo de La Habana—Ortiz condemns the *choteo*, some
fifteen years before Jorge Mañach's seminal meditations on the matter, as the culprit that stifles the initiative to forge an autonomous
sense of collective being inspired by noble ideals.[55] The sovereignty
that he was so sure of only two years prior had not materialized,
which causes him to make a puzzling call for "cultural injections"
from overseas: "Culture! That is the import that we need the most."[56]

Ortiz had previously made his opinions regarding the inseparability of culture and Europeanness clear, as is evident in a 1906 essay,
"La inmigración desde el punto de vista criminológico," in which he
endorses white immigration to the Americas (which meant dissecting the specific parts of Europe he considered white).[57] Other Cuban
writers also heralded Spanish immigration to the island in the early
years of the Republic, and picked up where Ortiz left off vis-à-vis
Spanishness as a cleansing racial force. In José Sixto de Solá's retrospective look at Cuba since 1899 in his essay, "El pesimismo cubano,"
published in *Cuba Contemporánea* (1913), he identifies Cuba's history as a Spanish "colonia-factoría" as the culprit for a lingering

collective cynicism that foils the complete fruition of an independent "national personality."[58] Despite his repeated denunciations of
"coloniaje" inherited from the Spanish rule of the island, Sixto de
Solá finds racial perks in Spanishness: "Our population is, then, bigger and more and more homogenous; that increase in population is
constituted principally by births of Cubans and immigrants of Spaniards, and it is well known that when blacks come into contact with
Spaniards, they dissolve. And both the increase in population and
the large proportionality of white people are very important factors
for advancement."[59] Written a year after the massacre of thousands
of Afro-Cubans affiliated with the Partido Independiente de Color
in the summer of 1912, Sixto de Solá's assertions demonstrate that
Spanishness in the Cuban Republic was not exclusively a construct
in terms of nationalities or nationalism, but also a vital component
of a white racial project that harkens back to José Antonio Saco, and
certainly beyond.[60] At times retrograde, progressive at others, the
oscillating implications of Spanishness demonstrate the idealistic
qualities, racial selectivity, and temporal flexibility that the signifier
had with respect to the past (symbolized in the conquistador) and
the present (concretized in Spanish immigrants to the island).

As Anke Birkenmaier notes, Ortiz's adherence to Lombrosian
positivist criminology tends to get chalked up as a "problematic
first phase" of one of the most important theoreticians of race in
the Americas—most known for his formulations of the *ajiaco* and
transculturation in the 1930s and 40s.[61] Yet, Ortiz did not disavow
his early writings.[62] Perhaps this contradiction is the tacit understanding of the ellipsis and parentheses in the title *Entre cubanos . . .
(psicología tropical)*. Ortiz's initial outrage, which turned into willing petition of the very target of his criticism, reads like a hushed
or muffled confession. The first book was a performance, the second the inside story, the unfavorable but unavoidable conclusion
that 'real' Cubans reach if they take a hard look in the mirror. The
title of *Entre cubanos . . . (psicología tropical)* signals the confiden-
tial tone—almost like a whisper—of Ortiz's reversal on the role of
the conquistador (embodied in Don Quijote) and Spanishness writ
large. Not all displays, however, were as intimate.

PLAGIARIZING PENINSULARITY

While on assignment in Europe for the Buenos Aires magazine *Caras y Caretas*, Rodó pondered *Don Quijote*'s significance as the tercentenary of Cervantes's death approached in a chronicle entitled, "La filosofía del Quijote y el descubrimiento de América" (1916). For Rodó, the work symbolizes Latin America's spiritual, "eternal" solidarity with its "discoverers and civilizers."[63] But Rodó's reading of the ludicrous yet inspiring conquistador embodied in Cervantes's literary character becomes a motive to venerate a "new heroic type," that is, real-life conquistadors.[64] Far from stigmatizing the conquistador for laying the bellicose groundwork that would permeate Latin American countries for centuries, *arielista* writers attempted to normalize and attenuate that figure's culpability in order to reassert its fearless optimism, courage, and strength—heroic ideals, in other words, that they believed were sorely needed in the emerging so-called American century.

A curious case of transatlantic plagiarism shows the extent to which some *arielista* essayists in Latin America were invested in revising and redeeming the conquistador, as well as Cuba's centrality in those gestures. In a 1924 letter to Enrique José Varona and Manuel Sanguily, two Cuban intellectual powerhouses, Rufino Blanco-Fombona, a Venezuelan modernist writer living in Madrid, complains that "un señor Rodríguez" in Cuba has accused him of plagiarism, and asks that they offer a public rebuttal on the matter. The accusation is that Blanco-Fombona's *El Conquistador del siglo XVI* (1922) is lifted from Emilio Gaspar Rodríguez's *Los conquistadores: héroes y sofistas* (1917). In his letter, Blanco-Fombona clarifies that in 1922 Rodríguez had sent him a copy of *Los conquistadores*, which was delivered in person by a Cuban diplomat in Madrid, José María Chacón y Calvo, but that after thumbing through it Blanco-Fombona found only "innocuousness and clichés," and subsequently threw it away.[65] Blanco-Fombona's *El conquistador* was published shortly after that. Months later, according to Blanco-Fombona, he received a Cuban newspaper clipping in the mail that reported that he had conceded to plagiarizing Rodríguez's text, so he wrote to Rodríguez and asked him to denounce that accusation. But instead, Rodríguez ran with the allegation and wrote in the *Heraldo de Cuba* (July 1923) that in Blanco-Fombona's book, "there are paragraphs textually copied."[66]

The situation sent Blanco-Fombona off the rails, and he sarcastically denied Rodríguez's claim, writing—in his characteristic bitter wit—"He who plagiarizes a Rodríguez plagiarizes no one" and "To plagiarize that pinhead would be like claiming that the Orinoco River needs the water from a sewer to supplement its channel."[67] Repeating the phrase, "este hijo de . . . Cuba," Blanco-Fombona calls Rodríguez a parasite, an *arribista* who is only trying to get famous by hitching his wagon to a more talented writer.[68] Even though Blanco-Fombona's book was not published until 1922, he gives a meticulous account of parts of it that had circulated in magazines and literary reviews in Madrid, Buenos Aires, and elsewhere since 1919. At one point, he even flips the culpability, maintaining that it was Rodríguez who had the opportunity to crib Blanco-Fombona's work, not the other way around (and he goes as far as to call him a "pick-pocket").[69]

It appears that Varona and Sanguily did not take Blanco-Fombona up on his offer to get to the bottom of this matter. Other commentators, however, did intervene and try to clear the air. In a favorable review of Rodríguez's *Los conquistadores* published in *Listín Diario* in 1922, Cuban-Dominican writer Federico García Godoy opines that the book, which deals only briefly with the conquistadors themselves, contains

> certain points of similarity with another work published later, *El conquistador español en el siglo XVI*, by my illustrious friend Rufino Blanco-Fombona, to which I dedicated an extensive comment in one of the latest issues of the excellent review, *Cuba Contemporánea*. Such analogies are not due to, as some seem to think, an accentuated imitation or anything like that. I firmly believe that they stem from the same nature of the matter that compels them to turn to the same sources of information and make more or less similar judgements.[70]

Years later, in 1927, another Cuban writer, Enrique Gay Calbó rehashes the facts of the case as outlined in Blanco-Fombona's letter in *Cuba Contemporánea*, only to downplay the allegations. "The search to find the imitation or reminiscence," he argues, "is always a fruitless endeavor, of a fussy, stickler of a critic. In *Los Conquistadores* there is one part, the shortest, of twenty-four pages, that started the incident. The following chapter: "Cervantes y el siglo XVI español," is also related to the conquistadors. But the rest, entitled "Martí," "América," and an appendix to it, reduces the book's uniformity and excludes it for the most part from the polemic."[71] While Rodríguez has chronology on his side (but not by much), and the fact that he sent his book to Blanco-Fombona (which the latter acknowledges), the sticking point revolves around the length of their respective texts. It seems far-fetched that Blanco-Fombona's one-hundred-dred-and-fifty-page treatment of the conquistador would be overly indebted to Rodríguez's quick gloss.[72]

The point of revisiting this contentious issue of propriety resides not in who wrote what first, but rather in the fact that their respective treatments of the conquistador arrive rather late to the party, since others had already dealt extensively with the topic in the years coalescing around the centennial commemorations of Latin American independence in 1910. Francisco García Calderón, for example, considered the conquistadors, despite their problematic baggage, "professors of energy."[73] In *El porvenir de la América Latina* (*The Future of Latin America*, 1910), Manuel Ugarte registers a tepid admonishment of their cruelty that promptly gives way to an enthusiastic endorsement:

> Anything that tends to break the chain translates into enervation (*desmigajamiento*). It is for that reason that, even after the Revolution, we have to consider ourselves as a part of Spain, whose moral personality, remade by the climate and immigrations, we aspire to prolong triumphantly in the world. We do not date from 1810; we are children of a long and difficult process that starts in the darkness and brings us to light in reform, selecting shades throughout the centuries and successive and interminable transformations.

It is not possible to renounce a previous stage of existence without destroying the bridge that carries us from pole to pole in time.[74]

In addition to repeating the aforementioned takes on the conquistador, which were frequently excerpted in Cuban magazines and newspapers that Rodríguez read and knew well, it is also worth noting that he himself was susceptible to another kind of formula. Cuban writer Alberto Lamar Schweyer, for instance, sums up a critical tendency to consider Rodríguez a

> strong branch of that great tree named José Enrique Rodó, a tree under whose shadow American thought and feeling flourishes. Although he rarely hints at his admiration for Rodó, the author of "Los Conquistadores" is a faithful disciple of the great Uruguayan thinker. In form, delivery, and the same vision that he has about things, we can clearly see the influence exerted by the immense writer that was immortalized in "Motivos de Proteo." Rather than a disciple, it would be more accurate to call him an imitator, which does not detract from his work, nor diminish his talent. To imitate means to follow a course already outlined by someone else and to not go down an already beaten path; a disciple follows the teacher and the imitator tries to outdo him.[75]

Lamar Schweyer's assessment, which is meant to be flattering, but falls flat, confirms a long-standing propensity with which I take issue in this book: that once essayists are linked to Rodó, the latter's authority becomes the only thing that critics see in their work. Indeed, it is very rare to find Rodríguez's name mentioned without Rodó's.[76]

Rodríguez was a diplomat in India, Canada, and the Netherlands, who would write about pressing issues facing Cuba for many years, as evident in the title of his last book published the year before his death, *La crisis cubana: sus orígenes, sus factores contemporáneos* (1938). As an "original and passionate Cervantist," Rodríguez would return again and again to *Don Quijote* in books like *El retablo de maese Pedro* (1916), *Los conquistadores: héroes y sofistas* (1919), and *Puntos sutiles del Quijote: acervo histórico-sociológico de algunos pasajes* (1922).[77] In *Los conquistadores,* Rodríguez makes the requisite grievance by blaming the repercussions of the execrable acts of the conquistadors on the Latin American psyche, which is evident, he claims, in the recurring civil wars throughout the region. Yet, he also considers them the embodiment of heroic ideals whose impositions of their language and religion were not only laudatory feats, but part of a colonial "generous politics" (*política bienhechora*): "There is no exploit, let me repeat, greater nor more heroic in the history of humanity than the one that the Conquistadors of the new land of America achieved. [. . .] I do not know what to admire more, the force and heroism that they displayed or the power of resistance deployed to fight nature and humans at the same time."[78]

For his part, Blanco-Fombona deals with similar sentiments in *El Conquistador del siglo XVI,* albeit in a more developed, and ultimately forgiving way. A writer and diplomat known for, as is by now quite clear, his bombastic personality, Blanco-Fombona had lived in Spain for a decade before publishing *El Conquistador.* Therefore, he had no qualms in making clear that his book joins the Pan-Hispanist chorus of attempts to redeem the "relatively small group of Spaniards that discovered, explored, and conquered most of the New World [that] have been considered until now, with almost unanimous injustice, as a series of monsters."[79] His approach, however, goes beyond merely adding nuance, for he went to great lengths in order to downplay, rationalize, and ultimately dismiss the nefarious aura surrounding the agents and enterprise of conquest. For example, the conquistadors may have been individualist, arrogant, intolerant, and cruel, but Blanco-Fombona chalks those defects up to the fact that "They were very Spanish."[80] However, he cites their virtues—energy, action, and above all, sincerity—which let them off the hook, as evidenced in the following quote: "The conquistadors were truly champions of the faith. The religious spirit of Spain was in them. They were moved by the same feeling that imposed the unity of faith in the war against the Moors. The heavy-handed incentives of the Conquest of America allied with the most pure and disinterested religious ideal. This feeling of sincere piety ennobles the beheadings, rapes, and plundering, all the lowest instinctual activities brought into play by the human beast."[81] By now we are very familiar with the racism of revisionist gestures that disguise atrocity as adventure, and reframe brutality as compassion, which Blanco-Fombona certainly performs: "They rescue, for Caucasian and Latin civilization, that world that was in the hands of yellow races, mostly barbarous. That has been the civilizing transcendence of their action and Spain's ensuing action."[82]

That indigenous populations were on a primitive stage of civilization, that all conquests are merciless so why bother comparing them, and that we cannot hold past actors accountable by contemporary standards are among a taxonomy of absolving notions that Blanco-Fombona forwards in his book. For instance, he argues that reproach for the loss of lives, resources, autonomy, beliefs, customs, and languages should not be directed at the agents of conquest and colonization, but rather at "those who let themselves be defeated."[83] But he is not just talking about a historical process in the distant past: "the white race infuses its spirit [into the Indians] [. . .] In many of these societies the superior element, the Caucasian, has not been renewed in sufficient number to completely absorb all of them. Sooner or later, it will happen. In some countries it has already happened."[84] In lamenting that it is no longer a point of pride to trace one's genealogy to the conquistadors, Blanco-Fombona brings the past to bear on a present in a way that rhetorically reproduces the atrocious acts and abhorrent apologies of a white supremacist, colonial project intent on racial absorption, when not outright eradication.

Within this transoceanic airing of grievances and mutual accusations lies a strategy to combat the rhetorics and representations of Latin America as young, underdeveloped republics, which were particularly intense in Cuba. This is one of the reasons why the fascination with the conquistador became a default, circular source of empowerment, as evidenced in Cuban writer Mario Muñoz Bustamante's novel, which he died before completing, entitled *Gente de hierro* (1921), comprised of laudatory profiles of fifteen individual conquistadors, parts of which had appeared prior in *El Diario de la Marina*.[85] Shortly after Bustamante's death, Néstor Carbonell describes *Gente de hierro* as, "a work in which the men of the conquest, those titans for whom there were no obstacles, have been portrayed just as they were: ferocious, tireless, without a notion of time or distance; fearless in the face of danger, without fear of scaling a mountain or wading across high rivers, unshaken by fire from volcanoes or icy summits; they did not fear Nature, nor any man . . ."[86] Here, once again, we can appreciate the echo chamber qualities of fictions of conquest in Cuba, as Rodríguez described the conquistadors in precisely the same ways.

CHANNELS OF CONQUEST

Coincidentally, Sigmund Freud happened to be thinking about such gestures of returning to traumatic pasts at around the same time as *arielista* essayists were selectively appropriating the conquistadors' efficacious attributes. In "Remembering, Repeating, and Working-Through" (1914), Freud observed in his patients a "compulsion to repeat" past traumas in the present, which took predominance over an "impulse to remember" them.[87] Instead of "working-through" the conquistador with Freud's psychoanalytic method, that is, confronting and ridding its symbolic capital in a cathartic process of overcoming, Latin American *arielistas* looked back to the conquistador as a way to recast traumatic remembrance as contemporary clout. The preceding examination of recuperations, or re-enactments, of a problematic past in an era of exigent circumstances underscores what is at stake for, in Blanco-Fombona's words, "a scattered race that is looking for itself, even in its most controversial personalities."[88] The redemption of the conquistador, as I have suggested, appears as a paradoxical source of heroic agency that took on particularly significant contours in and through Cuba. Aside from charting a futurity rooted in, and in some ways restricted to, the distant past, the conquistador resurfaces as a disciplining force that empowers the white component of a lopsided *mestizaje* formula by disappearing racialized otherness in order to restabilize the centenary subject's imagined or desired autonomy in a new century and under new colonial tutelage.

Categorical appeals to Spanishness in the Americas after 1898, or convenient disavowals of it, fluctuate as attempts to identify the constitutive characteristics of a new phase of *cubanidad* grew more urgent and fraught. The irony, as I have pointed out, resides in the fact that just as Cubans turned away from Spanish colonialism, they also looked back toward its most problematic figure, the conquistador, as a heroic emblem of an Iberian past whose racial and temporal flexibility perform vital functions for bolstering *arielista* idealisms. As the following section makes clear, the stark raciology centering on blackness, and the personal aspirations and investments driving it, were not restricted to prior colonizers and the formerly colonized. We also see such maneuvers of white supremacy triangulated between Argentina, Italy, and Africa.

Engineering Superiority: Simulation and the Eth(n)ic Interpellations of José Ingenieros

"¡Raza blanca, hijos, raza blanca!" This was purportedly José Ingenieros's response to a group of Andean youth—conflicting accounts identify them as either Peruvian or Bolivian—who sought the Argentine physician and philosopher's advice on the key ingredient needed to set their country on the right path.[89] A polymath, Ingenieros was an authority on many matters; he was a psychiatrist, criminologist, and sociologist who, as his surname suggests, engineered many aspects of Argentine, and by extension Latin American life.[90] During his time in charge of a clinic for the insane at the turn of the century and as the director of the Institute of Criminology in the Buenos Aires penitentiary (1907), Ingenieros personally put many people under the psychological, physical, and moral microscope, and wrote about it in texts like *Dos páginas de psiquiatría criminal* (1900), *Hipnotismo y sugestión* (1903), *La psicopatología en el arte* (1903), *Histeria y sugestión: estudios de psicología clínica* (1904), *Nueva clasificación de los delincuentes* (1907), *Las bases del derecho penal* (1910), *Patología de las funciones psicosexuales: nueva clasificación genética* (1910), *La psicología biológica* (1910), *La formación de la conciencia* (1910), *Principios de psicología genética* (1911), *Criminología* (1913), and *Principios de psicología* (1916). As evidenced in these book titles, Ingenieros was a key player in developing "new state mechanisms of vigilance, control, and production of knowledge."[91]

The confluence of *fin de siglo* moral discourses of degeneration and scientific diagnostics was a potent regulatory formula that fueled the flames of anxiety in a Buenos Aires densely populated by European immigrants. In addition to marking the centenary, 1910 was also the year with the highest number of immigrants to Argentina.[92] Furthermore, the labor movement, which since the 1890s had been driven in large part by European anarcho-socialist immigrants, would clash with the State at a symbolic moment for the latter entity to remember and reinforce its legitimacy.[93] What "foreign agitators" dissolved, from the State's point of view, was the moral and racial integrity of "real" or "legitimate" Argentines, which is to say descendants of Hispanic criollos and mestizos whose presence in the New World predated that of more recent arrivals. Those anxieties came to a head at the centenary as heated discourses surrounding "authentic" versus "aberrant" subjects played out in political arenas, the popular press, and also in Ingenieros's clinic, where his complicity with state mechanisms of surveillance, inspection, and disciplining was primarily concerned not with immigrants per se, but rather with the pathological conditions of delinquency, perversion, and insanity.

In fact, as Fernando Degiovanni points out, Ingenieros advocated a more capacious vision for an Argentine nationality not solidified but rather "in formation," renewed by fresh reserves of European whiteness, which had been a constant proposal throughout nineteenth century Argentina, not to mention elsewhere in the Americas.[94] The reasons for Ingenieros's stance are understandable, given that he immigrated to Buenos Aires from Sicily when he was a child and, moreover, was a staunch supporter and former leader of the Socialist Party (the very sectors that were demonized by the state). Born Giusep[p]e Ingegnieri in Palermo, he eventually changed his name to José Ingenieros. It is ironic that someone who dedicated such time and resources to analyzing the nefarious effects of simulation in Argentine society—most notably in texts like *La simulación en la lucha por la vida* (1903), *Simulación de la locura ante la sociología criminal y la clínica psiquiátrica* (1903), and *Locura, simulación y criminalidad* (1910)—would ultimately adopt it as a "strategy of integration."[95] As Jorge Salessi indicates, "it seems that, especially during the first decade of the twentieth century, Ingenieros deflected attention away from his immigrant and Sicilian origin and copied, in an exaggerated way, the tics and defensive reactions of the class to which he wanted to be admitted, but could not."[96] In the following pages, I examine Ingenieros's rhetorical deployment of whiteness as a strategic construct that he uses to simulate and separate himself from the immigrant hordes and their negative racialized connotations relating to blackness.

SICILY AND SIMULATION

A month after a 7.1 magnitude earthquake and its ensuing tsunami devastated Messina, Sicily, and surrounding coastal regions on December 28, 1908, the following story about an incident in the Argentine city of Santa Fe was reported in *Vanguardia*, the newspaper of the Partido Socialista in Buenos Aires:

> Santa Fe, 30—The news about the attempt to poison the water has been completely verified. At least that is the word on the street, but the police are keeping their lips prudently sealed on the matter.
>
> There is talk of a conspiracy cooked up by twenty Sicilians (rescued from the earthquake in Sicily?) that attempted to take advantage of the confusion of that incident in order to pillage the city. It is said that four of them were surprised inside the ground, when they were about to throw the poison into the filters.
>
> A desiccation of the filters has been ordered, which will be carried out today.[97]

In addition to providing a sense of the transatlantic ripple effects of an Italian natural disaster in Argentina, this dispatch of Sicilians literally poisoning the well in Santa Fe also sums up the negative racial connotations of Sicily globally. As Jennifer Guglielmo explains,

> Italy's history of African, Arab, Greek, Norman, and Spanish settlements defied all theories of racial purity, but southerners' dark complexions and "primitive" cultural practices were, to many

northerners, evidence of their racial inferiority. Southern Italy . . .
was a metaphor for anarchy, rebellion, poverty, and the lack of
"civilization." Indeed, the saying "Europe ends at Naples. Calabria,
Sicily, and all the rest belong to Africa" can still be heard throughout Europe, and these ideologies of southerners as backward continue to inform national political movements.[98]

Ingenieros himself was aware of the two Italys, where "A southerner
is, in the north, as foreign as a Paraguayan and infinitely more so
than a Parisian.[99] Southern Italy's peripheral status also extends
beyond national borders, as its too-close-for-comfort location to
Africa was viewed with suspicion throughout the Western world.

In *The Races of Europe: A Sociological Study* (1899), for example,
American academic and scientific racist William Z. Ripley identifies
three European races—the Teutonic, the Alpine, and the Mediterra-
nean (which correspond to north, central, and south, respectively).
Examining subjects in a mug-shot format that Ingenieros would
have found quite familiar, so as to take into account each subject's
height, stature, skin, hair, and eye color, Ripley charts a hierarchy
in which the Norwegian reigns supreme, the Austrian gets the silver medal, and the Sicilian subject (from Ingenieros's hometown
of Palermo, no less) is at the bottom.[100] In fact, Ripley repeatedly
points to Sicily as a negative example: its inhabitants' dark features
signify a lack of purity, evidenced in the fact that its "people speed-
ily degenerate into mixed types."[101] The stigma of Sicilianness figured prominently in realities and representations of immigrants in
the United States and Argentina. As Matthew Frye Jacobson points
out, Sicilians in the United States were frequently depicted in similar dehumanizing ways as African Americans.[102] As a matter of fact,
"[t]he epithet *guinea* . . . was used by whites to mark African slaves
and their descendants as inferior before it was applied to Italians at
the turn of the twentieth century."[103] Of course, it is important not
to conflate the racial politics that Italian immigrants experienced
in the United States and Argentina, but at the same time we should
recognize that they were also hemispherical and global in nature. In
other words, even though Sicilians had to confront and negotiate

racist associations with blackness to a greater degree in the United States, particularly in the Deep South, Sicilians in Argentina would also be very aware of such comparison, even if there they did not operate to the same degree.[104]

There is no example that better illustrates the xenophobic anxieties surrounding Italian immigration to Argentina than Carlos Néstor Maciel's *La italianización de la Argentina* (1924). Employing a blend of psychology and evolutionary concepts similar to the one that Ingenieros himself had systematized in Argentina, Maciel's racist tirade reproduces clash of civilizations rhetoric and decries the sinister infiltration of "el peligro itálico," or "the hidden power of Italianization," which seeks to "strengthen its transoceanic domination" and "intensify we do not know what shameful action in the development of the destinies of our country."[105] The vagueness of the Italian threat is a technique that leaves the door open for anything. At stake for Maciel's call for "Argentina for Argentines" is "our Hispanic-Creole racial character," which he believes Italians will undermine.[106] Predictably, southern Italians bear the brunt of his attacks: In Naples, "Assassinations and poisonings . . . had become so frequent, that abroad the word 'Italian' was a synonym for a poisoner." Not only that, in Sicily, "Some have seen murderers drink or lick the blood of their victims, like cannibals."[107] Maciel also emphasizes their connection to blackness when he contends that any success Italian immigrants and their descendants enjoy is due not to their own merits, since even "los negros de Jubaland" could have done the same given the fertile soil and favorable climate that Argentina offers.[108]

For someone like Ingenieros, Maciel's most damning accusation would be the notion that Italian immigrants fake assimilation for nefarious and unspecified purposes. Maciel avers that Italians are not interested in becoming Argentines, since they continue to speak and read in Italian, form communities and clubs, and retain their customs from the old country. They are, in short, "infusionables," even when they profess their willingness to acculturate: "It is false that those naturalized Italians and their descendants are sincere Argentines. They will appear to be when it is to their advantage."[109] "The art of dissimulation, the gambit," he goes on to write, "is an outstanding feature of the Italian character," which Maciel describes as their chameleonic malleability.[110] It is remarkable that Maciel would use Ingenieros's criterion of simulation against him (although not directly, of course). As Sylvia Molloy points out,

> Simulation, for Ingenieros, is born of a flaw, a maladjustment, a weakness. A strategy from the margins toward the center defined by the author as "pathomimicry," it allows the simulator to pretend to be what he or she is not in order to pass, to be successful, to achieve a goal. The criminal pretends to be mad to escape punishment; the fabricator pretends to be someone else to achieve prestige; the proletarian immigrant pretends to be middle-class to achieve acceptance. For Ingenieros, one cannot, like Oscar Wilde, simulate (pose as) what one is: to pose, for Ingenieros, is necessarily to lie.[111]

How, then, does Ingenieros, who deploys the very diagnostics from which he himself is somehow exempt, navigate such a predicament of duplicity? One way to unpack these fraught politics of authenticity resides in how he capitalizes on a rhetorical strategy of whiteness as a way of distancing himself from the negative biological and racial connotations of Sicilians.

(IN)VISIBILITY AND ANTI-BLACKNESS IN CAPE VERDE

We can look to *Crónicas de viaje, 1905–1906* for clues to how Ingenieros might have distanced himself from the racist specter of black associations to his Sicilian origins. Among his writings during stints in Italy, France, Spain, London, Monte Carlo, and Berlin is a chronicle composed from San Vicente, Cape Verde entitled, "Las razas inferiores" (1905). As locals approach his ship in their own small boats to ask tourists for money, Ingenieros expresses nausea and promptly points out their natural inferiority as indisputable and corroborated by "all the scholars who have *seen* black populations" (original emphasis).[112] The trauma of seeing, and perhaps in some way seeing his own (nonwhite, inferior) Sicilianness reflected back at him, may in part explain why he goes to such extensive lengths to disqualify blackness on so-called scientific principles. Ingenieros's vicious attacks on blackness also echo the outlandish notion that black people were better off and happier when enslaved than they are post-emancipation:

> It is a coarse error, however, that falsifies the interpretation of the historical role of the black race in the formation of American nations and character. The blacks imported to the colonies were, in all probability, similar to those that populate San Vicente: an ignominious scum of the human species. Judging harshly, it is necessary to confess that slavery—as a protective function and as an organization of labor—should have been maintained for the benefit of those poor wretches, in the same way that civil law establishes a ward for all incompetents and with the same generosity with which the alienated are afforded refuge in colonies, or animals are protected. Their slavery would be the political and legal sanction of a purely biological reality.[113]

Ingenieros sees the black people in front of him—and by extension all black people—as indigent, filthy, lazy, drunk, illiterate, and ultimately unable to even comprehend the concept of human rights, all of which situate them on a subpar stage of civilization. For these reasons, Ingenieros argues that "People of colored races should not be our political and juridical equals; they are inept for the exercise of civil capacity and they should not be considered 'people' in the legal concept of the word."[114]

Predictably, Ingenieros bolsters his total disqualification of black people with recurrent zoomorphic arguments that even deny them their humanity: "People of white races, even in their most inferior ethnic groups, are worlds apart from these beings, which seem closer to anthropoid monkeys than to civilized whites."[115] To be sure, Ingenieros goes to great lengths to dehumanize black people, from pointing to what he considers signs of their "genuinely animal mentality" evidenced by all of their "attitudes, gestures, language, tastes, aptitudes, and feelings of a domesticated beast," to arguing that "Lamenting the disappearance of races that are inadaptable to white civilization is the same as renouncing the benefits of natural selection. Cattle ranchers strive to select and refine their breeds, preferring well-bred cattle and establishing enormous differences of price between them and others. [. . .] The sociologist who uses their brain to observe human races instead of their heart, is obligated, at the very least, to think the same way as a breeder of horses or sheep."[116] As the enforcers of natural selection, "las razas blancas" benevolently usher black people to their demise and ultimate disappearance, which he deems a scientific inevitability:

> Anything that is done in favor of inferior races is anti-scientific; at most they could be protected so that they die out pleasantly, facilitating the provisional adaptation of those exceptions that are able to do it. It is necessary to be merciful with these scraps of human meat; it is advisable to treat them well, at least like a century-old tortoise in the London Zoological Gardens or like trained ostriches that parade in Antwerp's Zoo. We would not give our vote to the harsh Mississippi tribunal that, in the town poetically named Magnolia, just condemned a white woman named Theresa Perkins to ten years of forced labor for having married a black man. But it would be absurd to support their indefinite conservation, as well as contribute to the cross of blacks and whites. Argentines' own experience is revealing just how harmful the influence of *mulataje* has been in the mortar of our population, which acts as a yeast of our most ill-fated fermentations of the masses.[117]

SIMULTANEITY AND ETH(N)IC INTERPELLATIONS

Ingenieros's heavy investment in (his own) whiteness would continue in *Sociología argentina* (1913), a text in which "raza(s) blanca(s)" appears more than fifty times.[118] By no means a new formula, Ingenieros proposes a literal racial formation that echoes Domingo Faustino Sarmiento's civilization and barbarism dichotomy: "the only remedy to obviate the ills of South American nations: assimilate the culture and work of more civilized European nations: regenerating the primitive Hispano-Indio blood with an abundant transfusion of new blood, of white race."[119] This replenishment from a white European reservoir will racially cleanse a mixed Argentine nationality. It is telling, however, that the whiteness that Ingenieros conceptualizes is by no means as dissected as we have seen previously.[120] Proposing a capacious whiteness, free from the deterministic physiognomical and geographical cornerstones of the very positivist diagnostics which he more than anyone else in Latin America helped craft, shifts the microscope back onto racialized others: "The question of races is absurd when it is raised about people that are diverse branches of the same white race; but it is fundamental when it comes to certain races of color, absolutely inferior and inadaptable."[121] The convenience of this exemption is not lost on Theodore Allen, who avers that "when an emigrant population from 'multiracial' Europe goes to North America or South America and there . . . incorporates itself as the 'white race,' that is no part of genetic evolution. It is rather a political act: the invention of 'the white race.'"[122] As *Sociología argentina* progresses, the more categorical Ingenieros's insistence on white supremacy becomes:

> There is a fact uniformly accepted in ethnography: white races have shown in the last twenty or thirty centuries a superiority in the social organization of work and culture; their special nuclei are called civilized nations. The gods and heroes of the *Iliad* belonged to the white race, just as did the statesmen, philosophers, and poets of Greece and Rome; the so-called barbarians who repopulated the Roman world were white; so too were the Christian and heretic peoples of medieval Europe; just like those who provoked the Renaissance of science, literature, and arts, which initiated a new era in the history of humanity.[123]

Underlying this matter-of-fact tone is what could be read as a compensatory gesture for his own racial insecurities. While Rodó avoids explicit racialization in *Ariel*, and Ingenieros follows suit, in showcasing Greco-Roman genealogy as a warm blanket of reassurance, both writers disassociate "white" Latin Americans from being looped in with racialized others.

My point here is not to describe Ingenieros's well-known racism, even though it is important to read it in his own words. Instead, revisiting his racializing maneuvers suggests that Ingenieros not only passes, but gets a pass in literary history, which situates him largely in terms of his philosophical writings. Charles Hale, for example, identifies an ethical turn in Ingenieros's work after 1915, during which time he dethroned Rodó as the "maestro de la juventud" with ethical interpellations such as *Hacia una moral sin dogmas: lecciones sobre Emerson y el eticismo* (1917) and, posthumously, *Las fuerzas morales* (1926), in which the term *youth* appears fifty-seven times.[124] But his ethical writings predate 1915 since *El hombre mediocre*, his first *"arielista"* text, was published in 1913, the very same year as *Sociología argentina*. Rather than view Ingenieros's ethical turn in an asynchronous way—that is, in terms of a neat split between, on the one hand, his scientific racism and, on the other, his moral pedagogy—I would like to consider the implications of their overlap.

Written in self-exile in Switzerland after Argentine president Roque Sáenz Peña denied him a professorship that Ingenieros assumed was rightfully his, *El hombre mediocre* replicates *Ariel* in numerous ways. The book, which is comprised of Ingenieros's lecture notes for a 1910 course on the psychology of character, has a pedagogical scope and tone. Much like Rodó's essay, it is an ethical call to arms for young idealists of superior rectitude ("the small nucleus of sensible spirits") to develop their own personalities based in pursuit of the Ideal—"that particle of fantasy that puts you on top of the real"—and thereby rise above and reform their environs plagued by routine, emulation, and resignation.[125] "Beings of your stock," Ingenieros insists to his target audience in the book, "whose imagination is filled with ideals and whose feeling polarizes their entire personality, form a separate race of humanity: they are idealists."[126] This project of personal development, which prefigures a brighter, more perfect future is unmistakably *arielista*, and this idealist foundation made it Ingenieros's most popular text, not to mention required reading in schools throughout the Spanish-speaking world for many years.

Although Ingenieros diagnoses the differences between "inferior" and "superior" humans in *El hombre mediocre*, those classifications are seemingly devoid of the racist connotations that permeate the bulk of his writings. But this cannot be attributed to some sort of epiphany or renouncement of his racist thinking. Rather, other concurrent texts would perform that racializing labor, such as *Sociología argentina*, whose 1918 edition included a section on "La formación de una raza argentina" that merges talk of morality and ideals with the racist evolutionary rhetoric characteristic of his work. This temporal synchronicity in which both texts, not to mention others, simultaneously circulate and continually update should prompt us to question their independence and ponder their possible consanguinity. Such a critical gesture can help shed light on the wider implications of Ingenieros's ethical texts, as well as on the racial contours of his target audience. I highlight the particular situatedness of purportedly universalist discourses like *El hombre mediocre* not in order to merely catalog or reify Ingenieros's well documented white supremacist views. Rather, I do so to suggest that those views are implied in the concept of the ideal that his ethical and philosophical writings promote and that, as Alfred J. López notes, is virtually synonymous with whiteness.[127]

Since *El hombre mediocre* has influenced generations of Latin Americans, it is worth questioning what we implicitly consume in such a text. While there are no strict correlations between ethics and eugenics in *El hombre mediocre*, the two phenomena, if read in conjunction with other coetaneous texts, suggest that they are never as far apart as we may think. Although reading race where it is purportedly absent, as well as rehashing blatant racism from a century ago could generate accusations of artificiality or obviousness, such critiques would only reproduce the two claims that, respectively, call into question the very existence of racism or its contemporary relevance. However, delving into racist ideologies of yore through the lens of simultaneity can enhance critical repertoires that respond to Paula Moya's call for the "social imperative" of close literary readings of race.[128] It is incumbent, then, to scrutinize the dynamics—both explicit and implicit—of race-making strategies which, in the case of Ingenieros, means appreciating his complicity in developing and deploying repressive state apparatuses in his role as a criminologist while unveiling his personal stakes in making (his own) whiteness homogeneous, normalized, and superior. Similar ironies and conveniences also operate among Peru, France, and Haiti in the following section of this chapter.

Votre América: Blackness and Pan-Latinism in
Les démocraties latines de l'Amérique

In *Indian Given: Racial Geographies across Mexico and the United States*, María Josefina Saldaña-Portillo writes, "Geography is not only a discipline for mapping the world to be seen: it is also a way of disciplining what we see, of disciplining us into seeing (and knowing) mapped space as racialized place."[129] Saldaña-Portillo's examination of racial geography takes into account the invested rhetorics and imagined representations that underlie physical cartographies. In other words, race-making is concomitant in place-making, which strategically situates adjacency and distance in order to designate a here and a there, an us and a them. Such logics of proximity, as Ann Twinam underscores in *Purchasing Whiteness: Pardos, Mulattos, and the Quest for Social Mobility in the Spanish Indies*, were key features of whitening petitions (*gracias al sacar*) that racialized others used to bolster their claims of successful close interactions with white people and which were in turn used as proof that they could be, or already were, white (enough).[130] In Latin America, the legacy of petitioning whiteness, as both a racial formation and geographic formulation, extended far beyond the eras of conquest and colonization. In fact, such geo-racial strategies were paramount in centenary surveys of Latin America, such as Peruvian writer Francisco García Calderón's *Les démocraties latines de l'Amérique* (1912). In the remaining pages of this chapter, I contend that García Calderón's foregrounding of whiteness as a precondition of pan-Latin identity hinges on calculated manipulations of racial anxieties—including anti-blackness, yellow peril panic, and anti-German sentiments— meant to convince the French state (his intended readership) that only Latin Americans can safeguard the waning prestige of the "Latin race" as the impending inauguration of the Panama Canal presaged its definitive demise. The foreboding prognostications and forlorn pleas that comprise García Calderón's pitch shed light on the selective arrangements of racial machinations of *latinidad* in the *arielista* archive, which, I argue, reveal that the consolidation of *arielismo*'s racial ambitions is contingent on inculpation of racialized alterity in the Americas in conjunction with a genuflection to Europeanness.

Hailed as Rodó's "favorite disciple," García Calderón, along with his brother Ventura, lived in Paris for decades, where they assumed consular posts for the Peruvian government and wrote extensively— in both Spanish and French—about world literature, philosophy, art, culture, and politics. *Les démocraties latines de l'Amérique* is one of the most wide-ranging analyses of Latin American history and culture of the time.[131] However, unlike Rodó's *Ariel*, García Calderón's examination of Latin America and its place in the contemporary world was not intended for a Spanish-speaking audience, but for a French reading public, first, and, with the English translation published in New York and London in 1913, for readers in the United States and Great Britain. A Spanish translation did not appear until 1979. Largely dedicated to political history, *Les démocraties latines de l'Amérique* is divided into seven parts. The first section explores the colonial, independence, and industrial eras of Latin American history and begins with a psychological analysis of the conquering and conquered races. Section two deals with political ecology in Venezuela, Peru, Bolivia, Uruguay, and Argentina. Part three offers the same approach to Mexico, Chile, Brazil, and Paraguay. Part four examines Colombia, Ecuador, Central America, the Dominican Republic, and Haiti. Section five expands its scope to political, literary, and philosophical ideas in Latin America. Part six cements García Calderón's Pan-Latinist ideology and highlights the various geopolitical threats Latin America faces, that is to say, imperialism from the United States, Germany, and Japan. The last section lays out four principal problems afflicting Latin America: the problems of unity, race, politics, and economics. The conclusion weighs a variety of possibilities and predictions about the future of Latin America, its culture, and its pivotal geographical location in the years leading up to the opening of the Panama Canal, an event that symbolized the triumph of US imperialism while bringing nations of the world closer together and possibly into conflict. An in-depth engagement with each of the seven books of *Les démocraties latines de l'Amérique* is beyond the purview of this study. Therefore, my objective here is to focus on the complex racializations through which García Calderón imagines Latin America as an essential part of Pan-Latinity and assesses its place within a global paradigm. For these reasons, my approach to *Les démocraties latines de l'Amérique* centers on the foreword, section six (Pan-Latinity, geopolitical dangers), section seven (Latin America's problems), and the conclusion.

Evident from the onset of the text is a hemispherical dichotomy with incongruous features:

> There are two Americas. In the north, the "Outre-Mer" of Bourget, is a powerful industrial republic, a vast country of rude energies, of the "strenuous life." In the south are twenty leisurely states of unequal civilization, troubled by anarchy and the color problem. The prestige of the United States, their imperialism, and their wealth, have caused those restless Latin republics of the South to be forgotten and underestimated. The name of America seems to be applied solely to the great imperial democracy of the North.[132]

This subaltern positioning of Latin America is a frequent trope in García Calderón's essays and plays a fundamental role in the design of *Les démocraties latines de l'Amérique*: "We propose to draw up the balance-sheet of these Latin republics: this is the aim of this book. We interrogate the history of these states, the reasons for their inferiority and their prospects for the future."[133]

Blackness is the primary malefactor in the numerous problems (geographical, racial, political, and economic) that he insists explain Latin America's inferiority with respect to the United States and the world. Race, he posits, is the cause of other political and economic impasses that block Latin America's progress: "[Race] explains the progress of certain peoples and the decadence of others, and it is the key to the incurable disorder which divides America."[134] By treating race as a metonymy of a series of ills, García Calderón follows in the footsteps of French social psychologist Gustave Le Bon, Latin American sociologists Carlos Octavio Bunge and Alcides Arguedas, and English eugenicist Karl Pearson, whose racist theories he cites and adopts in order to forward idealized notions of racial purity.[135] Furthermore, he does not hesitate to embrace theories of degeneration and the various categories yielded by this well-known line of thinking and apply them directly to what he considers to be inferior races in the region, which is to say, indigenous people, members of the African diaspora, and their descendants.

Although indigenous people are portrayed as isolated, exploited, and decaying populations that learn to love their oppressed condition, it is blackness that bears the brunt of García Calderón's racialized accusations: "The black race is doing its work and the continent is returning to its primitive barbarism."[136] Indeed, blackness is the central player in his envisioned race war that so-called degenerate races supposedly wage on white and *mestizo* Latin Americans. According to García Calderón, enslaved Africans transported to Latin America are the epitome of barbarity: they are "primitive creatures, impulsive and sensual. Idle and servile, they have not contributed to the progress of the race."[137] Not only does García Calderón blame blackness for not contributing anything to an idealized notion of Latinity—which overlooks, of course, the variegated ways in which slavery and other forms of exploitation benefitted upper-class, white families and their descendants—but he also presents what Santiago Castro-Gómez calls an "aristocratic imaginary of whiteness," which connotes "civilization" as under attack from "barbarism" (read "blackness").[138] The racialized and gendered description of the colonial origin of blackness in Latin America that García Calderón offers is revealing: "The African woman satisfied the ardor of the conquerors; she darkened the blood of the race."[139] This is not only a grotesque description of sexual violence perpetuated against enslaved women by their enslavers; it also inverts the active/passive, or transgressor/victim, dichotomy and attributes the transgressive role to the enslaved person. Despite being enslaved, the African woman is portrayed as actively infecting her white-skinned enslavers with her negativity, that is, her dark skin color. Additionally, the dichotomous description projects a multitude of negative traits associated with blackness onto a lone slave woman, but recognizes plurality in enslavers, thus endowing the latter with individuality while constricting the former to an archetypical status.

Race as a category has a double metaphorical resonance for García Calderón, both as an illness that invades bodies and as a disruptive political force that invades nations. However, the adjectives he uses to describe blackness oscillate between, as I just pointed out, ascribing them the status of active assailants or assigning them passivity. For example, in noting the relationship between blackness and its "depressing influence on the American imagination and character," García Calderón maintains that people of African descent corrupt bloodlines with "elements of idleness, recklessness, and servility, which are permanent."[140] Other negative characteristics, he avers, include weakness, ignorance, an absence of "moral feeling," violence, and anarchy.[141] Of course, the standards that García Calderón sets for enslaved peoples in the past, whose descendants experience discrimination in the present, are quite unattainable. Not only are enslaved peoples with painful histories of colonialism, degradation, and genocide blamed for somehow frustrating the modernizing projects of their oppressors, but García Calderón also suggests that they are "revenged for their enslavement in that their blood is mingled with that of their masters."[142] One of the many discrepancies in *Les démocraties latines de l'Amérique* is the incongruity between, on the one hand, a portrayal of blackness as a steadfast force that stubbornly persists in skin color and personal attributes, and, on the other, as the epitome of inferiority and weakness. For a supposedly vitiated, "degenerate" element, blackness is described as so vital and invigorated that it corrupts and overpowers the race that García Calderón frames as superior. In this way, he projects onto blackness both biological inferiority and power, a paradoxical diagnosis of deficiency and consumption.

For García Calderón, the so-called "race problem" is primarily a problem with blackness, which becomes an emblem and cause of a range of sociocultural and economic problems. Basing his observations on the law of concomitant variations elaborated by John Stuart Mill in *A System of Logic* (1843),[143] García Calderón identifies "a necessary relation between the numerical proportion of blacks and the intensity of civilization."[144] While glossing over the profitable venture of slavery that enriched white Latin American oligarchs and funded the national projects they spearheaded, he correlates the presence of blackness with economic insecurity. This is another example of the contradictory weak/vital dichotomy in *Les démocraties latines de l'Amérique*. The logic is as racist as it is simplistic—the presence of African diaspora begets economic instability:

> Wealth increases and internal order is greater in Argentina, Uruguay, and Chile, and it is precisely in these countries that the proportion of blacks has always been low; they have disappeared in the admixture of European races. In Cuba, Santo Domingo, and some of the republics of Central America, and certain ones of the States of the Brazilial [sic] Confederation, where the children of slaves constitute the greater portion of the population, internal disorders are continual. A black republic, Haiti, demonstrates by its revolutionary history the political incapacity of the negro race.[145]

The negative appropriation of Haiti is revealing in that it recasts political agency (the Haitian slave revolt that defeated French forces, gained independence, and successfully fended off encroachments by the British and the Spanish) as "political incapacity."[146] As Sibylle Fischer's work illustrates, the narrative of Haiti's political legacy has long been subject to refusals to acknowledge the significance of the Haitian Revolution as anything other than an illegitimate revolt, a fluke, or, to use James Martel's phrase, a misinterpellation of the tenets of the French Revolution.[147] In addition to downplaying and distorting the magnitude of Haiti's revolutionary history, García Calderón also neglects to mention the widespread sociopolitical and economic marginalization of Haiti by other nations around the globe after the Haitian Revolution—an ongoing process in which his own essay participates.[148] As Arlene Torres and Norman E. Whitten Jr. point out, there is a long history of using Haiti as the negative end of the dialectic against which *blanqueamiento* (whitening) in Latin America is constructed and refashioned:

The concept of Haiti as a nation within the popular culture of these regions by those self-identifying as "white" or "light" includes the idea of impoverishment to the point of creating an island of infra-humans. It also contains the imagery of revolts out of control, of a revolution not completed that could someday overwhelm the democracies of mainland South America. The imagery of black Haiti held by mainland South American whites (*mestizos*) suggests an undesirable power of blackness within *mestizaje* that is to be feared and controlled.[149]

To be sure, García Calderón's strategy of *blanqueamiento*, an "economic, political, and personal process," relies on a reductive dichotomy of blame (a racial scapegoat for the economic and political challenges facing Latin America) and remedy (*blanqueamiento* through Western European immigration to Latin America): "In South America civilization is dependent upon the numerical predominance of the victorious Spaniard, on the triumph of the white man over the mulatto, the black, and the Indian. Only a plentiful European immigration can re-establish the shattered equilibrium of the American races."[150] Here, García Calderón revives—not that it was by any means extinct at the time—a nation-building discourse that calls for the Europeanization of Latin America. García Calderón's advocacy for whitening the Latin American continent exemplifies Aníbal Quijano's concept of the coloniality of power in which, following independence, white elites kept in place the racial hierarchies established during the conquest and colonization and envisioned themselves in the image of Europe.[151]

As we have seen, race and economics are interconnected phenomena in *Les démocraties latines de l'Amérique*. Despite the facility with which he equates blackness with cultural barbarism and economic turmoil, García Calderón also recognizes the role played by the influx of foreign capital in the economic challenges facing Latin America. Here, García Calderón highlights the paradoxical coexistence of abundant natural resources and a lack of capital and economic autonomy in Latin America due to foreign investment and monopolization.[152] Therefore, García Calderón does not ignore the genealogy of financial colonialism in Latin America. The paradox resides in the fact that foreign loans funded revolutions for independence from Spain, but the subsequent debt burden was so great that, coupled with the unwise use of the loans by political elites, it afforded foreign interests "privileged positions" in Latin American politics and economics. He admits that European capital is responsible for the modernization of infrastructure and political stability where they exist in Latin America, however, he also recognizes that "the new continent, politically free, is economically a vassal."[153] These critiques, if we read them as such, come off as discordant when juxtaposed with the seemingly unmitigated praise García Calderón projects onto Western Europe. Nonetheless, he does recognize that without Europe, Latin American countries would not be independent or have any vestiges of stability such as transportation and trade. Furthermore, he proposes *more* European involvement in Latin America, through immigration, as the remedy for both the "problems" of race and economics, which he views as largely one and the same.

This idea illustrates what Slavoj Žižek calls the paradox of the chocolate laxative. Given that one ingests laxatives to relieve constipation, yet chocolate is an ingredient that causes constipation, Žižek argues that the product "contain[s] the agent of its own containment."[154] By framing Europe as an economic exploiter of Latin America as well as its vehicle for development, García Calderón seems to paradoxically prescribe the agent of the continent's containment. In their seminal work, *Empire* (2000), Michael Hardt and Antonio Negri summarize this mentality of economic development: "Since this is how the dominant economies developed, it must be the true path to escape the cycle of underdevelopment. This syllogism, however, asks us to believe that the laws of economic development will somehow transcend the differences of historical change."[155] García Calderón does not advocate total autonomy from outside entities, but rather promotes a Pan-Latinist ideology in order to not only reconstruct Latin American identity as white, Latin, and European, but also, in more materialist terms, improve Latin America's place on the slope of "the pyramid of global constitution" at a moment of geopolitical change.[156]

LOCATING LATINITY IN CULPABLE GEOGRAPHIES

Pan-Latinism, the idea that all Latin peoples (speakers of Romance languages) share a common culture and therefore constitute a race, was an ideology advanced with great alacrity by French and Latin American intellectuals throughout the nineteenth and early twentieth centuries. In *The Idea of Latin America*, Walter Mignolo explains that Pan-Latinism in France was inextricably bound to the politics of empire. The Louisiana Purchase (1803) and the triumph of the Haitian Revolution (1804) dealt a major blow to the French imperial project in the Americas. From the perspective of the French elite, Pan-Latinism provided a low-cost avenue to retain or regain some semblance of its former imperial prestige in the Western Hemisphere. Furthermore, it was marketed to newly independent nations as an identity based on a shared spiritual and cultural legacy capable of empowering the Latin countries on each side of the Atlantic to resist, and perhaps convince themselves that they could rival, the powerful Anglo empires of the United States and Britain.[157] For Mignolo, Latinity operated as a perplexing anti-colonialist strategy utilized by Latin American elites to "civilize" their nations by aligning their identities, histories, and interests with the prominence of Latin culture.[158] This explains why Mignolo problematizes viewing Latin American independence movements as decolonizing processes. Instead, Mignolo interprets Pan-Latinism as a mental recolonization deliberately orchestrated by specific class interests that simultaneously turned away from Spain and toward other imperial models like France.[159] In effect, some Latin American elites appropriated this imagined and idealized cultural alliance as a way of constructing themselves and the nations they supposedly represented in a more amenable way to European empires, with the objective of expediting the financial benefits and class privileges that could result from that association.

Among the first Latin Americans to publicly support the idea that Latin America was indeed "Latin" was a Colombian intellectual and diplomat living in France named José María Torres Caicedo.[160] In an 1856 poem entitled, "Las dos Américas," Torres Caicedo established a polarity of Latin peoples of Latin America defending themselves against the Anglo-Saxons of the United States. This racial binary, which was reinvigorated at the end of the nineteenth century by Paul Groussac, Rubén Darío, and Rodó, became a ubiquitous, if not dominant, paradigm that Latin American intellectuals used to think through geopolitics and cultural debates in the early decades of the twentieth century. For example, prominent figures like Rodó, Blanco-Fombona, and García Calderón, who were acutely aware of the significance of the juxtaposition of the centenary celebrations of Latin American independence and the flagrant economic and political imperialism orchestrated by the United States throughout the continent, embraced a Pan-Latinist ideology due in part to, as Carlos Alonso reminds us, "a desire to affirm a spiritual essence shared by all Latin American nations in order to oppose Pan-Americanism."[161] In other words, Pan-Latinism provided a way for Latin American intellectuals to "write back" against emerging US imperialism.[162] In addition, Pan-Latinism was, as we have already seen, a vehicle for some Latin American intellectuals and politicians to "clean up" or "whiten" their national identities, effectively circumventing their shared history of colonization, and to imagine themselves as an extension of Western Europe.

Les démocraties latines de l'Amérique received a powerful endorsement in a laudatory preface written in December of 1911 by Raymond Poincaré, a French statesman who became the prime minister of France the following month. Ernest Flammarion, the founder of what would later become Groupe Flammarion, a large publishing house in France, published García Calderón's essay in Paris a few months later in 1912. In 1913, Poincaré was elected president of France, a post he held until 1920. But Poincaré's role in García Calderón's essay is not limited to the preface: Poincaré and other members of the French political elite turn out to be the ideal readers of *Les démocraties latines de l'Amérique*.

While the benefits of Pan-Latinism were clear for Latin American intellectuals, in that they could imagine themselves as part of a prestigious and highly selective cultural heritage in order to legitimate their "acceptance on the stage of nations," what was the advantage for

Europeans to see Latin Americans as an extension of themselves?[163] As Esther Aillón Soria points out, Pan-Latinism was a strategic, not to mention paternalistic, attempt to better France's global position in the face of US hegemony.[164] García Calderón's text forwards that agenda in overt ways. However, one wonders why Western Europeans, particularly French elites, would identify with what García Calderón repeatedly refers to as a continent plagued by racial "inferiorities" and political and economic instability. In other words, how does García Calderón motivate Europe to recognize itself and its interests in Latin America?

The Pan-Latinist rhetoric in *Les démocraties latines de l'Amérique* is more complex than just emphasizing the cultural commonalities between Western Europe and Latin America. Rather, García Calderón exploits familiar racial and nationalist antagonisms in hopes of persuading his European readers, which included the soon-to-be president of France, to concern themselves with the geopolitical and economic affairs of Latin America. By strengthening ties with its cultural and spiritual kin, he maintains, Europe can benefit economically from Latin America's strategic geographical location. If Europe does not act, he insists, then other nations (the United States, Germany, and Japan) will successfully position themselves in the region and emerge as global leaders.[165]

Getting European readers to invest themselves in a purportedly inferior continent requires that García Calderón construct a creative cartography of Latin America's racial lines. First, he attempts to show that those racial, economic, and political "inferiorities" do not exist everywhere in Latin America by highlighting countries that exemplify development and progress. For example, he cites Argentina, Brazil, Chile, Peru, Bolivia, and Uruguay as countries where "wealthy peoples" (an unsubtle code for white) enjoy economic and political stability. As I have already indicated, he further emphasizes a shared Latin culture by setting it in opposition to blackness. Although recommending European whitening was perhaps intended to flatter his French readers, García Calderón also has to locate the "Latin" parts of Latin America and distinguish them from other areas where blackness and mestizaje exist (even though he glosses over or downplays the existence of non-white populations in countries like Brazil, Bolivia, and his native Peru). Therefore, the aforementioned white and developed countries "must not be confused with the republics of Central America, Haiti, or Paraguay."[166] It is no coincidence that García Calderón equates the economic and political stability of the Southern Cone countries with what he sees as their racial homogeneity, thus pitting them against other areas of Latin America in which political unrest existed.[167]

Here it is pertinent to reiterate that his treatment of Haiti in the essay is central to his argument. In fact, it participates in an ongoing process that Paul Farmer terms the "geography of blame."[168] In *AIDS and Accusation: Haiti and the Geography of Blame*, Farmer, a medical anthropologist, deconstructs the racism and processes of "exotification" that underlie discourses that blame Haitians for "infecting" the United States with HIV and AIDS.[169] We see a similar gesture, albeit in a very different context, in *Les démocraties latines de l'Amérique*. García Calderón's recurrent denigration of Haiti as, once again, a "black republic [that] demonstrates by its revolutionary history the political incapacity of the negro race," could be read as a compliment to France, whose imperial power in the Americas was truncated by the Haitian Revolution (1791–1804).[170] In this way, his critique of Haiti is a gesture meant to express his solidarity with imperial France. García Calderón motivates Europeans to identify with Latin American by divorcing the region from the African diaspora in Haiti and by giving the French economic incentives. He accomplishes the latter by emphasizing the precarious nature of Latin culture's prestige in a rapidly changing world in which countries are contending for economic and geopolitical leverage and global dominance.

Neo-Imperialism, Racial Antagonism, and Latin Displacement

Although geography makes contact between Latin America and the United States inevitable, the role of the latter grew increasingly imperialistic after the Monroe Doctrine in 1823. "Everywhere," García Calderón writes, "the Americans of the North are feared."[171] Drafted not long after Costa Rica, El Salvador, Guatemala, Honduras, Nicaragua, Ecuador, Peru, and Brazil achieved independence from Spain and Portugal in 1821–22, the Monroe Doctrine threatened military action against any European country that sought to involve itself in Latin American affairs. Emboldened first by the Platt Amendment in Cuba in 1901, and later by the Roosevelt Corollary of 1904 that stated that the United States had the right to intervene in the Western Hemisphere at any moment in order to quell any perceived instability that might facilitate or entice European interest in the region, subsequent US presidential administrations converted what was initially marketed as a defensive measure into a justification for expansionism and hemispherical hegemony. Between 1898 and 1912, the year when García Calderón published his essay, the United States had intervened politically, militarily, or financially in Cuba, Puerto Rico, Colombia, Panama, the Dominican Republic, Mexico, and Honduras: "Warnings, advice, distrust, invasion of capital, plans of financial hegemony—all these justify the anxiety of the southern peoples."[172]

García Calderón's target audience could interpret the precariousness of Latin America in a flattering way, that is, as evidence of the kind of devastation and barbarism that take place in the absence of Western European powers. But this blandishment of an imperial past, if it was indeed read as such, is by itself insufficient for convincing a European reading public—and, especially, the French political elite—of why it should concern itself with a seemingly hopeless situation across the ocean. For that reason, García Calderón frames the issue in a way that makes Latin America the center stage for an approaching global conflict, the results of which could very well determine who controls the world economy. In addition, he also suggests that the rich historical and cultural legacy of Latinity is at stake. Even if the obsolescence of Latin culture and the possibility that the nations identified with it might be left behind in the wake of modernity were credible threats, García Calderón still had to explain how Europe could possibly challenge the burgeoning industrial and military hegemony of the United States. Such a persuasion seems even more implausible if we take into account the implications of the Panama Canal, opened in 1914. Its completion symbolized the rise of the US empire and the fading of France's influence in the world, as the Compagnie Nouvelle du Canal de Panama failed to complete the project and went bankrupt in the late nineteenth century, which gave the United States the pretext to finish building the waterway.

To make matters worse, García Calderón points out that Germany and Japan also recognized the strategic importance of Latin America and were poised to challenge US hegemony in the Western Hemisphere. The mention of the geopolitical ambitions of Germany and Japan would resonate with French readers, as they were no doubt aware of English geographer Halford Mackinder's so-called "Heartland Theory" (1904), which predicted a soon-to-be empire (Germany) would take control of a "pivot area" (Asia), from which a German/Russian alliance would emerge as the world's new superpower.[173] Although he does not use Mackinder's terminology, García Calderón's sleight of hand transposes Latin America as the pivot area that "conquering and plutocratic powers" from all corners of the globe vie to occupy in order to expand their empires.[174] Moreover, he describes the convergence of competing imperial projects in Latin America in an anxious, apocalyptic tone. This "future clash" is by no means restricted to a South/North dialectic; it is conceptualized in terms of race. According to García Calderón, large-scale German immigration to the Americas since the nineteenth century could effectively defy US economic monopolization because Germans and Americans "resemble one another by race and in energy."[175] Across the other ocean, "the mysterious Orient [sends] its legions of Pacific invaders into the New World."[176] Emerging as a formidable imperialist force after its victories over China (1894–95) and Russia (1904–05), Japan, which for García Calderón is the embodiment of the "Yellow Peril," is driven by an animosity toward the United States due to territorial and commercial disagreements involving the latter nation's usurpation of the Philippines and Hawaii.[177] García Calderón warns that this tripartite onslaught—in addition to the process of impairing political sovereignty that was already evident by 1912 in various parts of Latin America—has the potential to put the intellectual and cultural legacy of Latinity in jeopardy. For that reason,

> America is . . . an essential factor of the future of the Latin nations. The destiny of France, Spain, Portugal, and Italy would be different if the 80 millions of Latin Americans were to lose their racial traditions; if in a century or two America were to pass under the sceptre of the United States, or if the Germans and Anglo-Saxons were to attack and oppress the nucleus of civilization formed by Argentina, Uruguay, and Southern Brazil.[178]

García Calderón was aware that framing Latinity as under attack from Germany, not to mention the ever-convenient alterizations of blackness and Asians, would resonate with the memories of French politicians and readers of the not-so-distant Franco-Prussian War (1870–71), a relatively brief conflict that brought about a significant shift of power in European affairs. Prussia and the North German Confederation joined forces against the French, and their victory, coupled with internal social strife in France, brought an abrupt end to the Second French Empire and its leader, Napoleon III. The Treaty of Frankfurt ended the Franco-Prussian War in May of 1871 and unified the German Empire under Wilhelm I. Included in the terms of the treaty was the relinquishment of large areas of the Alsace and Lorraine regions of France. Raymond Poincaré was a boy in Lorraine at the time of the Franco-Prussian War and chronicles his resentment toward Germany in various diary entries.[179] Thus, García Calderón, an avid student of history, was acutely aware that framing another bout of imperialism against the Latin "spirit," especially by Germany, would probably not fall on deaf ears in France.

The essay identifies the planned opening of the Panama Canal in 1914 as the powder keg capable of igniting the next major battle between imperialist powers. The route to the next important chapter in globalization and modernity, then, would run right through the middle of Latin America. This transformative event, García Calderón predicts, will essentially shrink the world by altering its trade routes, thereby "displac[ing] the political axis of the world" away from the

Atlantic Ocean and Europe toward the Pacific and whichever nations dominate it.[180] To put it succinctly, whoever controls the Pacific, controls the future. The Pacific, then, is capable of decentering a Eurocentrist interpretation of history, as well as its Latin cultural legacy. Therefore, García Calderón affirms that Latin America's geography and its large population can make significant contributions to an imagined Latin community. Since the conflict will be global in nature, he stresses that the Latin race will need as many "heirs of the Latin spirit" as possible.[181] It is noteworthy that despite the neospiritualist literary tendencies he embraced in his youth, which tended to elude the subject of race, García Calderón was also, as we have seen, obsessed with racialized scientism. Moreover, he conceptualizes the protagonists and antagonists in the approaching imperialist rivalry in terms of race. This change in perspective, he insists, is a sign of the times, as other countries around the world are uniting and seeing themselves as races instead of as nations:

> Flourishing on every hand, we see Pan-Slavism, Pan-Islamism, Pan-Asianism, Pan-Germanism, Pan-Latinism—barbarous words which give an indication as to the struggles of the future. . . . Slavs, Saxons, Latins, and Mongols are contending for the possession of the world. It is thus that the drama of history becomes simplified; above the quarrels of precarious nations are rising the profound antagonisms of millennial races.[182]

Transatlantic Latinity, then, is an inevitable reality of the current geopolitical climate. It is important to note that García Calderón is not the only voice championing the cause of Pan-Latinity in the text. French politicians of the highest offices also lend their support. In addition to Raymond Poincaré's laudatory preface, García Calderón cites the favorable impressions of South America by the former prime minister of France Georges Clemenceau. After concluding his first term as prime minister (1906–09), Clemenceau traveled to South America in 1910, where he was dazzled by the prominence of French culture in Buenos Aires, Montevideo, and Rio de Janeiro. In his essay, García Calderón cites Clemenceau's admiration of Latinity in South America, and insists that "[a] new energy, undeniable material progress, and a creative faith announce the advent, in the new continent . . . , of wealthy nations, rich in industry and agriculture; of a continent in which the exhausted Latin world may renew itself."[183] For García Calderón's project, which above all proposed Latin America as a necessary pillar for a global Latin alliance, referencing Clemenceau was an effective maneuver.

Like Poincaré, Clemenceau was staunchly anti-German and his relentless efforts to disarm and defund Germany during the Paris Peace Conference years later earned him the nickname *Le Tigre*.[184] García Calderón, of course unaware of what would be Clemenceau's key role in World War I in the coming years, takes advantage of the revanchist attitudes and policies of distinguished figures of the French state by floating the possibility that Germany, which still retained French territories from the Franco-Prussian War, could occupy other "Latin" lands overseas, thereby placing the proverbial nail in the coffin of the Latin race. *Les démocraties latines de l'Amérique* is thus bookended by the soon-to-be president of France's prologue and a conclusion that incorporates a recent French prime minister. The Peruvian is not making the case for Pan-Latinity by himself, for his essay is in direct contact and dialogue with the highest powers of the French state.

The *arielista* imaginary in García Calderón's essay points to a Latin Americanism whose locus of enunciation emanates from within, and seemingly for, the French government; is written in French; and, moreover, criticizes US, German, and Japanese imperialism in Latin America while at the same time advocating for Western European cultural and economic interventions.[185] The paradox of this "neocolonial pact" suggests that *Les démocraties latines de l'Amérique* is not an anti-imperialist text, if we understand the label as connoting an "us" versus "them" scenario (or "our autonomy" in the face of "their imperialism"), but rather the embodiment of variegated forms of colonial domination that persist in modernity.[186] In fact, at several moments in the text García Calderón cites favorable examples of the Latin imperialist spirit, such as Christopher Columbus and the French colonization in Africa. The question for García

Calderón is not Latin American sovereignty, but rather whose economic intervention can usher Latin America into a more prominent global standing. In other words, García Calderón seems to reinforce the periphery as such in exchange for "the promised admission of Latin America as the belated guest in the feast of Western civilization"—or, perhaps, as Ramón Grosfoguel suggests, in the hopes of attaining a semiperipherical status in the world-order system.[187] When García Calderón employs the idea of Latinity in order to connect Latin America's historical trajectory to that of Europe, he subscribes to what Enrique Dussel has called the "developmental fallacy" that holds that Latin America's autonomy can one day become a reality only by following—which is to say being dependent on—"developed" European nations.[188] As we have seen, García Calderón promotes Pan-Latinism as a way of reanimating, and indeed idealizing, the imperial pasts of France and England, which strengthens an Occidentalist geopolitical imaginary mutually reinforced by modernity and coloniality.

Despite García Calderón's attempt to exploit the cultural and geopolitical antagonisms between France and Germany that had existed since the Franco-Prussian War, as well as those between French imperialism and the Haitian Revolution, it appears as if his intended audience, the French power brokers, resisted seeing Latin America as an extension of European Latinity. Even Poincaré admitted that he was unconvinced by García Calderón's suggestion that a metropolis in the Southern Cone could one day become the center of the Latin world: "a Frenchman may be forgiven for refusing to believe that the capital of classic culture will ever pass from Paris to Buenos Aires, as it has passed from Rome to Paris."[189] In fact, much of Poincaré's preface talks about the Peruvian's Pan-Latinist convictions, not his or his country's support of them. Furthermore, Poincaré, whose platform focused largely on financial and social stability, even if only in appearance, was not persuaded by the idea that strengthening a transatlantic Pan-Latinist pact could advance France's economy in any significant manner.[190] It is important to note that only five years earlier Poincaré, as a member of *L'académie française*, was actively involved in promoting Pan-Latinist projects in Latin America.[191] However, those projects were aimed at strengthening cultural and academic ties, not economic ones. As a result, García Calderón's project seems doomed from the start. The authoritative eclipse carried out by Poincaré's preface, which praises García Calderón's Pan-Latinist sentiments but does not endorse them financially or politically, can be read as a manifestation of the European hegemony for which García Calderón actively calls throughout his essay. This gesture undermines García Calderón's Pan-Latinist negotiations before the reader has the chance to consider them on their own terms.

In this way, García Calderón's deployment of Pan-Latinity back-fires, revealing its insufficiencies, and, above all, its paradoxes. In addition to the racist rendering of blackness, which he framed as a cultural and economic void to be filled by Latinness, his essay also performs a divisive brand of Latin Americanism that disrupts the unifying goals of that identity discourse by advancing blackness as a disqualifying criterion of Latin belonging. At the same time, the Peruvian essayist fails to see how his own text contradicts the political objectives of sovereignty inherent in Latin Americanist projects of the time. Even though García Calderón affords importance to Latin America by casting it as ground zero for *the* large-scale geopolitical conflict of the new century (the opening of the Panama Canal), he imagines the region primarily through the imperialist mediations of other nations. In short, he critiques one imperialist gesture while petitioning another. In other words, *Les démocraties latines de l'Amérique* promotes a subaltern position for Latin America by repeating a pattern of alterization originally carried out during conquest and colonization by which racialized diagnostics and developmentalist ideologies, as Ramón Grosfoguel contends, "concealed European and Euro-American responsibility in the exploitation of these continents. The construction of 'pathological' regions in the periphery, as opposed to the 'normal' development patterns of the West, justified an even more intense political and economic intervention from imperial powers."[192]

Les démocraties latines de l'Amérique certainly evidences a "nostalgia for the greatness of empire" based on, as I have argued, an economy of Pan-Latin whiteness.[193] This ideology of whiteness is an intermediary space striving to distance itself from blackness in Latin America, while at the same time seeking to strengthen ties with the imperial source of its imagined Latin cultural identity. In other words, blackness is utilized as an antithesis against which Latinity (in France as well as in Latin America) constructs and reinforces itself. The idea of unity in García Calderón's text discounts blackness, indigeneity, and *mestizaje*, in order to imagine a Latin American identity that is, or desires to be, exclusively Latin and white. While in *Ariel* Rodó avoids delving into the dissonant racial past and present of Latin America in order to advocate a selective, harmonious vision for the continent, García Calderón's approach is more racially focused, global in scope, and seemingly less concerned about cultural autonomy in a strict sense. Race, in other words, is an axis that transcends other categories. Yet, for García Calderón, race and geopolitics are inseparable phenomena, and modernity and development rely on racial scapegoats that reinforce a shared currency of Pan-Latin whiteness. Speaking through a code of an idealized imperial past recreates and bolsters colonial racialization, centered on paradoxical uses of blackness and racial antagonisms involving Germany and Japan, at a significant historical moment for thinking about the Latin American continent, its identity, and its place in the world—that is, the time between the centenary of Latin American independence and the completion of the Panama Canal. Read against this backdrop, García Calderón's essay underscores the ways in which the economy of whiteness functions as a racial strategy that depends on the blatant devaluation of blackness in order to reinvigorate idealizations of a Eurocentric imperial past that blur the lines between autonomy and alterity.

As we have seen, in addition to commemorating a formal political milestone that set Latin American apart from Europe, the centenary was also a racial project that recentered Europeanness. Paying close attention to the personal and collective investments in transatlantic processes of proximity, simulation, and disavowal evidences a will to whiteness rife with insecurities from subjects whose own white identities were perceived as less than or suspect. In order to stack the deck in their favor, *arielista* intellectuals marketed their respective associations with chimerical racial purity as antithetical to global blackness. Therefore, so-called white Latin American countries are really an extension of France since they are not like Haiti. Sicilians are Argentines because they are so different from Africans. Where would whiteness be without such comparative, not to mention convenient, stipulations? Dissecting such pursuits of the "Latin ideal"—which meant navigating being, seeming, believing, and desiring in conjunction with the politics of imperialism, nationalism, and immigration—brings into focus the hemispheric distortions and transoceanic reconfigurations of white supremacist ideologies and imaginaries in the *arielista* archive.[194]

CHAPTER 2

Tethered Transcendence

Juvenescence, Introspection, Illumination

No strong education of intelligence can be founded
on naïve isolation or on voluntary ignorance. [. . .] The
strength of our heart should test itself by accepting the
Sphinx's challenge, not dodging its formidable questioning.

JOSÉ ENRIQUE RODÓ, *Ariel*

IN A SERIES of lectures collected under the title *The True Life*
(2017), Alain Badiou asks what an old man like him, and philosophy in general, has to say to young people today. Badiou speaks of
change rather than consent and urges students to find the "true life"
of disinterestedness, which stands in opposition to the "false life"
constituted by money and power.[1] Badiou's words, which unambiguously echo Rodó's visionary project of youth agency in the very same
year as the centenary of the latter's death, manifest the distinction
between interpellation and self-articulation at the heart of *arielismo*.
On the one hand, *Ariel* is a monologue disguised as a dialogue, a
lecture or sermon that the students in the fictionalized classroom
silently consume. At the same time, it was pivotal in fueling student

activism and political protagonism throughout Latin America in the twentieth century. Such a contrast between the prescriptive and the emancipatory, the illusory and the real, is also evident in Walter Benjamin's early writings (1910–1917) targeting the "new youth" of Germany, which parallel—both in terms of chronology and content— the spiritualist campaign associated with *arielismo* in Latin America.

In articles written between 1912 and 1915, Benjamin, who was in his early twenties, argues that the thoughts and actions of young people are not their own, but rather residuals from those that came before them. As such, it is incumbent that youth develop a new consciousness, find their own voice, and "by means of knowledge, . . . liberate the future from its deformation in the present."[2] The university, then, must be transformed into "a site of permanent spiritual revolution" founded in freedom and "new ways of questioning."[3] Enacting a "deeper life," no doubt analogous to Badiou's "true life," requires a spiritual awakening and recognition that "from youth alone radiates new spirit, *the* spirit."[4] In Benjamin's articles, the mind joins forces with the spirit as catalysts of reform, rather than adversarial sources of cynicism or relativity: "[T]here is truth, even if all previous thought has been in error."[5]

The interplay of introspection, illumination, and ideals that emerges in Badiou and Benjamin's respective exhortations were also central tenets of *arielista* emancipatory discourses that targeted young people. In addition to commemorating the past, the centenary was also a moment for intellectuals to encourage youth to modify or replace outdated ideas, doxa, and norms. Of course, this recommendation did not appear out of nowhere in the early twentieth century. Andrés Bello, for example, emphasized the importance of young people's "independence of thought" back in 1848, a recurring trope of what Rafael Rojas terms, in relation to Rodó's *Ariel*, the "language of youth."[6] What is noteworthy, however, is how frequent and fervent those calls for epistemological integrity became around 1910.

Executing such a monumental endeavor required interpellating a new young subject whose multidimensional characteristics Rodó clearly outlined in *Ariel*:

Ariel is the empire of reason and feeling over the base stimulus of irrationality; it is generous enthusiasm, lofty and disinterested motive in action, the spirituality of culture, vigor and grace of intelligence, the ideal objective to which a select portion of humanity rises, rectifying in the superior man the tenacious vestiges of Caliban, the symbol of sensuality and dimness, with the persistent chisel of life.[7]

This often-cited passage shows that Rodó attempts to synthesize the rational and the spiritual into a utopic corrective. In other words, the "superior" subject hailed in *Ariel* must integrate both the mind and the spirit in their vitalist undertaking. Yet, in identifying the sources of empowerment and exemplarity, the spiritual takes precedent over the epistemological, both in terms of the text's handling of those two phenomena as well as in the reading public's reception of Rodó's project. While the longevity of this intrinsic, and notoriously unresolved, feature of *Ariel*—that is, the middle ground between, on the one hand, the integrity of the truth value of ideas and, on the other, reclaiming the "spirit of religiosity" that operates outside of materialist conceptions of existence and morality—can be attributed in part to Rodó's mystical rhetoric, that issue also ripples through *arielista* essays in less magical ways.[8]

While the routine reading of *Ariel*, and by default of *arielista* essays, understands them as harmonizing forums through which vague concepts like truth, rationality, spirit, introspection, intuition, illumination, and ideals seamlessly merge to form a totalizing project of superior self-fashioning, and collective development, I pay special attention to the particular inflections and tensions in *arielista* texts that reveal not the limitless potential and unflawed nature of transcendent discourses aimed at youth, but rather their precarious constructions. The essays by Carlos Arturo Torres, Manuel Ugarte, Carlos Vaz Ferreira, and Antonio Caso that I examine in this chapter attempt to create a secular, discursive, empowering space for youth to recognize the need to diminish the Catholic Church's monopoly on the discussion and practices of moral conduct and an ethical life for youth and the masses, which leads them to emphasize integrity, transcendence, heroism, superiority, truth, and futurity, all components of that era's "cult of the Ideal."[9] Whereas at the turn of the century *Ariel* projected an optimistic aura of coalescence, the *arielistas* grappled with putting their respective political and pedagogical strategies into practice in a straightforward and symmetrical way. Since the expectations and exigencies that politicians, radicals, and professors made on young people's mind, spirits, and conduct at the centenary are replete with compromises and contradictions, the centenary subject had to decode mixed messages with respect to combatting ideology, performing introspection, and achieving autonomy.

Therefore, this chapter seeks to discern and demystify both the rational and spiritual stipulations at play in *arielismo* with respect to negotiations of reason, religiosity, instinct, and intuition—the routes through which *arielista* intellectuals advise young people to activate exemplary illumination in an empowering quest toward truth. Spanning hyperpartisan political climates in postwar Colombia, antiimperialist campaigns from Buenos Aires to New York, and university classrooms in Montevideo and Mexico City, the following four parts of this chapter delineate how epistemological imaginings and spiritual interpellations of the centenary subject replaced religion with ideals and ethics, which offered only a "fragile transcendence," as another Uruguayan renaissance man, Alberto Methol Ferré, pointed out in 1969.[10] Rather than repeat insistent claims about the sublime character of *arielismo*'s transcendence, this chapter brings to light its discontinuities and tenuous enactments that reframe the ways in which the quintessential tropes of enlightenment and empowerment are construed in the *arielista* archive.

This chapter is divided into two interrelated yet discrete sections, each of which make evident how *arielista* political and pedagogical programs rhetorically tether the lofty goals they envision to the very phenomena they seek to amend, overcome, or resolve. In the first section, I argue that Colombian politician Carlos Arturo Torres, whose place in the pantheon of the history of ideas is solidified as a model of dispassionate rationality and tolerance, replicates the class antagonisms that his work proclaims to expunge, which, following Wendy Brown, suggests that tolerance is not transcendence, but rather another form of aversion. Next, I deconstruct Argentine anti-imperialist crusader Manuel Ugarte's begrudging acquiescence to religiosity, despite having previously railed against its nefarious influence in Latin American life. This dramatic shift, I argue, is reminiscent of Friedrich Nietzsche's retrograde step, which holds that breaking with the past by means of secular enlightenment is a form of heroism that strives for absolute epistemological autonomy, but ultimately recognizes the impossibility of its collective enactment. Reconsidering both the equanimous character of Torres's reconciliatory avowals and the efficaciousness of Ugarte's radical aims brings much needed nuance to established scripts of Latin American intellectual history.

The second section of this chapter juxtaposes the free-thinking pedagogies of two prominent *arielista* university professors, Carlos Vaz Ferreira (Uruguay) and Antonio Caso (Mexico), whose influential lecture notes–turned books came about during a period of intensified Pan-American evangelical missions that actively sought to shape the character of young men in Latin America according to Protestant principles. My argument here is that the disparate introspective paths to enlightenment that they model for their students, while meticulous, harbor opacities and absolutisms that are at odds with the transcendent desires we attribute to *arielista* pedagogies. In the first part of this section, I scrutinize how Vaz Ferreira, who identifies two ideological hinderances to disinterested pursuits of knowledge and facts (immediacy and mystification), proposes "good hyperlogical sense" as a remedy for unraveling the knottiest epistemological and ethical quandaries, but does not offer specific guidelines for students to develop that instinct, thereby leaving the key to illumination enigmatic and ultimately inconclusive. In contrast, I illustrate how for Caso intuitive immediacy is the mainstay of an introspective pedagogy that eschews impartial epistemological truth in favor of a mystical logic that binds the subject to intransigent notions of Christian faith and sacrifice.

Carlos Arturo Torres: (In)tolerance and Affirmation

In the lead-up to the 1910 centenary celebrations of Colombia's independence, there was little doubt about which historical figure would mark and memorialize the occasion: "The Liberator" Simón Bolívar. At that pivotal moment of remembering and reckoning, Colombian writer and diplomat Carlos Arturo Torres wondered if such a monument contradicted the very events, qualities, and ideals that it meant to symbolize. Citing a "mental tendency" to conflate Bolívar and independence, which overlooks all of the anonymous people who thought, fought, and made possible the achievements that get attributed to a lone representative figure, Torres underscores the need to curb this type of monolithic "herolatría," or hero worship.[11] As such, Torres sees the centenary not as a moment to remember and revere his nation's foundational myths and figures—and by extension the ideas, opinions, and facts of what we believe and know to be true—but rather to actively interrogate them in *Ídola fori* (1909), which Aníbal González classifies as the "first serious study of the role of ideology in Spanish American culture and politics."[12]

In the prologue to *Ídola fori*, Francisco García Calderón refers to Torres as a "director of free thinkers" who is part of a "small prophetic group" of elevated philosophers in Latin America (presumably the *arielistas*).[13] *Ídola fori* borrows its title from one of the four "idols of the mind" (*idola mentis*) that English philosopher Francis Bacon scrutinizes in his *Novum Organum* (1620): the idols of the marketplace, which comprise "those formulas or ideas—real political superstitions—that continue to prevail in the spirit even after a rational criticism has proven their falsity."[14] The primary problem facing Colombia, and by extension Latin America, that Torres addresses is the "mental stagnation (*anquilosis*) . . . that rejects any modification, correction, analysis, and progress," which he insists can be remedied through "liberat[ing], to the extent possible, the human mind from the iron molds of preconception."[15] In his lengthy treatise, Torres dissects two competing categories of the epistemological contours of the Latin American mind: *inconsciencia*, constituted by superstitions and hardline convictions, and, conversely, *conciencia*, which prioritizes mental independence rooted in evolutionary logics of change and flux. Relativity and tolerance are correctives to what he considers a "misfortune of our mental formation [that] exists in us as a native impulse the tendency to elevate to the category of indisputable truth whatever idea is consecrated by trends or by the hermetic faith in the preaching of our spiritual directors."[16]

At the center of Torres's project is the cultivation of a "principle of critical independence." This impartial gauge for rendering disinterested judgment on any matter, he writes, rises from the ashes of the prestige of scientific certainties of yesterday "full of vigorous youth."[17] Youth is both the rhetorical axis and intended audience of *Ídola fori*, since, Torres points out, each generation forges new ideas, which lead to new truths that are a reflection of the "authentic mark of their mentality."[18] In other words, young people are uniquely positioned to create new ways of thinking and doing that are not beholden to cynical motives, traditional formulas, and restrictive paradigms. For a book that is credited as a pioneering, extended analysis of ideology in Latin America, and one that so unambiguously emphasizes the necessity for youth to forge epistemological autonomy and integrity, there appears throughout the pages of Torres's book a tension between modernizing the mind, on the one hand, and moderation, on the other. This issue comes into particular focus through the circuitous and contentious implications of his treatment of the concept of tolerance as it relates to the masses and their role in democratic reforms in postwar Colombia, which, I argue, sheds light on the internal strains of *arielista* synthesis, thereby complicating *Ídola fori*'s reputation as a model of serenity.

CIVIL WAR AND CENTENNIAL COLOMBIA

Torres's ambitious objective of modernizing the mind is not an abstract exercise. Rather, it emerges from a period of national reckoning stemming from sectarian splits between tradition and modernity, as well as conflict and cooperation. The Colombian political landscape of the second half of the nineteenth century was defined by hyperpartisan conflict between Conservatives, who favored a centralized, religious state, and a traditional agrarian economy, and Liberals, who preferred stronger regional governments, separation of church and state, and a modernized monetary and trade system. Those scuffles, however, were by no means restricted to rhetorical posturing in the legislative chambers. Rather, they played out in numerous regional revolts and six civil wars (1860, 1875, 1876, 1885, 1895), and culminated in the devastating Guerra de los Mil Días (1899–1902), which claimed upward of 100,000 victims and ravaged the country's already waning economy.[19] The Conservative party's policies of *Regeneración* (1878–1898), which blended positivism and Catholic fundamentalism into one absolutist governing formula, instituted an extreme centralism that gave the head of state virtually unchallenged authority to appoint local and national officials. This essentially wiped Liberals off the legislative map for many years. President Rafael Núñez codified the *"regeneracionista"* vision in a new Constitution in 1886, a document drafted by his predecessor, Miguel Antonio Caro, who continued this policy until *los Mil Días*. The Constitution of 1886 affirmed the power of the Catholic Church in national matters such as education and censure of dissidence. Excluded from politics, targeted as dissidents, and frustrated by the Conservative party's refusal to update antiquated monetary and trade systems that had stifled the country's import/export economy, many radical liberals took up arms against the government.

As the latter stages of the conflict became concentrated in the liberal stronghold of the Colombian isthmus of Panama, the United States, citing article 35 of the Mallarino-Bidlack Treaty of 1846 that allowed it to ensure free transit, intervened. Of course, President Theodore Roosevelt realized the strategic importance for the United States in the Panama Canal, which by that point was well under construction by a French company. In fact, ownership of the Canal was one of the most important facets of the peace accord of 1902, which, significantly, was signed on board the US battleship Wisconsin. On the heels of the peace accord, in January 1903, the United States quickly negotiated and signed the Hay-Herrán Treaty, which granted the United States sole jurisdiction over the canal zone for a

century. However, due to disagreements about monetary compensa-
tion and the nation's compromised sovereignty, the Colombian sen-
ate rejected it. Momentarily deterred, the United States sought an
alternate route by supporting an uprising in Panama, which seceded
from Colombia in November of 1903. Within two weeks, the Hay-
Bunau-Varilla Treaty secured US ownership and control of the canal.
Years later, in 1909, the Root-Cortés-Arosemena Treaties—which
formally recognized Panamanian independence, set terms for border disputes, compensations, and Colombian usage of railways and
the future canal—generated public outrage and increased already
fervent anti-American sentiments in Colombia. This culminated in
the resignation of conservative president Rafael Reyes (1904–1909),
whose platform of peace and harmony was undermined by his auto-
cratic ploys, which explains why Torres seized that moment to make
a plea for national reconciliation.

Peace and harmony as redemptive, albeit elusive, remedies for
Colombia could not be flatly relinquished. Nor could they be nothing more than hollow concepts. Instead, Torres's treatise recommended a dose of rationality in order to see beyond empty gestures,
interrogate invested words, curb recurring authoritarianisms, and,
ultimately, reconstruct a nation with fissured ideological and geopolitical contours, and recast it in a calmer and more discerning
mold. Rodó was a productive source for him to do so. But deci-
phering competing truth claims, and legitimating the authority that
derives from them, is not an issue so easily solved. After all, the
Regeneration claimed to be the sole purveyor of the big picture, "la
verdadera verdad," the real truth, which amounted to a totalitarian
system in which the State and the Catholic Church became an inseparable entity.[20] Such a political tactic by conservatives made any challenge to the State's authority tantamount to an allegation against
the legitimacy of the Catholic faith, or at least this was the counter
argument conservatives had in their quiver. Liberals were outraged
at the constitutionalized persecution of scientific and intellectual
thought, the censorship of newspapers expressing anti-conservative
ideas, as well as the Church's stewardship of public education, and
saw the Regeneration's "Christianization" or "Catholicization" of the

Colombian government as counterproductive to the cultural and economic aims of a modern democratic society.

The centenary was an auspicious moment to mitigate the fanaticisms that had defined the preceding decades, take critical stock of how people think and what they believe, and elevate, on the base of rationality, tolerance as the pinnacle of national aspirations. As a moderate liberal writer who served as a diplomat for conservative administrations in Paris, Liverpool, Madrid, and Caracas, Torres was uniquely suited to address such issues, and *Ídola fori* is the exemplary forum where these initiatives take shape.

BETWEEN RECONCILIATION AND ROTATION: APORIAS OF RELATIVITY AND EVOLUTION

Ídola fori targeted mental atavisms, interrogated the ties that bind knowledge, truth, belief, and accuracy, and recommended updating outdated ideas.[21] Above all, this insistence on the urgent need for "mental evolution" recognizes the centrality of the notion of historical relativity.[22] Since even the most definitive conclusions are constantly subject to scrutiny, alterability, and exhaustion, it is inevitable that "Yesterday's truth thereby becomes today's disturbing preconception; the invigorating and productive principle degenerates into a kind of dark prison of the mind."[23] Times change, and so too do the truth narratives that accompany and define them.[24]

Even though the very notion of truth is at stake, Torres is far from oppositional in his critiques. Rather, "The emblem of the spirit of correction is a chisel, not a pickaxe; its message is one of improvement (*perfeccionamiento*), not destruction (*aniquilación*)."[25] Since Torres is easily one of the most recognizable *arielistas*, it is no coincidence that the word "chisel" (*cincel*) appears twice in the opening scene of Rodó's *Ariel*. As other critics have pointed out, the violent effects of Prospero's authoritative delivery, which sculpts the ethical contours of his young subjects, do not really gel with the teacher's purported serene methods and aims.[26] But the same cannot be said about Torres, whose stance is unwaveringly rooted in the spirit of "tolerance and liberty."[27] While it is true that "correcting" or "rectifying" unambiguously imply updating or replacing things that are no longer accurate or viable, and would perhaps therefore inherently include a sense of justified disdain for what preceded them, *Ídola fori* insists on "conciliation and harmony" (*conciliación y concordancia*), which make Torres's essay a sterling example of *arielista* serenity and idealism.[28]

Rodó even wrote an enthusiastic article supporting *Ídola fori* entitled "Rumbos nuevos," in which he praises Torres's message of tolerance. Yet, Rodó affords relatively little space to a direct analysis of *Ídola fori* and instead explicates, as he had done in *Ariel*, neospiritualist tendencies in Latin America that seek to supersede the realms of positivism. Although Rodó enumerates various criticisms against positivism, he does not remain silent about its favorable contributions to Latin American thought:

The positivist initiation left in us, in speculative matters as well as practical and action-oriented ones, its powerful sense of relativity; the exact consideration of earthly realities; the vigilance and insistence of the critical spirit; mistrust of absolutist affirmations; respect for the conditions of time and place; the careful adaptation of means and ends; the recognition of the value, of the act itself and the slow and patient effort evident in every type of endeavor; scorn for gullible intentions, sterile outbursts and futile anticipations.[29]

Yet, as a sole analytical lens, positivism was insufficient, which is why Rodó mobilized a young generation of Latin Americans to seek higher spiritual ideals outside of its confines: "Positivism, which is the cornerstone of our intellectual formation, is no longer the crown that defines it."[30]

However, counteracting positivism's hegemony with neospiritualist idealism is not a case of simply substituting the former for the latter, but rather of complementing positivism's advances while curbing its excesses. But as *Ídola fori* unfolds, modernizing the mind takes a backseat to moderation, which generates a recurring centrism: "there is religious fanaticism as well as irreligious fanaticism;

superstitions of faith as well as those of reason; idolatry of tradition as well as of science; intransigence of the old as well as of the new; theological despotism and national despotism; conservative and liberal incomprehension."[31] This hesitancy to stake a claim accounts for some rather noteworthy discrepancies over the course of his essay. For example, whereas early in the text Torres asserts that "Any conviction is slavery," he later advocates, "rational and perfectible convictions."[32]

Straddling the fence is a neospiritualist calling card, but it is noteworthy how often and overtly Torres's prioritization of relativity as a guiding principle curtails his otherwise staunch advocacy of critical thought and mental autonomy. On the one hand, this tendency to oscillate, without resolving or even addressing the ensuing incongruencies between claims, could be read as part of what he calls "The rotation of ideas" which "implies . . . successive and incessant demolitions and restorations."[33] To demolish ideology, only to bring back, reinstate, repair, and return it to its former condition (all the significations of *restaurar*), suggests that the nature of the "rotación" has more to do with shuffling than overturning. This could explain why he goes to such lengths to avoid interrogating one of the primary ideological dimensions of religion. As we will see, instead of divesting religion of its dogmatic effects, as he does so explicitly with politics, Torres suppresses his rational criteria, which value autonomy and accuracy, by lending staunch support for religiosity.

But he does not go it alone. His preferred method for circumventing a clear stance with respect to the rift between reason and religiosity, which is ultimately a matter of truth and belief, is to let other philosophers do it for him. In addition to tapping the usual neospiritualist stalwarts like William James and Henri Bergson, whose work offered idealistic antidotes to positivism's rigid materialist and deterministic explanations of human life, *Ídola fori* also takes its cues from other European thinkers who walk a fine line between rational critiques of religious dogma and a profound reverence for religiously derived mindsets, affects, and practices. One of his constant reliances is British sociologist Benjamin Kidd, whose *Social Evolution* (1894) stresses the civil importance of religion, in the form of the pursuit of higher ideals, and not the veracity of its doctrines. Similarly, Ernest Renan's theological rejections of Christianity and the divinity of Jesus Christ, coupled with his defense of the social utility of religious feelings, help Torres engage critiques of religion without denigrating its historical, sociological, and psychological value to human existence. But what of the issue of accuracy of religious beliefs and the authenticity of the moral codes that derive from them? For this, Torres turns to Belgian writer Maurice Maeterlinck, whose essay, "Our Anxious Morality" (1907), reflects on the secularizing trend of the modern era:

> The hour seems to be striking at which many will ask themselves whether, by continuing to practice a lofty and noble morality in an environment that obeys other laws, they be not disarming themselves too artlessly and playing the ungrateful part of dupes. They wish to know if the motives that still attach them to the older virtues are not merely sentimental, traditional and illusionary; and they seek somewhat vainly within themselves for the supports which reason may yet lend them.[34]

The dilemma of veracity, then, centers on reason as, on the one hand, a source of productive doubt and, on the other, an insufficient mechanism for conclusively resolving it.

In such a conundrum, one option is to forgo truth in favor of belief. Or, to put it another way, ideals rely not on their verity, but rather the act of affirming their possibilities. At the same time, hegemony thrives on consent to artificial constructs. For Torres,

> It can be affirmed that between a wrong belief and the total lack of all belief, a comprehensive spirit will never hesitate; in the bright red, fertile plains of our rivers, not yet cleared by the colonist's axe, depraved plants and damned herbs poison the air with their aroma of death; however, a day will come when the plow will penetrate there and from the lush ground that the laborer's work transformed, a harvest of blessing will emerge; such is the promise of the future.[35]

Implied in this *arielista*-tinged language is the idea that "un espíritu comprensivo"—a telling label for Torres's targeted subject—should prioritize understanding in the sense of tolerance of belief, not accuracy of truth. In the concluding chapter of his book Torres justifies this choice—believe anything over lack of belief—by ironically maintaining that the goal of contemporary thought is precision not paralysis. Much to the detriment of his stated objective of cultivating an autonomous critical mindset, Torres insists that neospiritualist philosophy seeks to "show the atom of truth that can exist even in the most absurd of beliefs."[36] The unresolved ambiguities in Torres's argument not only point to an unraveling of his primary thesis in *Ídola fori*, but also indicate that perhaps verisimilitude, and not truth, suffices. For a project intent on expunging idols and dogmas, the relativization of truth, which subsequently gives way to its near obsolescence, presents an unresolved quandary.

Likewise remarkable is his credulous position with respect to how contentious ideological and religious issues get resolved. He seems to underestimate the power of ideology, arguing that "the *Idols of the Forum* will disappear to the extent that it is necessary for the progress of the human spirit."[37] Similarly, "Religious problems tend to find ample solutions of enlightened tolerance and of mutual respect for the intimate jurisdiction of consciousness."[38] A silver bullet of sorts, tolerance is a hands-off antidote, seemingly subject only to the unforeseeable whims of historical evolution. This time heals all wounds approach is akin to punting the ball on putting tangible reforms into motion. Moreover, under the pretense of rationality, tolerance offers a way of saying everything abstractly, but ultimately very little tangibly (which is an issue at the heart of neospiritualism's disagreements with positivism). Maeterlinck reinforces this porous middle ground in *Ídola fori* by amalgamating the lines that divide rationality from other phenomena: "that strange fluid that we call thought, intelligence, understanding, reason, soul, spirit, brain power, virtue, beauty, knowledge, because it goes by a thousand names, even though it is only one essence."[39] Dissolving mind, spirit, and matter into one ambiguous category exemplifies a neospiritualist stance careful not to rock the boat in the wake of a choppy era of hyperpartisanship.

But at what point does quiescence itself take on contentious aspects of ideology? In *Regulating Aversion: Tolerance in the Age of Identity and Empire,* Wendy Brown examines such suspicions, and avers that "tolerance does not offer resolution or transcendence, but only a strategy for coping."[40] The exigencies for a person in Torres's situation—a diplomat seeking a middle ground, urging tolerance so as to turn the page on decades of brutal civil strife—are understandable, but they need not be taken solely at face value. Before we hasten to laud Torres as a progressive man of the people, we should consider the possibility that what is intended as an inclusive and harmonious remedy to a contentious sociopolitical situation, can instead be read as a postponement of those very aims.[41] In fact, there is an ominous undercurrent to Torres's deployment of tolerance, which, as Brown points out, is an ineludible facet of that concept: "The cultivation of tolerance as a political end implicitly constitutes a rejection of politics as a domain in which conflict can be productively articulated and addressed, a domain in which citizens can be transformed by their participation."[42]

Ídola fori's stature—as a text that seeks to balance respect for differing beliefs, dispel outdated superstitions, and galvanize wider democratic representation and participation—seemingly flies in the face of Brown's assertions. However, even though Brown's scrutiny of tolerance focuses on its usage in contemporary multiculturalist settings, its applicability to Torres's text and time facilitates looking behind what appearances conceal, just as *Ídola fori* purports to do. Perhaps tolerance is the means to combat ideology whose endgame is itself a return to closely related tenets. According to Brown, tolerance should not be confused with gleeful acceptance. Conversely, "Despite its pacific demeanor, tolerance is an internally unharmonious term, blending together goodness, capaciousness, and conciliation with discomfort, judgment, and aversion. Like patience, tolerance is necessitated by something one would prefer did not exist. It involves managing the presence of the undesirable, the tasteless, the faulty—even the revolting, repugnant, or vile."[43] Dislike, then, is an inherent facet of tolerance, no matter how serene the tone or vision, which may account for Torres's problematic treatment of the masses in *Ídola fori.*

CONSTRAINTS OF COMMONALITY

In "Rumbos nuevos," Rodó applauds Torres's emphasis on equilibrium, but also criticizes his lagging support for the implicit authority of "legitimate aristocracies of the spirit, for the orientation and government of the collective conscience."[44] Such an assertion may make one wonder just how closely Rodó read *Ídola fori.* Torres takes issue with venerating lone figures to the detriment of all those who tend to be omitted from national narratives, and even refers to the masses as "the essential grain of the greatness of nations."[45] However, his positive views on the masses prove to be momentary exceptions. Far more frequent are portrayals of the masses as incapable of transcending their retrograde instinctive impulses.[46] His dehumanizing description is anything but serene and inclusive: "the impulse of the masses represents how much thoughtlessness and irrationality there are in human actions; . . . to want to put an atom of reason near those instinctual impulses would be like trying to argue with an earthquake or convince a hurricane."[47] Basing his assertions largely on Gustave Le Bon's widely influential study on social psychology, *Psychologie des Foules* (1895), Torres reveals a fear of the crowd's unbridled desires, and therefore disqualifies their ability to understand, much less chart, reasonable, moral, and nonviolent courses of action within a national framework.

According to Torres, the masses "are a shapeless spirit and an obscure and primitive conscience from where truth and justice do not emanate except in rare cases, in momentary gusts, in fickle and ephemeral inspirations."[48] Given these mental and metaphysical negations of the masses, it only seems natural that Torres argues that throughout history the task of steering civilization toward higher ideals has been the obligation of "superior minds that have dared to be right against everyone else."[49] Such outstanding individuals are capable of envisioning the future and therefore their primary task is to pass "the torch of truth over the thick cloak of darkness in which the masses stubbornly cover themselves in order to deny light."[50] It is striking just how closely these remarks, even though Torres insists the contrary, resemble Carlyle's unmitigated praise of "great men" in *On Heroes and Hero Worship* (1840):

> [The hero] is the living light-fountain, which it is good and pleasant to be near. The light which enlightens, which has enlightened the darkness of the world; and this is not as a kindled lamp only, but rather as a natural luminary shining by the gift of Heaven; a flowing light-fountain, as I say, of native original insight, of manhood and heroic nobleness;—in whose radiance all souls feel that it is well with them.[51]

Despite his professed distaste for the mythologizing tendency to project onto the select few all the accomplishments of a collective effort, Torres echoes Carlyle's heavy-handed emphasis on exemplary illumination. This paradox, when paired with Le Bon's denial of group agency, takes us back to Brown's aforementioned skepticism of the benevolent aspects of tolerance. For Brown,

> tolerance involves neither neutrality toward nor respect for that which is being tolerated. Rather, tolerance checks an attitude or condition of disapproval, disdain, or revulsion with a particular kind of overcoming—one that is enabled either by the fortitude to throw off the danger or by the capaciousness to incorporate it or license its existence. Thus, tolerance carries within it an antagonism toward alterity as well as the capacity for normalization.[52]

The middle-of-the-road approach in *Ídola fori* turns out to have deceptively circuitous implications. As we have seen, tolerance does not entail collaboration, but rather a limited inclusiveness that ultimately reinstates the very "aristocratic superstition" that Torres looks to alleviate. But if the argument goes that the masses are too easily swayed to support and violently defend parties and platforms that they do not fully comprehend, such as the religiously invested Regeneración, then how can the chosen intelligentsia, who refuse to confront the ideological features of religiously derived belief, effectively enlighten them?

Reason and truth are evasive criteria in projects of national reconciliation, as becomes evident when Torres negates even "an atom of reason" to the larger citizenry, while remaining steadfast in his commitment to locate "an atom of truth . . . even in the most absurd of beliefs."[53] Needless to say, if mental evolution and autonomy are the goal, these ironies complicate their viability. Opening Torres's text is Bacon's definition of the idols of the forum, but the clearly demarcated terrains of reason and the spirit in the English philosopher's account—"those formulas or ideas—real political superstitions—that continue to prevail in the spirit even after a rational criticism has proven their falsity"—unravel as the essay progresses and give way to a "criterio cultivado" (cultivated judgement) aimed at avoiding or, when possible, harmonizing extremisms.[54] Yet, as the following excerpt from Rodó's *Liberalismo y jacobinismo* (1906)—which Torres includes in his text—confirms, neospiritualists may indeed purport to strive toward equity, but more often than not they only reinforce rigid class dynamics due to a hesitancy, when not an outright unwillingness, to actively interrogate their own roles as ideological agents:

> In art, as in morals, and as in any type of ideas, the absence of intuition with respect to the nuances is the limit of the spirit of the crowd. [. . .] There where critical judgement will notice twenty shades of feelings and ideas, in order to choose among them the one that is the spot of equity and truth, vulgar judgement will see nothing more than two extreme hues: the one of *yes* and the one of *no*, the one of absolute affirmation and the one of complete negation, in order to toss to one side the weight of blind faith, and to the other that of irate hatred.[55]

Entwined in complexity, the middle ground is a defining feature of *arielista* essayists who embrace neospiritualist approaches. Fluctuating and evasive criteria, aims, and outcomes, typically nestled in paradox rather than coherent resolution, are inherent to the *arielista* enterprise, not deviations from it. Torres illustrates the *arielista* predicament of navigating the ambiguities between carving out a place for rational accuracy and autonomy and validating the legitimacy of the spirit.

Yet, electing intricacy over conflict does not translate into an entirely soothing undertaking. In his prologue to the second edition of *Ídola fori*, García Calderón cites the "example of an imperial race" on Torres, whom he considers an "austere fighter" that "[a]rrives to Colombia full of puritanical fervor, a traveler on a new Mayflower," intent on delivering a "tenacious corrective of common sense."[56] However, Torres's vision for dispelling mental illusions and political ideologies is hardly "common sense," as it relegates the bulk of the citizenry to a naturalized, inferior role in society at the very moment when routes to more robust participation were being charted.

Liberation Teleology: Compromise and Manuel Ugarte's Continental Campaign

If Carlos Arturo Torres enjoyed the reputation as a serene thinker, Argentine writer Manuel Ugarte was, according to American proselytizer Samuel Guy Inman's *Problems in Pan Americanism* (1921), "the most persistent and most active of all the Yankee haters in Hispanic America."[57] While there are certainly others whose animus toward the United States surpassed Ugarte's criticisms, Chilean writer Francisco Contreras emphasizes his importance as an antiimperialist stalwart: "Twenty-five years ago, José Enrique Rodó launched, in his famous treatise *Ariel*, the first word denouncing the danger and highlighting, in the idea of unity, the way to ward it off. But the writer Manuel Ugarte is the one who has in this sense done the most intense, sustained, and, it must be said, self-sacrificing labor."[58] There is no question that Ugarte's work, which synthesized *arielismo*, socialism, and anti-imperialism in an aspirational vision toward continental unity, documented and denounced like few others the methods and outcomes of US interventionism in the early twentieth century.[59] Texts like "El peligro yanqui" (1901), "La defensa latina" (1901), *El porvenir de la América Latina* (1910), "Carta abierta al Presidente de los Estados Unidos" (1913), *Mi campaña hispano-americana* (1922), and *La Patria Grande* (1922) made him a leading anti-imperialist voice and visionary. But his popularity as a "great whistleblower of America's conscience" (*gran alertador de la conciencia de América*) reached epic proportions when he embarked on an ambitious (not to mention self-funded and promoted) speaking tour throughout Latin America between 1911 and 1913. Ugarte traveled to Latin American countries to condemn US incursion and call for a unified resistance. Predictably, he was not welcomed with open arms in countries bearing the brunt of US influence (such as Mexico, Guatemala, El Salvador, and Nicaragua), and even received death threats in Costa Rica.[60] Support from students and workers was fervent, even though Ugarte was denied access to some countries and venues and his speeches and articles were censored. He even took his message to New York City in 1912, where he spoke frankly about "Los pueblos del sur ante el imperialismo norteamericano" at Columbia University. Speaking in Spanish, but distributing English translations of his speech, Ugarte states that what began as a research trip, ended up sparking "an emanation of collective consciousness."[61]

In contrast to Torres's efforts to effectuate national reconciliation, Ugarte's activities as an anti-imperialist crusader promoted cultural solidarity in a decidedly regional ambit. Unity is a prominent theme in Ugarte's essays, as well as, I suspect, one of the reasons for the relatively lackluster interest in his work. In other words, since US interventionism tends to be imagined in an intractable way, as a sort of blueprint that was laid out in Cuba in 1898 and subsequently reapplied, with minor modifications, in other locales, there is likewise an assumption that Latin American responses to that phenomenon are indistinguishable, which flattens and conflates a myriad of challenges, strategies, and perspectives. As a result, the ideal of unity becomes a requisite starting point in the *arielista* essay genre that gets suspended in limbo both rhetorically (they all say the same thing) and logistically (how feasible is a united front comprised of some twenty countries?). Therefore, this section offers a new reading of the discourse of unity in Ugarte's work, one that takes into account the intricacies of what it proposes rather than solely what (we assume) it opposes. This renewed consideration brings to light overlooked or oversimplified features of Ugarte's continental writings, particularly the idea that anti-imperialism is not solely a geopolitical issue, but also an epistemological imperative that requires a modernized pedagogy to help young people break with the past. Geopolitical precarity, then, does not stem exclusively from brute imposition or cultural fascination, but rather is facilitated by mental obstacles and their resulting ethical conventions derived from stifling intellectual atmospheres, antiquated educational approaches, and a fragmented cultural conscience that negatively impact Latin American youth.[62]

In *Vernacular Latin Americanisms: War, the Market, and the Making of a Discipline*, Fernando Degiovanni shows how Ugarte explicitly rejected moral approaches to anti-imperialist resistance that merely reproduced the cliché-ridden spiritualist/materialist dichotomy of difference between Latin American and US cultures that Rodó popularized, to the detriment of economic and political conditions and considerations.[63] In recapping Ugarte's animus toward *Ariel's* figurative personae, Degiovanni adds nuance to the often-conflated dynamics of the Latin American anti-imperialist landscape of the early twentieth century. However, it is important to note that, despite his professed antipathy toward what he considered Rodó's reductive, spiritualist rallying cry, Ugarte also had to negotiate the role of the spirit in his own anti-imperialist platform. In the following pages, I trace the trajectory of strains and discrepancies in Ugarte's work, from his resolute stance in favor of carving out a mental autonomy free of the psychological and pedagogical impediments posed by superstitions and traditionalisms, to a softening of his views toward religiosity and Catholicism as cultural stimulants in *El porvenir de la América Latina* (1910), a text published at the centenary and in the midst of an avalanche of imperialist incursion.[64] Registering this shift in perspective with respect to secular illumination and the sacred, I argue, helps us recenter the pragmatics, as well as reconsider the radicalism, of Ugarte's anti-imperialist project.

RATIONAL NONCONFORMITY

Published in his *Crónicas del bulevar* (1903), Ugarte's "La juventud sud-americana" ("South American Youth") reads like an abridged *Ariel*. The chronicle opens with a conversation between Dr. X, a renowned professor at the Sorbonne, and an Argentine university student, who briefly discuss the need for Latin American youth to overcome indifference, inform themselves, and get involved in reforming the political and moral landscape of their democracies. Although Ugarte mildly disparages Dr. X's expertise in this field, he agrees that: "It is beyond discussion that our character has been until now too vehement and not meditative enough. We are not accustomed to reasoning, and we get everything wrong due to instinct or imitation. Only on very rare occasions do we stop to analyze an idea to form our own justified opinion. Our native laziness leads us to adopt the version that circulates or to give in to the first impetus. That is where the origin of our defects begins."[65] This atmosphere of "compliance" (*acatamiento*) persists due to a lack of a "will to know," which converts youth into "beings of impression, and not of reason."[66] The remedy for this epistemological crisis resides in a reason-based education that encourages youth to question everything in the pursuit of truth, a pursuit Ugarte summarized in the following maxim: "It is better to drag around the disparagement of telling the truth, than be applauded for knowingly repeating common error."[67] In conjunction with other requisite *arielista* tropes—such as generosity, enthusiasm, and futurity—Ugarte defines youth as "the blind push towards the ideal, the rebellion of thought against the absurd, and the cheerful shouts of those who are in agreement with their conscience."[68] An effective intervention into politics—"a decisive push towards emancipation"—entails effectuating a comprehensive rupture: "For youth, history, nor tradition, nor ancestors should exist. Truth should be enough for us. We have to make a completely new life for ourselves."[69]

While certainly evocative of Rodó's trilogy, *La Vida Nueva* (1897), Ugarte's blanket statement regarding interrupting the historical continuity of tradition and ideology implies a militant stance that

Rodó's elitism precluded him from sharing. This radical slant grows more vigorous in *Las ideas del siglo* (1904), a transcribed speech published by the Centro Socialista de la Circunscripción in Buenos Aires, in which Ugarte outlines socialist proposals that seek to eradicate the "thousand atavistic, philosophical, political, and social superstitions [that] keep almost all humans in an inferior state, tied to things whose value is conventional and fictitious."[70] The question, then, is whether or not young people are condemned to "remain immobile in the middle of the widespread renovation, tied to their forebearers' formulas and condemned to relive and continue eternally living what others already lived."[71]

Ugarte's emphasis on secular self-determination as a vehicle for overcoming superstitions takes center stage in *Enfermedades sociales* (1907), where he argues that educational praxis in Latin America is essentially the implementation of the panoptic fear promulgated by religious authorities. In Ugarte's estimation, "To impose scientific, religious, or social dogmas is to *enter killing*, it is to prepare nations for faith and not for free examination" (original emphasis).[72] Such orthodoxy persists due to the traditional reverence paid to religious institutions and teachings, as well as the temerity in replacing them with new truths. Since the products of that educational system are ill equipped to carry out rational reforms, their only recourse resides in a deceptive optimism—a byproduct of faith—that "substitute[s] the living reality and visible certainties with the desires and aspirations of dreams."[73]

Revamping traditional pedagogical methods and outcomes involves purging an "Ancient morality based on inexact propositions and supported by antiquated syllogisms" because "it is in undeniable contradiction with our experimental epoch, in which science destroys day after day what still subsists of the gullible interpretations that pleased our parents, and in which our interrogative activity specifies the true essence and exact purpose of all things through deductions and approaches."[74] Positivist precision, in which veracity is contingent on verifiability, illuminates the path for the subject to shuck off its inaccurate, and therefore inimical, ideological inheritances. But it takes a toll: "We are born into intellectual life restricted by a past that, of course, is not impossible to shake off, but that sterilizes our first impulses, forcing us to waste our best energies in the task of unlearning."[75] Identifying incompatible ideas and distancing oneself from the normativities the derive from them, both empower the subject and leave it in another predicament. How sustainable is a free-thinking, secular self-formation for Latin American youth in an era of aggressive imperialism? To better understand how such a question is pertinent to Ugarte's project, I turn my attention now to elucidating how his secular impetus toward critical autonomy gives way to a more moderated and affirming accommodation of religiosity in *El porvenir de la América Latina*.

SENSING THE CENTENARY

In *El porvenir de la América Latina*, Ugarte explains, "I have written this book because I think that after a century of independence, when we are beginning to gather the fruit of our best fights, when the progress we have made makes us think constantly in a future of light, we have the obligation to collect ourselves for a moment to measure our muscles and dialogue with our conscience."[76] Published in the wake of a series of geopolitical challenges to Latin American sovereignty and on the brink of what would be an avalanche of US interventionism in the region, *El porvenir de la América Latina* takes a measured look at the psychological, moral, and pedagogical obstacles that Ugarte feels have prevented Latin American countries from mobilizing as a "homogenous whole" (*conjunto homogéneo*).[77] This concern for integrality, as we will see, takes precedence over Ugarte's prior calls for rational integrity. The centenary was an irenic catalyst for fomenting collective empowerment in the face of foreign intrusions. Dedicated to "youth who are thirsty for ideals," the book shifts from thinking *about* what hinders young subjects to speaking *to* them directly, which causes Ugarte to chart a more aggregate course in which metaphysics, ideals, morality, and religion outweigh frank epistemological interrogations.[78] Ugarte's softened tone and concessions to the spiritual coincide with the overall tenor of the centenary, which itself seemed to draw from Rodó's conciliatory temperament in *Ariel*.

The crux of the matter for Ugarte involves a nuanced analysis that walks a tightrope between, on the one hand, "the respect that sincere convictions demand" and, on the other, "the liberty of judgment that the state of modern knowledge imposes."[79] Abating his strong advocacy for rational and secular criteria does not, however, mean that Ugarte inhabits a mere neutral position, which is evident in his inclusive definition of religion as "The enormous mass of beliefs, observances, traditions, idealisms, ceremonies, and hierarchies that we have decided to call religion."[80] This quote is suggestive for two reasons. First, the emphasis on the vastness of diverse elements converging into one phenomenon can be read as an edifying counterweight to what he frequently bemoans as the "fractured" borders and collective conscience of Latin America. Even though some of the components—"beliefs, observances, traditions, . . . hierarchies"—undoubtedly instantiate the normative aspects of religion that Ugarte rejects in his earlier essays, the inclusion of idealisms and ceremonies signals a willingness to move beyond them. Note how the constitutive features of religion are not normatively imposed but decided upon collectively ("hemos convidado en llamar religión"). Second, this subtle but important concentricity moves beyond an implicit critique of religion and toward an explicit accommodation of religiosity as a primordial cultural ingredient, a precursor of sorts to what Chilean philosopher Helio Gallardo would later term at another significant historical moment for Latin America—the quincentennial of the "Encounter"—a "spirituality of resistance."[81]

Whereas in his earlier essays Ugarte did not address religion other than to categorically spurn its nefarious influence on young minds and actions, in *El porvenir de la América Latina* he becomes more scrupulous in his examination of the four primary components of religion: deism, ritualism, clericalism, and morality, which span a chronological trajectory from antiquity to the contemporary age. First, he validates the psychological and existential factors that gave birth to deism (a belief in a supernatural creator of the universe that stays out of human affairs). Faced with fear and bewilderment, early humans created celestial explanations for their existence and surroundings. Despite the constitutive role of human psychology and cognition in this process, Ugarte does not denigrate the sentiments behind what Freud would later call the "psychical origin of religious ideas": "I do not know if we still have within us a spark of panic that stirred the amazed troglodytes in the middle of the jungle with supernatural signs, but I do not think that there is anything more noble out of all possible actions."[82] For Marx, however, simply pinpointing the provenance of religious experience is not enough. Without taking into account the socioeconomic conditions and agents that maintain and maneuver the façade of the compatibility between mind and emotions, religion's hegemony cannot be effectively interrogated and, ultimately, displaced.[83] Although Ugarte shared a similar intention in earlier texts, his validation of the primordial religious sentiments of deism skips over the material predicaments so central to Marx's critique of religion (including the false consciousness that stems from it) in order to recognize what Peter Berger refers to as the "world-building potential of religion."[84]

Even though Ugarte concedes that religious belief was a human fabrication (an understandable, even if inaccurate, reaction to the unknown), he nonetheless sees it as a useful force in animating its adherents to perform what Robert Wuthnow calls "socially integrative functions."[85] In other words, the enduring value of religion can be found in its civil inflections, instead of in institutional or idiosyncratic realms. In this way, religion builds community, rather than promises to decipher metaphysical quandaries or fulfill the individual's desire for spiritual reassurance. Therefore, primordial concepts like deism may be artificial, but they are not arbitrary. According to Ugarte, the passage of time and the repetition of rituals have cemented the psychological legitimacy and the social utility of deistic religiosity. "This is why," he explains, "in countries in which deism predominates in its most human and pure form they are the ones that lead the species, and also why southern nations where two forms of negation coexist—religious zealotry and atheism—they often lack the rigidity and austerity that are essential conditions for victory."[86] Here, Ugarte embraces what only a few years earlier he scorned, and he does so through a resemantization of the concept of stringency. In previous texts, for instance, he decried normative, immutable restrictions placed on the mind by what he labels "an enterprise of moral deformation" orchestrated by religious authorities and institutions.[87] Now, however, unmodifiable spiritual practices are opportune.

Although, as Peter Berger notes, ritualism "reminds" people about religion's legitimacy, Ugarte also underscores its capacity for deception and coercion.[88] On the one hand, religious rituals can serve as "support for humans and incentive for virtue."[89] But that does not mean that those words and actions have any basis in reality. In recalling Tolstoy's idea that "we teach as a sacred truth what we know is impossible and has no meaning at all for us," Ugarte gives a momentary, approbatory nod to a critical autonomy that recognizes the fabricated nature of religious belief and ritualism.[90] For that reason, he stipulates that as long as ritualism is contained within itself—which is to say, that it does not take on any other kind of significance or signification outside of the confines of the community of believers—it remains innocuous. Nevertheless, Ugarte links a consistency of religious rituals to a strong sense of nationalism.[91] In this sense, cohesion—whether national or regional—trumps doctrinal veracity and ritualistic efficacy, leaving the *arielista* subject to sort out the oscillations of Ugarte's mixed messaging.

A moment of consistency does surface in his ideas surrounding anti-clericalism, which condemn the impunity with which religious authorities and institutions corrupt and monopolize education and politics. Since religion is a sacred, spiritual realm and politics a quotidian one, Ugarte argues that they should be kept in their respective corners. Yet, it is important to keep in mind that morality, the last aspect of religion he examines, derives from, and indeed keeps largely intact, the codified norms propagated by the very same religious texts and agents. For example, he contends that those who negate possibilities and resign themselves to defeat (in the most general sense), would benefit more by believing in moral action and responsibility. This *arielista* credo of action dictates that one should buy into and do something they know is not true because it is better than not doing anything at all. Affirmation, not accuracy, is the starting point for morality. In Ugarte's case, interrogating the derivatives

of religious morality gives way to embracing their mobilizing qualities and possibilities. However, even Ugarte recognizes this is not
ideal: "between doctrinal errors and the ones of those who defend
it, we have to confess that there is no place right now in the South
for a morality that does not have as its base the doctrine that was
the cradle of our civilization."[92] The temporal caveat—"por ahora"—
signals a reluctance, but ultimately a resignation, to overlook the
critical foundation of his earlier projects in order to forge a "moral
nationality" around the time of the centenary that, at least until the
threat of US imperialism has subsided, must continue to be a Cath-
olically derived one.[93]

In a final curious turn, Ugarte states that the goal for religious
renovation in Latin America should not be combating its doctrines
(a position that contrasts with his earlier oeuvre), but rather sepa-
rating it from politics and thus reducing religion's clout on everyday
life. The discrepancy here, of course, lies in the fact that he repeatedly maintains that religion is a necessary mechanism of cohesion
and progress, yet at the end of *El porvenir de la América Latina*
he opines that its influence should be excluded from the political
arena. In this way, the spiritual is socially advantageous, yet appar-
ently politically harmful. It is worth noting, however, that these shifting stances are by no means aberrations in the field of the sociology of religion. In fact, it is remarkable just how similar they are
to Jürgen Habermas's own evolving trajectory concerning religion
in civil society. For instance, Habermas's early advocacy for unqualified secularization eventually cascaded into an appreciation of religion as a necessary phenomenon (albeit one that should not exercise
influence in political institutions), and ultimately into support for
it surpassing the merely private or personal arena.[94] For Habermas,
one of the preeminent philosophers on religion and society, bri-
dling the secularizing impulse took several decades of meticulous
inquiry and gradual modification. In contrast, Ugarte, who anticipated Habermas by a half century, faced a pressing and fraught geopolitical landscape, which assuaged the ideals of a rational rupture
with religious hegemony that he professed before embarking on his
notorious hemispheric campaign. As a result, Ugarte glosses over

the critical gaps in his analysis and admits religion's usefulness in combating imperialist efforts: "In the campaign to oppose North American infiltration, Catholicism has to be one of the forces of resistance and support. Conquering nations that want to denationalize and absorb other groups start by attacking their beliefs."[95]

Ugarte's predicament in parsing reason and religion illustrates the central premise of this chapter, that is, that *arielismo*'s discourse of transcendence is not as straightforward as it is made out to be. Moreover, the close readings and contextual specificity that I outline here show the concrete challenges that *arielismo*'s abstract messaging of empowerment is not able to simply supersede, which also prompts us to look at Ugarte's radicalism in a different way.

DISAVOWAL AND THE RETROGRADE STEP

Slavoj Žižek's idea of disavowal may shed light on Ugarte's pronounced, practical evolution on the nature and roles of rationality and religiosity. For Žižek, disavowal is the idea that "I know very well, but I act as if I don't know."[96] Disavowal, then, functions as both a recognition and an abnegation, which Žižek calls "one big fetishistic denial."[97] As a subjective instrument to deal with catastrophic experiences, disavowal does not necessarily imply transcendence or an achieved alternative remedy. In fact, as Žižek argues, "While crises do shake people out of their complacency, forcing them to question the fundamentals of their lives, the most spontaneous first reaction is panic, which leads to a "return to basics": the basic premises of the ruling ideology, far from being put into doubt, are even more violently reasserted."[98] This is not to say that Ugarte pivots from radical to reactionary near the centenary. His backtracking is for the sake of something bigger, which is an action quite in line with the centenary spirit.

In this way, knowingly curtailing the rational base of his early intellectual project demonstrates strength in compromise, which, although it leaves something to be desired from a radical point of view, is not a critical gesture entirely devoid of heroism. In fact, Nietzsche advocates such an action in *Human, All Too Human* (1887):

A few steps back.—One, certainly very high level of culture has been attained when a man emerges from superstitious and religious concepts and fears and no longer believes in angels, for example, or in original sin, and has ceased to speak of the salvation of souls: if he is at this level of liberation he now has, with the greatest exertion of mind, to overcome metaphysics. Then, however, he needs to take a retrograde step: he has to grasp the historical justification that resides in such ideas, likewise the psychological; he has to recognize that they have been most responsible for the advancement of mankind and that without such a retrograde step he will deprive himself of the best that mankind has hitherto produced.[99]

Ugarte effectuates a similar retrograde step, ironically in a book entitled *The Future of Latin America*, in which futurity implies not necessarily propulsion, but rather a sort of regression or retention of the very phenomena and forces that required such exertion from which to distance himself (and by extension other Latin Americans). This is the tragic aspect of Nietzsche's "free spirit," whose choice to return and reintegrate—to "go under"—signals a surprising circularity: "for one may well want to look out over the topmost rung of the ladder, but one ought not to want to stand on it. The most enlightened get only as far as liberating themselves from metaphysics and looking back on it from above: whereas here too, as in the hippodrome, at the end of the track it is necessary to turn the corner."[100]

Such a counterintuitive gesture comes with considerable implications for the endgame that the centenary subject worked so diligently to bring about. On the surface, it provides little incentive to pursue such goals. Yet, in the end, the subject finds value and purpose outside of attaining and maintaining individual autonomy. The retrograde step evidences the fluctuating contours and objectives of Nietzsche's heroic process of questioning and overcoming—even Zarathustra appears at the end of *The Gay Science* (1882), a year before *Thus Spoke Zarathustra*, to happily descend the mountain.

If Nietzsche is susceptible to, or even willingly embraces, the retrograde step, then that should prompt us to question what we can realistically expect of Ugarte's radicalism at the centenary. His reversion can be attributed to a particular cause, US imperialism in Latin America, and not a confrontation against the whole of metaphysics as we see in Nietzsche's work. Moreover, Ugarte does not seem pleased with the choice he must make, but feigns it for the sake of the utilitarian ideal of unity: "If South American youth want to save the future, they will have to moderate their absurdities and greed, and balance obligation and ambition in a system that, without being a copy of that which prevails among the Yankees, marshals an equivalent social efficacy."[101]

A closer look at how Ugarte is out of step with his own modernizing criteria—such as rescuing primitive religiosity after insisting on its demise—suggests a paradoxical centenary message that can be read as follows: "Break the chains of the past! Now put them back on because they will unite us!" These shifts are not unique to the *arielista* archive—after all, strains are constitutive to any archive. However, instead of reading those moments as mere contradictions or failures, they afford us valuable glimpses into the tenuous, temporary solutions that responded to US incursion and reflected the early twentieth century climate of negotiating the roles and authority of church and state, especially with respect to notable sociopolitical shifts in issues like civil rather than religious marriage, divorce, and abortion. Furthermore, they instantiate a version of heroism located not in complete rupture with the past, but rather in a willingness to consent to a tethered transcendence in which the ideal is postponed in favor of the practical. In the end, for Ugarte, religiosity as a stimulus for collective self-determination may be what Herbert Marcuse calls "the irrational element in its rationality."[102] As we will see in the following two sections of this chapter, these politics of irrationality are also at play in introspective pedagogies that seek to parse instinct and intuition in the university classroom, *arielismo*'s primary fictionalized and actual stage.

Epistemological Alcoves and Soul-Searching in Prospero's Classroom

Frequently hailed as the "Maestro de la juventud de América," Rodó is rightly credited with crafting a spiritual call to arms that inspired Latin American students throughout the hemisphere to collectively organize (most notably in the Congresos de Estudiantes Americanos, the first of which took place in Montevideo in 1908, where Rodó was invited to speak) and achieve university reforms (such as the Reforma de Córdoba in 1918). In this way, *arielismo* can be understood in part as a shared youth code, ethos, and doctrine that resonated outside the enclosed walls of the fictionalized classroom in which Prospero imparts his lesson. Students certainly made *Ariel's* platform into their own and renovated the very spaces of their intellectual and sociopolitical empowerment. But what messages were they receiving in the classroom? In the remaining pages of this chapter, I juxtapose the work of two professors, Carlos Vaz Ferreira (Uruguay) and Antonio Caso (Mexico), both members of an exclusive club—comprised of Alejandro Octavio Deústua (Peru), Raimundo de Farias Brito (Brazil), Alejandro Korn (Argentina), Enrique José Molina (Chile), and José Vasconcelos (Mexico)—that Francisco Romero baptized the generation of contemporary Latin American philosophy's founders.[103] Their texts, which are edited transcriptions of their lecture notes from university seminars they taught, bring into sharper focus the epistemological and ethical shaping of *arielista* subjects in their natural incubators, university classrooms. Those "personalists"—a term meant to signal their inquiries into the human condition with an emphasis on personal development—take deep dives into the nuances and snares of the subjective and the spiritual and recommend two distinct paths to enlightenment for young people to pursue.[104] For his part, Vaz Ferreira recommends that students develop a special instinct capable of detecting misinformation and effectively resolving epistemological impasses. In contrast, Caso endorses an intuitive methodology that has a mystical slant. In what follows, I assert that both circumscribe the painstaking formulations and illuminating aims of their respective programs in ways that impair their effective enactment. In Vaz Ferreira's case, I underline how he withholds the key to implementing his pedagogical model, which leaves students in an unproductive limbo. With respect to Caso, I show how his purported ideals of disinterestedness promptly give way to adamant reinscriptions of Christian doxa. Those discrepancies, I argue, trouble perfunctory claims about the transparency of *arielista* pedagogies, while also shedding light on the tacit and dogmatic aspects of philosophical curriculums in Latin American university classrooms during the centenary.

CARLOS VAZ FERREIRA: THE "AUTHENTIC ARIEL"

The luminary featured above the caption praising "the highest spirit of superior culture in Uruguay" on a December 1929 cover of the Buenos Aires magazine *Claridad* was not José Enrique Rodó, but rather another eminent Montevidean philosopher, Carlos Vaz Ferreira.[105] Rodó and Vaz Ferreira were the most revered "maestros de juventud" of their generation—just as there was a Centro de Estudiantes "Ariel," so too was there an Agrupación Juvenil "Vaz Ferreira." Both were instrumental in shaping the educational landscape in Latin America (particularly in Uruguay), yet it is ironic that there has been a preference for Rodó's fictionalized classroom, imagined students, and masquerade as an old professor when Vaz Ferreira's many books derive primarily, when not entirely, from his lecture notes as a professor at the Universidad de la República in Montevideo.[106] If, as one newspaper article in San Salvador maintained, "Rodó, with his book *Ariel*, marked a new path for Latin American youth, elevating it towards more ample ideals," then "Uruguayans owe their freedom of thought from verbal conceptualism to Vaz Ferreira."[107]

In contrast to the hemispheric reach, ornate style, and generational resonance of Rodó's succinct, self-marketed gospel, Vaz Ferreira's actual pedagogical interventions were more localized, pragmatic, and impactful, which is perhaps why even the most vociferous critics of *arielismo* considered him the "authentic Ariel."[108] As a young professor who spearheaded educational reform in his country and encouraged students to pursue disinterested inquiry in their studies and lives, Vaz Ferreira embodied the introspective ideals that he taught in courses on psychology, logic, and philosophy, which he modeled in public venues. Transcriptions of his public lectures were disseminated in newspapers and magazines throughout Spanish-speaking countries.

If Rodó inspired young people to explore the inner recesses of their minds and souls, Vaz Ferreira dissected the epistemological and ethical problems they would encounter in doing so. His pedagogical method, which one student likened to a scalpel of "deep ideation," meticulously examined dense problematics in an impartial way.[109] For instance, in a speech that Vaz Ferreira delivered to mark the construction of the Facultad de Enseñanza Secundaria in Montevideo and that appeared in the first issue of the monthly publication of the Federación de los Estudiantes del Uruguay, *Evolución* (1905), he noted how falsity and fluctuation thwart the productive and progressive aims of educational pursuits.[110] Ever attentive to the particulars, but never deferential to foregone conclusions or impregnable opinions, Vaz Ferreira's pedagogical theory and praxis were attuned to the provisional, rather than universal, nature of ideas, facts, and truth claims. Therefore, what Enrique Dussel labels Vaz Ferreira's "anti-positivist vitalist rationalism" targets the constructedness of conceptualism, that is, "the theory that universals exist, but only as concepts or ideas in the mind."[111]

In *Ariel*, Prospero advocated a methodology of illumination founded on an idyllic synthesis of rationalism and spiritualism. Vaz Ferreira, however, faced a more challenging task; he had to enact, rather than just encourage, the *arielista* aspiration of enlightenment, which, as the following pages demonstrate, entailed moving beyond abstractions of the spirit and tackling the knotty interstices of the mind. After reviewing Vaz Ferreira's singular contributions to the pedagogical and political landscape of Uruguay, as well as the propagation of Pan-American evangelism near the centenary, this section analyzes his asystematic methodology in two important lectures-turned-books—*Moral para intelectuales* and *Lógica viva*—and highlights the logical limitations of his freethinking project.

It would be difficult to overstate how much students adored Vaz Ferreira. According to a 1913 Montevidean newspaper article penned by "Student X," "If one were to ask the students what they most love, respect, and admire, they would all respond in unison: Dr. Carlos Vaz Ferreira."[112] A prodigy described as the "best mind of his generation" and "the most brilliant young personality that has arisen from the faculty," Vaz Ferreira was tasked with implementing a philosophical reform of the university in 1896.[113] Two decades of bitter polemics between spiritualists and positivists in the university, which increasingly played out in the press and fueled political antagonisms, necessitated a new educational model that toned down the divisive radicalisms that had characterized the intellectual atmosphere of the country, recognized the university's constructive role as a cultural catalyst, and recentered the pursuit of disinterested knowledge as a priority. Vaz Ferreira emerged from this process as a respected, transitional figure, and shortly after, at the age of twenty-five, he was appointed the Chair of Philosophy. Over the next half century—in addition to publishing his lecture notes as books like *Ideas y observaciones* (1905), *Los problemas de la libertad* (1907), *Conocimiento y acción* (1908), *Moral para intelectuales* (1909), *El pragmatismo* (1909), *Lógica viva* (1910), *Lecciones de pedagogía y cuestiones de enseñanza* (1918), *Conocimiento y acción* (1920), *Estudios pedagógicos* (1921-1922), *Sobre los problemas sociales* (1922), among others— he served the university in numerous capacities, including curricular planning, chairing departments, founding the College of Humanities and Sciences, and served as rector of the University on two occasions (1928–1930, 1935–1941).

Suffice it to say that Vaz Ferreira was nothing short of a celebrity, a status rarely afforded to an educator. This explains why when Albert Einstein visited Montevideo in April of 1925 to elucidate his theory of relativity, he elected to discuss, in French, the nature of perception and reality with none other than Vaz Ferreira.[114] Their famous encounter was initially captured in a photograph, and later enshrined in a 2008 monument in the Plaza Artola, both of which depict the two philosophers sitting close to one another on a bench, Einstein with one hand resting on his crossed knee and his arm around Vaz Ferreira, who faces Einstein with one hand raised toward his chin and a folder resting in his lap. The scene exudes a sense of camaraderie and equality, which only elevated Vaz Ferreira's already revered status as an intellectual powerhouse that could hold his own with a heavyweight like Einstein.

Vaz Ferreira's rapid ascension to important posts in the educational system was not due solely to recognition of his talents by those in positions of power. Rather, it stemmed primarily from public campaigns that were launched by students themselves. In addition to constant nominations for vacant posts, *homenajes*, and letters of support, students organized an initiative that petitioned the Uruguayan government to create a "cátedra superior universitaria" specially for Vaz Ferreira.[115] This "cátedra libre" would allow him to impart lectures in an open forum where he could spontaneously explore and debate ideas with students, unbound by curriculum, topics, allegiances, or approaches. The initiative was successful and Vaz Ferreira assumed the post of Maestro de Conferencias in 1913 and held it until his death in 1952. His *conferencias* were nothing short of a cultural phenomenon in Uruguay.

Another revered Uruguayan writer and educator who started his career in the early twentieth century, Alberto Lasplaces, describes Vaz Ferreira's pedagogical method modeled in his lectures as exemplary:

> It is no longer a matter of teaching according to a certain number of questions, of training disciples in a certain number of answers. It is something infinitely loftier and more transcendental. The professor makes his own path and does not obey anything other than his own will, his own free preferences. The disciple does not attend class driven by the threatening phantom of an exam, anxious to learn quickly in order to forget later on. No. With the utilitarian calculation removed, what remains is the pure and noble eager-

ness to improve oneself, to broaden the horizons of life through contemplation and contact with superior spectacles. The professor knows that they listen to him with interest; the disciples speak sincerely to him. Where can one find anything more perfect, closer to such a pedagogical ideal?[116]

Vaz Ferreira captivated jam-packed audiences, and year after year students aired complaints in the local press about the urgency to find more accommodating venues, since so many people had to be turned away to due space restrictions. In addition, they made appeals for his lectures to be transcribed, typed, and printed in newspapers and magazines so that those not able to enter or attend would not miss out. Students, and the public writ large, craved and consumed Vaz Ferreira's lectures, which fueled the reformative spirit of university movements.[117]

There was an awareness that the effects of this extraordinary collaboration between university students and the Uruguayan State would reverberate outside of legislative chambers and public venues. As one supporter of the initiative put it, "In the interest of our nation the State should facilitate the educational action of the teacher [Vaz Ferreira] consecrated by the youth as the axis of a fruitful spiritual renovation."[118] Chosen by the very constituency to which he dedicated his life, this "spiritual director of the legions of young people" made it clear in his first *conferencia* that he would strive to "achieve an optimization (*superiorización*) of the cultural environment."[119] Bringing about such transcendental aims—a spiritual project that links nation, education, and culture—relies on, to quote Vaz Ferreira's lecture at the Ateneo de Montevideo in 1911, replacing "pedagogical exclusivism" based on systematization with "pedagogical experimentation."[120] Students reacted positively to his experimental methodology, as evidenced in a 1910 issue of *Evolución* (dedicated to the Segundo Congreso de Estudiantes Americanos that had just taken place in Buenos Aires), where they underscored the young professor's "serious and profound footprint" while also crediting him for having created "new ways of thinking."[121]

Vaz Ferreira's project of free thinking, which tackles logic, meta-physics, ethics, psychology, and pedagogy, prompts centenary sub-jects to examine dichotomous thinking and other epistemologi-cal hurdles that they will face in their lives, in hopes that they will develop a critical independence capable of carrying out an impartial search for truth. This requires a thorough examination of epistemo-logical grey areas. As we have seen, in addition to remembering a nation's past and celebrating its accomplishments, the centenary was also a pretext for polemics surrounding ideas and truth in education. It is no coincidence that Vaz Ferreira's most important texts—*Moral para intelectuales* (1909) and *Lógica viva* (1910)—appear in the midst of a secularizing era of Uruguayan politics and society, spearheaded by the reformist liberal policies of José Batlle y Ordóñez, who served two terms as the president of Uruguay (1903–1907, 1911–1915). The separation of church and state, which involved removing references to God and the Bible from official documents, was an important ini-tiative in Batlle's first term.

In 1906, the Comisión de Caridad y Beneficencia Pública (Char-ity and Social Welfare Commission), in order to "guarantee a com-plete liberty of conscience against impositions or suggestions that may undermine it," removed all crucifixes from hospital walls, which sparked an extensive public debate about progressive liberalism and religious freedom.[122] Rodó reacted to this "intolerant" act by urg-ing moral tolerance and respect for religious sentiments of charity that were inseparable from the figure of Christ.[123] The relationship between the Batlle administration and the Catholic Church became more divisive in the leadup to the centenary festivities, especially with regard to their respective roles in creating and maintaining national identity and overseeing education. A 1909 law forbidding religious instruction and practices in public (which is to say, State-run) schools sidelined religious authorities and institutions at the very moment that they were keen on being prominently featured in the centenary celebrations as a way of clutching onto their histori-cal importance and contemporary relevance.[124]

Some of those disputes coalesced around Vaz Ferreira. In a 1909 column of *El Liberal*, the editors address the critiques that another Uruguayan newspaper, *La Razón*, directed at them for having endorsed Vaz Ferreira as the next rightful dean of *preparatorios*. The competing publication favored a staunchly religious candidate, Eduardo Monteverde, and alleged that *El Liberal* was anti-religious. Pointing out that their endorsement, unlike *La Razón's*, has nothing to do with religion and everything to do with the fact that the professor is a "free thinker," *El Liberal* asserts that Monteverde would bring counterproductive religious thinking into the classroom. In contrast, Vaz Ferreira pursues "the understanding of truth" (*el conocimiento de la verdad*) and therefore is capable of "inspiring the love of speculation without the mental reservations of a believer."[125] While this episode may seem like little more than a local squabble about differing ideas on how to most effectively shape the character and ideals of youth in Uruguay, it actually forms part of larger landscape of competing pedagogical and spiritual projects aimed at young people in Latin America during the centenary era.

A well-respected math professor, Eduardo Monteverde was also one of the most important figures of an emerging and robust evangelical movement that sought to influence the intellectual and spiritual development of young men in Latin America. Converted to Protestantism by an American pastor, Monteverde was elected as the director of the Montevideo branch of the Young Men's Christian Association (YMCA) in 1910. Beyond its stated mission—to form the minds, bodies, and morals of young men—the organization also sought to counteract what Monteverde considered the over-secularization taking place in Uruguay. The YMCA was perhaps the most effective organization in promoting evangelism in Latin America. Under the auspices of branches in Argentina, Brazil, Chile, and Uruguay, the first international missionary conference ever held in South America took place in Montevideo in June 1914. The organization was also gaining traction in Mexico, Cuba, and the Panama Canal zone, all hotspots for US intervention at the time. In a profile on "Monteverde of Montevideo" in *Association Men*, the monthly magazine published by the YMCA, the Uruguayan educator expresses what could be characterized as an anti-*arielista* sentiment as he embraces a new era of Pan-Americanism:

> Thank the people of North America for the Young Men's Christian Association and for what it is doing for any country. Its influence for good is greater than the schools and greater in a sense than the church or any institution in South America. It is the one form of Americanism which we love and honor. It typifies to us the best American ideals. When we hear it said that the dollar typifies the American people we know it is not true. Our northern neighbors have sent us the best manifestations of their ideals of character and service through the Young Men's Christian Association.[126]

As the centenary of Latin American independence approached, there was increased mobilization of evangelic campaigns, which operated as corollaries to the politics of Pan-Americanism. Founded in 1906 on Madison Avenue in New York, the Laymen's Missionary Movement (LMM) was one of the most active and influential organizations that sponsored countless congresses and conventions to help churches with foreign missions in Latin America. Beginning in 1909, the LMM's monthly publication, *Men and Missions*, set its sights on converting young people, an urgent objective encapsulated in one of that organization's mottoes: "This is the only generation we can reach." In addition to reporting on missionary work throughout the hemisphere (including their own profile on Monteverde in Uruguay), *Men and Missions* also opened its pages to the agents of Pan-Americanism, such as John Barrett, director general of the Pan American Union in Washington, DC.[127]

The timing for evangelism was opportune, since Pan-American political networks, commercial routes, and military deployments were by then well established and only expanding further through increased US occupation of Latin American and Caribbean countries. Citing the "utter breakdown of the moral and spiritual leadership" in Latin American countries, an American Methodist missionary in South America named Homer Stuntz took to the pages of *Men and Missions* in 1913 to insist that, since the Monroe Doctrine and the Roosevelt Corollary to it have shut out Europe from further "civilizing" the continent, "We must recognize that North America must give the Gospel to South America."[128] Similar appeals to a moral imperative of the United States to save Latin American countries from themselves grew more frequent as the Panama Canal neared completion. For instance, months prior to its opening in August 1914, Theodore Roosevelt chronicled his travels throughout South America for *The Outlook*, a popular magazine that reported on Latin American countries and supported the United States' civilizing burden.[129] In addition, the Panama-Pacific International Exposition in San Francisco (February 20 to December 4, 1915) generated even more interest in Latin America, particularly from a Pan-Americanist angle. Weeks later, the Second Pan-American Scientific Congress, where Monteverde was a delegate, was held in Washington, DC (December 27, 1915–January 8, 1916).[130] One month after that, the Congress on Christian Work in Latin America (February 10-20, 1916), the first Protestant missionary conference in Latin America, took place in Panama.[131]

The idea for a missionary congress dedicated to the study of Latin America came at a conference in New York in 1913, which also included plans for subsequent regional conferences that would take place in Lima, Santiago, Buenos Aires, Rio de Janeiro, Havana, Mexico, and other locations. The organizing committee received support from the Pan-American Union in Washington, DC, as well as from Secretary of State William Jennings Bryan. Monteverde was elected president of the Congress and was a featured speaker at the unprecedented event attended by some five hundred delegates (including businessmen, men of industry, statesmen, preachers, and heads of Christian organizations, evenly split between Latin America, the US, and Canada, with smaller numbers from England, Spain, and Italy). Another pivotal figure, a Brazilian Presbyterian educator from São Paulo named Erasmo Braga, wrote a report on the many formal lectures and informal discussions during the Congress that the Missionary Education Movement of the United States and Canada published, and Monteverde translated from Portuguese into Spanish as *Pan-Americanismo: aspecto religioso. Una relación e interpretación del Congreso de Acción Cristiana en la América Latina celebrado en Panamá* (1917).

The Congress, in the words of Samuel Guy Inman, achieved the "most comprehensive survey of the social, educational, and religious conditions of Latin America ever attempted."[132] Braga makes it clear that the purpose resided in a mission to spread a personal Christianity, and that its participants were not there to judge different faiths (even though there were healthy doses of critique centered on Catholic doctrines and superstitions) nor be antagonistic toward Latin Americans. However, the genre of the report's title (*relación*), not to mention its overall content and tone, are reminiscent of colonial-era texts of conquest and colonization. The *relación* was not an objective form through which missionaries merely narrated what they experienced in the Americas. Rather, missionary agents (be they political, military, or religious) drafted *relaciones* in order to examine conditions on the ground and communicate administrative opportunities and potential hazards to official authorities as they considered the most effective way to exercise influence over other peoples and places.

Just as in the colonial era, Braga's *Pan-Americanismo* emphasizes the "imminent spiritual danger" of Latin America and the need to "infuse" what it lacks, which, as it turns out, are many things, including ethical ideals, moral order, and an educational system that forms character.[133] Therefore, those evangelicals in attendance, as Monteverde stipulated in his speech, sought to "initiate a new era of Christianity" and achieve the "spiritual elevation of America."[134] Some in attendance, such as the aforementioned Stuntz, thought this was a feasible objective, citing the "plasticity of the Latin American," which works to the advantage of evangelical missionaries who wish to "inculcate" a democratic spirit.[135]

The spiritual contours of Latin Americans were not the only thing that those at the Panama Congress aspired to reshape; they also revised the continent's history so that the very figures of independence that Latin American countries were celebrating at the centenary milestones were reframed as evangelists whose emancipatory campaigns were not unlike those that the Protestant missionaries in Panama were undertaking. Moreover, they proposed evangelical

Christianity as a vital source of civilization, morality, democracy, liberty, and culture in Latin America's history since the nineteenth century, and subtly converted Bolívar and San Martín into allies of contemporary US intervention when Latin American democracies were under siege.

This revisionist sleight of hand accentuated the Pan-American ideal that the two Americas are not different. However, for as much talk as there was about the spiritual salvation of Latin America, Charles L. Thompson, a chairman of the Missionary Education Movement who was present at the Panama Congress, reminded the audience that missionary work in the region is "for our own protection."[136] This explains why the English-language report on the Congress— *Christian Work in Latin America. Survey and Occupation. Message and Method. Education* (1917)—which was published for the Committee on Cooperation in Latin America by the Missionary Education Movement of the United States and Canada, was written like a military report that reviewed the natural resources, religious life, education system of Latin America, and evaluated the statics, problematics, and possible courses of action and outcomes of missionary activity. The tenor of subsequent reports on missionary congresses grew more bellicose two months later, with the publication of *Men and World Service. Address Delivered at the National Missionary Congress Washington, D.C., April 26–30, 1916. A Survey of Achievement. A Council of War. A Summons to Advance.* President Woodrow Wilson attended the first day of the National Missionary Congress and threw a reception for its attendees in the White House.[137]

Reverend Samuel Guy Inman, a Texan missionary in Mexico, was the secretary general of the Committee on Cooperation in Latin America (founded in 1913), which sponsored the Panama Congress and was entrusted with continuing the work that it began.[138] In an article in *The Outlook*, Inman wrote that "the survey unquestionably showed that the existing moral and spiritual life of these young nations demands help from the outside for its proper development, and that the Latin-Americans, far from resenting such help, earnestly welcome its coming through evangelical missionary agencies."[139] It is remarkable just how similar the rhetoric and aims of evangelism and *arielismo* were. Both currents were vying to shape the personal and spiritual development of young men in Latin America (albeit in opposite geopolitical directions). Just as *arielista* intellectuals were modernizing their pedagogy around disinterested inquiry, evangelical missionary organizations flooded the market with books and pamphlets, began educational campaigns to convert students to Protestantism, and collected funds to sponsor professorships in universities in Latin America. Although far away from the threat of US military intervention, Uruguay was on the evangelical radar because of its reputation as a center of free-thinking, which missionaries considered an inroad for pitching the intellectual, individual aspects of their evangelic beliefs. Therefore, although there is a longstanding tendency to read Vaz Ferreira's work in a restrictive, national context, his labor is not just a local issue.[140] Rather, it is embroiled in and responds to a larger Pan-American and *arielista* landscape.

MYSTIFICATION AND THE HYPERLOGICS OF GOOD SENSE

When Vaz Ferreira assumed his post as Maestro de Conferencias in 1913—the same year in which the Committee on Cooperation in Latin America was founded and plans were being made for the Panamanian Congress on Christian Work in Latin America—his initial idea was to "make philosophy." However, he quickly realized that his most pressing task was to address the "problem of youth," which, since he was attentive to students' concerns regarding curricular and administrative issues and a reliable ally of university reform movements, did not refer exclusively to the sociopolitical mobilization of young people.[141] Rather, it entailed cultivating in youth a new consciousness based on disinterested truth. Far from abstract treatises on philosophy, Vaz Ferreira's lectures-turned-books *Moral para intelectuales* and *Lógica viva* emerge as counter discourses to the missionary exploits that were ramping up and targeting Latin American youth around the centenary. While American evangelicals were preaching a Christ-centric message of revelation and salvation, university students throughout Latin America heralded *Moral para intelectuales,* alongside *Ariel,* as their own secular "gospels" that, rather than predicating monolithic sources of enlightenment, encouraged young people to constantly interrogate the spiritual and the rational in their daily lives.

As its title indicates, *Moral para intelectuales* reviews epistemological and ethical quandaries that the future leaders of Latin American nations will encounter in their personal and professional lives. Evangelists targeted the same audience, since they realized that their agenda could not be achieved solely by foreign missionaries, but rather by local converts. Rather than a normative manual of conduct, *Moral para intelectuales* highlights "a special intellectual and moral *anesthesia,* for the absurdities and ills that we breathe, that are in the current atmosphere, and in which we have grown accustomed to think and feel."[142] In this illusory environment, the thinking subject with "superior character" lives a problematic existence because they see everything in terms of degrees and shades, while there are those who buy into "certain optimistic fictions . . . that explain to us the fulfillment of an obligation . . . as an act that, not only does not stir up any doubt, but that is done in every case in an almost mechanical way."[143] This "mystification"—a term Marx also used to describe an ideological phenomenon that covered up the real dimensions, investments, and maneuvers of those forces exercising dominance in society—equates the uncritical fulfillment of a moral act or obligation with its validity or precision.

Since young people were on the receiving end of a barrage of competing character-building discourses—primarily *arielista* ideal-laden interpellations, Catholic traditionalism, and American evangelic campaigns—Vaz Ferreira elucidates the perils of religious thinking by sidelining religion as "simply a series of formulas, rites, practices: some purely verbal, vulgar, deformed beliefs that are found on the surface of the spirit; and I do not think that they tend to produce any overly deep effects neither in the sense of evil nor in the sense of good."[144] However, he stipulates that, if intellectualized, religion can take on nefarious attributes. In other words, when religious proponents attempt to modernize "mystification" vis-à-vis scientific methods so as to embody a "superior" morality, it forces people to engage in a dangerous kind of mental gymnastics that loses sight of the truth.[145]

Comprised of excerpts for his lecture notes from a course that he taught at the Universidad de la República in 1909, *Lógica viva* takes a deeper dive into how this "psychologically falsifying tendency" carries over into education.[146] Framed as a "study of the way that people think, discuss, get things right or get them wrong—particularly the ways in which they get things wrong," *Lógica viva* reviews a variety of sophisms that mislead young people's minds.[147] Such errors include false oppositions, expediency, pursuit of precision, and "verbo-ideological fallacies," or the relationship between ideas and the words used to represent them. He identifies systematicity as the culprit that binds all of those phenomena: "to believe in the existence of the only formula, to hope for and desire it, as some do; to long for 'the one that will come' (*el que vendrá*), for the one that will bring the formula: *the* formula; everything is a manifestation of the exclusivist paralogism into which even the best spirits fall."[148] Here the criticism of Rodó is unmistakable. In *El que vendrá* (1896), Rodó writes of a "yearning to believe" and awaits the arrival of a singular, almost supernatural, leader who will specify a new formula to guide artists out of the doubt and emptiness of the modern era.[149] Rodó predicated a redemptive hope, crystalized in his messianic "the one who will one day arrive." For Vaz Ferreira, systems—no matter their purview—are not accurate solidifications of disinterested knowledge obtained through meticulous inquiry, but rather stifling obstacles for mental emancipation.

In opposition to educational methods that shy away from scrutinizing "reality itself" (*la realidad misma*) only to elevate "simplified schemas," Vaz Ferreira conceptualizes his pedagogy as "ideas to keep in mind" that are subject to modification.[150] This "living" facet of his project appreciates striving for the ideal of accuracy while also refusing to sacrifice intellectual integrity which would only make analysis conform to a pre-conceived conclusion or conviction. In fact, he puts the same stipulation on reason that he puts on metaphysics: their value resides in their capacity to suggest not subject, to be partial and provisional.[151] Such an assertion goes against the common assumption that each individual is equipped with an instinctual radar that instantly and effectively detects fallacy. Instinct (as an innate reaction) is insufficient, which is why Vaz Ferreira recommends cultivating a special kind of instinct, an "experimental" or "empirical" instinct that picks up where reason alone leaves off.[152] According to Vaz Ferreira,

> But there is another good sense that comes after reasoning, or, more accurately, together with it. When we have thoroughly examined the reasons for and against that exist in almost all cases; when we have made all logic (the good logic) possible, when the issues become a question of degrees, there is a moment in which a type of instinct—what I call the good hyperlogical sense—is the one that clears up for us the questions in concrete cases. And it would be good that logic would not deprive people of this superior form of good sense.[153]

In contrast to the concept of instinct as a hardwired, unpredictable, and dangerous impulse so impetuously disparaged by diagnostics of modernity—especially when it referred to racialized masses, which it almost always did—"good hyperlogical sense" is distinctive in that it dwells within the superior subject and plays a role that is both crucial and secondary. For what purports to be a "positively practical" guide for introspection, comprised of numerous concrete examples, *Lógica viva* offers little clarity as to how the interpellated subject is to access or develop "good hyperlogical sense." The irony here resides in the fact that the primary mechanism to counteract "mystification" is itself mystifying. Rationality certainly does the vast majority of the legwork, which tasks a vague concept of instinct with inexplicably resolving difficult issues only when all other logical recourses have been exhausted. This special variety of instinct, then, reads less like an equitable synthesis of neospiritual aims and methods, and more like a stipulative, when not speculative, gesture to them.

   Although his pedagogical project warns primarily against expeditious introspection and truth assertions, in the end Vaz Ferreira's reworking of instinct as a last resort in a meticulous intellective process ultimately leaves the most important matters indefinitely deferred. The pedagogical aim of this type of deep learning, Oscar Martí points out, is "to clarify rather than solve."[154] Yet there were other *arielistas* for whom intuitive immediacy was not a symptom of mystification, but rather the only viable method for reclaiming a vast universe of imperceptible forces and intangible phenomena that constitute our subjective experiences in the world.

Introspective Immediacy and the Sacrificial Subject

In the summer of 1909 philosopher and educator Antonio Caso delivered a series of lectures at the Escuela Nacional Preparatoria in Mexico City in which he promoted metaphysical speculation in the heart of the most prominent positivist institution in the country, founded by none other than Comtean disciple Gabino Barreda. In October of the same year, after being named director of the Escuela Nacional Preparatoria, Caso founded the Ateneo de la Juventud (1909–1914), a group comprised of young intellectuals including José Vasconcelos, Alfonso Reyes, and Dominican writer Pedro Henríquez Ureña, that ushered in a "new era of thought" forged in the values of spiritual humanism of a "superior culture" to contrast positivism's restrictive clutch on Mexican politics and education.[155] While by no means uniform in their political leanings during the Mexican Revolution—Vasconcelos supported revolutionary Francisco I. Madero's presidential bid against Porfirio Díaz, while Caso voted for the latter's reelection—the constitutive members of the Ateneo did share an unabating faith in the renovating power of metaphysical possibilities, higher ideals, and subjective experience, all of which were invalidated by the institutionalized positivism of the Díaz regime that had dominated Mexican education, politics, and culture for over three decades.[156]

Rodó was a source of inspiration for the *ateneístas'* cultural project.[157] In the introduction to the first Mexican edition of *Ariel* (1908), Pedro Henríquez Ureña explains Rodó's significance to the youth of the region:

By releasing *Ariel* in Mexico, where until now only echoes of its influence had arrived, we believe we are doing a service to Mexican youth. We do not intend to declare that Rodó offers the only nor the most perfect teaching suited to young people. In the philosophical sphere, many can take issue with what he says; in the field of social psychology, they may ask from him a deeper conception of Greek life and a more ample vision of the North American spirit, but nobody can deny the essential virtue of his doctrines, which is fundamentally about the most sublime of superior spirits of humanity, nor the energetic virtue of stimulus and conviction of his sermon, nor, in short, that *Ariel* is the most powerful inspiration of ideals and efforts directed at the youth of our America in the future.[158]

In August and September 1910—on the verge of the outbreak of the Mexican Revolution—members of the Ateneo organized a series of *conferencias* to commemorate the centenary of Mexican Independence, which were subsequently transcribed and published as *Conferencias del Ateneo de la Juventud* (1910). Henríquez Ureña spoke about the importance of Rodó's *Ariel* as the "most powerful voice of truth, ideals, and faith directed at America in recent years."[159] But the bulk of his talk centered on the Uruguayan's recently published *Motivos de Proteo* (1909), a highly anticipated, monumental undertaking that boosted Rodó's prominence as the centenary neared. For instance, in Mexico the *Revista Moderna*, whose pages chronicled *modernista* aesthetics and sensibilities, published thirty of the one hundred and forty-eight chapters of *Motivos de Proteo*, until its publication was interrupted in November 1910 due to the tumultuous circumstances of the Revolution.[160] The guiding maxim of *Motivos de Proteo*—"Reformarse es vivir" (To renew oneself is to live)— prompts young people to realize that the introspective process that they must pass through in order to attain subjective and ethical enlightenment is constantly mutating, and that they themselves are in a state of perpetual becoming.[161] According to Henríquez Ureña, Rodó's new book promoted a form of heroism rooted in a more personal way of thinking ("pensar personalmente"), and 'personality' is the most referenced concept in *Motivos*.[162]

The ethical and introspective dimensions of this heroic personality were also central concerns for Caso, who dedicated his *conferencia* to dissecting Puerto Rican educator Eugenio de Hostos's *El Moral Social* (1888). Whereas Hostos's collection of essays outlines a sociology of ethics in which reason is the glue that binds the individual, society, and the nation, Caso argues that rationality by itself cannot animate the spirit of sincerity, love, and generosity necessary for a heroic subject to emerge in its full potential.[163] The rest of this chapter examines how this axis of Casonian philosophy forgoes intellectualism for intuitive immediacy and a mystical logic in two of his lectures-turned-books, *La filosofía de la intuición* (1914) and *La existencia como economía y como caridad: ensayo sobre la escencia del cristianismo* (1916). In addition, I underscore the coercive stipulations that blunt the emancipatory potential of those two cornerstones of Caso's aesthetic spiritual project of moral heroism, which is founded on the notions of charity and sacrifice.

MYSTICAL INTUITION

José Vasconcelos became the rector of the Universidad Nacional Autónoma de México (UNAM) in 1920. He would pass the reins to Caso in 1921, but not before he designed a new seal and motto for the university: "Por mi raza hablará el espíritu" ("For my people, the spirit shall speak"). According to Enrique Krauze, the aspirational adage evidenced *arielismo*'s patent influence.[164] For Vasconcelos, the phrase embodied the mission of the Ateneo and that of subsequent university reform movements to forge "a culture of new tendencies, spiritual and absolutely free in essence."[165] In order to enact a culture of spiritual autonomy in both Mexican civic society and institutions, members of the Ateneo also drew from American psychologist and philosopher William James's valorization of the "reality of the unseen" and mysticism in *The Varieties of Religious Experience* (1902), which proposed a more capacious spiritual alternative to the intellectualist and material determinisms espoused by positivism.[166] Yet, it was French philosopher Henri Bergson's work—especially *L'Évolution créatrice* (*Creative Evolution*, 1907)—that charted an intuitive method of introspection that tapped into the spontaneous, vitalist impulses to which Spencerian evolution was blind. The ripple effect of Bergson's inward turn is clearly evidenced in a short (eleven-page) essay written by Caso entitled, *La filosofía de la intuición* (1914), which ponders the "secular conflict between mysticism and intellectualism" and seeks its resolution in combining "scientific methods and results with intuitive truths."[167]

However, his nod to synthesis is rather fleeting since it admittingly favors "metaphysical truth."[168] For Caso, intuitionism is "the only means capable of overcoming the conclusions of agnostic intellectualism."[169] This intuitive vanquishment of the intellect stands in stark contrast to their purported integration, and it quickly becomes clear that Caso has no intentions of pursuing such a merger. Instead, anticipating Vasconcelos's cosmic focus by a decade, Caso proposes a Bergsonian-heavy synthesis that sidesteps positivism altogether, "a metaphysical, cosmological synthesis: *creative evolution*, speculative vitalism *sui generis*."[170] Unlike Vaz Ferreira's weariness of expediency, Caso's brand of vitalist philosophy values subjective immediacy:

> Immediate intuitions are the base of all knowledge, the premises of all proof. The analytical and synthetic method of the logicians is not able to produce the simultaneity of knowledge, the integration of scientific truths in concrete universal truth. In order to achieve the latter, it is necessary to once again resort to the only method that drives the simultaneity of knowledge, that is: intuition. One must immerse its abstract facts in intuition.[171]

But this is no ordinary intuition, as evidenced in its shifting nomenclatures throughout the text, such as "real philosophical intuition," "synthetic and disinterested intuition," and "intuition of immediate spiritual reality."[172] In contrast to Vaz Ferreira's critiques that target mystification, Caso's special intuition relies on a mystical logic, "a diverse logic, the logic of imagination and feeling, the logic of instinct that, for the pure intellectualist . . . would be the negation of all logic."[173] However, Caso overlooks the *a priori* compromise of mysticism when he insists that the mystic "does not choose or eliminate: he speaks his spiritual interiority and imposes it as *his* truth, as a symbolic truth, as the only possible truth."[174] It is worth noting that the mystic is not free of religiously-derived spiritual frameworks and discovers them independently through introspection. Rather, the mystic is already a devout person who tends to disdain the material world and therefore seeks solace or truth in psycho-spiritual pursuits. Even though "God does not speak through everyone's lips," this does not mean that the philosophical intuition that Caso advocates is therefore an individualist practice.[175] In fact, just as *La filosofía de la intuición* prompts the subject to make an inward turn toward a dynamic, introspective source of truth, it does so through the guise of a spiritualist logic that signals the sacrificial disposition of the superior subject in *La existencia como economía y como caridad* (1916).

THE WILL TO SURRENDER

Just as it is important to remember that Arthur Schopenhauer took more than one crack at *The World as Will and Representation*—given the differences between the editions published in 1818, 1844, and 1859—so too must we recognize the multiplicity of Caso's *La existencia como economía y como caridad: ensayo sobre la escencia del cristianismo*. First published as forty pages of continuous text in 1916, the 1919 edition expanded not only its length (to five chapters) but also its title, *La existencia como economía, como desinterés y como caridad*, which the 1943 edition retained, along with adding four new chapters.[176] Derived from lecture notes for a course he taught in 1915 at the Universidad Popular Mexicana, an institute of *libre enseñanza* conceptualized as an adult extension school founded by the Ateneo de la Juventud that operated from 1912 until 1920, Caso's book is redolent of *The World as Will and Representation* in important ways. Reminiscent titles and evolving reeditions aside, each text scrutinizes the epistemological, ontological, aesthetic, and ethical facets of human experience. Moreover, both philosophers concur that introspection is not governed by rationality and life is overwhelmingly driven by Will (in Schopenhauer's case), or *economía* (which for Caso is synonymous with egoism). Unlike Schopenhauer's pessimistic take on metaphysical will, however, Caso locates the core of his "philosophical Christianity" in the ideal of charity.[177]

Billed as "a *tribute to the heroes and the heroism of the history* of the most important event in the evolution of humanity: the development of evangelic ideas and feelings throughout time" (original emphasis), *La existencia como economía y como caridad* proposes an affective, altruistic heroism as an alternative to strict understandings of existence as struggle, survival, and extinction, notions that are succinctly captured in French biologist Félix Le Dantec's epigram, "To exist is to struggle, to live is to conquer."[178] Against deterministic conceptions of life espoused by Le Dantec, Haeckel, and Darwin, Caso advances one of the strongest reverberations of *arielista* ethics rooted in immaterial aesthetic and moral phenomena such as beauty, belief, love, and benevolence. In Caso's aesthetic project, intuitive introspection is not strictly an anti-positivist stance that validates a "multiform and diverse" reality; it also illuminates a path to "otro orden y otra vida."[179] That "other life" is a "supernatural" one of loving sacrifice and charity. But charity as the antidote to *economía* comes with important stipulations. Supernatural life is not just synonymous with metaphysics, which is to say an introspective or speculative terrain. In fact, charity—the cornerstone of accessing the supernatural—requires Christian beliefs and acts: "Belief in God is the direct consequence of acts on the behalf of good. If you all are not charitable you will not be believers."[180]

Whereas Torres, Ugarte, and Vaz Ferreira aim to rid young people of the psychological baggage derived from religiosity so that life, truth, and purpose come into sharper focus, Caso relocates the matter to another ideological plane of limitless compromise, as evidenced in his proposed formula for life (which he calls the "equation of good"): "*Sacrificio = máximum de esfuerzo X mínumum de provecho*" (Sacrifice = maximum amount of effort X the minimum of benefit).[181] The supernatural, then, is conditional on self-surrender (in addition to surpassing the tangible limitations derived from positivist paradigms). Instead of marketing this worldview as "you have to experience it to believe it," action is a prerequisite for evidentiality: "Your century is selfish and perverse. [. . .] He who does a good act knows that the supernatural exists. He who does not will never know. All the philosophies espoused by men of science are worthless when faced with the disinterested action of one man of good."[182] Here, reclaiming the subject's introspective turn, only to subsequently tether its newfound agency to external ethical obligations, demonstrates the ideological dynamics at play in the aesthetic as a "mediatory category."[183]

In *The Ideology of the Aesthetic*, Terry Eagleton indicates how the essence of self-determination at the center of both aesthetics and subjectivation is not entirely deregulatory. Eagleton's "affective" subject, which is "sensitive, passionate, individualist," ultimately "poses an ideological challenge to the ruling order, elaborating new dimensions of feeling beyond its narrow scope."[184] In a similar fashion, for Caso the aesthetic marks a transcendence of the normative confines of positivism vis-à-vis introspective and spiritual autonomy, which is short-lived since the subject voluntarily forfeits its newly acquired independence to "a disinterested commitment with a common well-being."[185] Eagleton questions to what extent this ethical impulse of "free consent" could be "the antithesis of oppressive power, or a seductive form of collusion with it."[186] While parsing this inherent contradiction in the concept of the aesthetic, Eagleton underscores that:

On the one hand, it figures as a genuinely emancipatory force—as a community of subjects now linked by sensuous impulse and fellow-feeling rather than by heteronomous law, each safeguarded in its unique particularity while bound at the same time into social harmony. [. . .] On the other hand, the aesthetic signifies what Max Horkheimer has called a kind of "internalised repression," inserting social power more deeply into the very bodies of those it subjugates, and so operating as a supremely effective mode of political hegemony. To lend fresh significance to bodily pleasures and drives, however, if only for the purpose of colonizing them more efficiently, is always to risk foregrounding and intensifying them beyond one's control.[187]

One certainly gets a similar sense of duality when reading Caso's *La existencia como economía y como caridad.* While his pedagogy promotes an introspective process that gets channeled outwardly in an altruistic fashion, which certainly aligns with Prospero's lesson in *Ariel,* Caso's stringent stipulations of virtuous consciousness and conduct, which go well beyond Rodó's reverence for religiosity, reveal the stakes of his Christian aesthetic and ethical project, which are as high as they are prescriptive. According to Caso, "One must live fundamental intuitions. He who does not sacrifice himself does not understand the world in its totality, nor is it possible to explain it to him."[188] Immediacy and totality would seem to be at odds in a disinterested pedagogical project, but here they constitute two sides of the same coin. Although Caso's critique of science is that its purview, methods, and conclusions can only ever be partial, his recommendation that the world, in its totality, can only be understood through intuitive immediacy is certainly not void of its own ideological ironies. In fact, one would be hard pressed to think of a more effective fulcrum to ideology than immediacy. The invitation to self-exploration quickly presents a stark choice, one that fights intolerance with intolerance: you can only understand the totality of experience through intuitive immediacy and sacrifice, and you will not sacrifice unless you are a practicing Christian. Locating empowerment in subjective experience, which for Caso is simultaneously expansive and restrictive, autonomous yet regulated, subsequently calls on the subject to curb individual desires and chart new affects while reverting to very old religious ideas of sacrificing one's self-interest to other magnanimous imperatives.

As we have seen, Caso's philosophical practice is by no means strictly speculative. Nor, of course, is his pedagogical role, which at times takes on sacerdotal contours: "Reader: what is said here is only philosophy, and philosophy is an interest of knowledge. Charity is action. Go and commit charitable acts. Then, in addition to being wise, you will be saintly. Philosophy is impossible without charity; but charity is perfectly possible without philosophy."[189] In Caso's formulation, heroism is aesthetic and altruistic, an act of self-abnegation, which emanates from the introspective depths of the subject. Such displacements first toward and then away from the subject are inherent features of the humanist pedagogy at the core of *arielismo*, which is predicated on an idealist vision of eventuality, a futurity that its interpellated audience will put into motion, but will likely never see come to full fruition. However, in Caso we see an urgency to act, with an immediate spiritual payoff. But such recompense is no less mystical than in Rodó's essay, whose denouement is replicated in *La existencia*: "the supernatural order [of love] falls on the biological one and floods it with its divine impetus."[190]

Accentuating the tensions and fault lines between reason and religiosity helps us appreciate with more clarity the vague, but aesthetically powerful, significations of the spiritual base of *arielismo*. As an aspirational youth ethos, *arielismo* was a call to action to reformulate introspective exigencies in tandem with sociopolitical realities into a myriad of projects that shaped the epistemological and ethical contours of a subject that should be critical, but willing to compromise and ultimately consent to being a constructive agent of reform, which, as we have seen, does not require rupture but rather retention. Instead of a matter of inconsistency or failure, the logistics of charting secular introspection and spiritual illumination at the heart of the *arielista* project are too tangled, totalizing, and transcendental to be actualized. Although the *arielista* politicians, radicals, and professors I examined in this chapter tell their young readers (or listeners) to overcome ideologies and superstitions of the past by confronting and integrating new facts and ways of thinking, their mixed messaging, which oscillates between autonomy and relinquishment, muddles their calls for balancing mental emancipation and spiritual empowerment. Following Herbert Marcuse, perhaps we can read this desired consummation of the mind and spirit as an ideological sleight of hand of bourgeois affirmative culture that "uses the soul as a protest against reification, only to succumb to it."[191] In other words, idealist inwardness frees the individual to, somewhat surprisingly, keep itself in check.[192]

The final scene of *Ariel* shows the youngest of Prospero's students—Enjolrás—emerging from his customary "reflexive introspection" ("ensimismamiento reflexivo") to notice the celestial stars looking down on the masses.[193] This significant moment in Rodó's essay—the only time when the students speak in the text— illustrates the introspective and affective duality of the *arielista* project. At the same time, Enjolrás's distant gaze into the heavens implies its postponement to an undisclosed future. In this way, the centenary subject targeted by *arielista* pedagogies is suspended in what German philosopher Ernst Bloch terms an "Ontology of the Not-Yet."[194] While this sense of eventuality produces a hopeful effect for those who subscribe to the *arielista* program, it also forms the base of the ontologies of Non-Being formulated by Latin American iconoclasts who rejected *arielismo*'s optimism and whose work I examine in the next chapter.

CHAPTER 3

Pedagogies of Dissent
Anarchist Eclipses and the Suicidal Subject

The strongest man in the world is he who stands most
alone.

HENRIK IBSEN, *An Enemy of the People*

It is, a thousand times more noble, to die for Hatred of Life,
than to live in fear of Death.

JOSÉ MARÍA VARGAS VILA, *Huerto agnóstico*

"ARIEL," WRITES VÍCTOR Pérez Petit, "is a gospel for South
American youth: it has baptized its sublime inspiration with a serene
osculation, the fragrance of nards, and the transparency of light.
Ariel is the voice and conscience of our race."[1] Indeed, *Ariel* became
a common code and inspiring creed throughout Latin America,
which elevated Rodó to the iconic status of a "parish priest" (*cura
de almas*).[2] As a moral project of affirmation and consent, *Ariel* was
effective in part because it condensed a plethora of vague keywords
like love, beauty, good, harmony, personality, and will into a mes-
merizing rhetoric that, on the one hand, could be used to talk to

and about young people and that, on the other, they could appropriate to conceptualize and express themselves. Moreover, Prospero's praises of youth as a divinized, magical force border on apotheosis, which made it easier to bequeath to youth a comprehensive sense of self, as well as an urgent historical mission rife with collective responsibilities. As we saw in the previous chapter, the heroism of young subjects interpellated in *arielista* discourses—in addition to its unproblematically assumed whiteness that was demonstrated earlier in this book—comes to fruition through an introspective praxis that empowers their individuality, only to circumscribe it to stipulations of serenity and sacrifice.

There were also, however, dissenting *arielistas* who openly rejected the normative, ethical baggage with which *Ariel* saddled young people. Writers like José María Vargas Vila (Colombia) and Fernando Lles y Berdayes (Cuba) enjoy much less fanfare than other *arielistas*. In fact, we could even question their designation as *arielistas* since they offer stark and surprisingly understudied rebuttals to the central precepts of *arielismo*. Despite their confrontational dispositions and styles, their pedagogies of dissent tend to get either overlooked, or worse, subsumed by the very moralizing *arielismo* that they reject. In other words, another feature of *arielismo*'s reach as a critical construct is that it metabolizes transgressive counter-proposals, thereby reframing openly hostile noncompliance as consonant with *Ariel*'s constructive vision and soothing ethics. In response to this conflating tendency, this chapter examines the corruptive, anarchic proposals for extreme youth individualism that lurk in the recesses of the *arielista* archive, and analyzes the metaphorical solitary and suicidal acts of epistemic resistance that essayists Vargas Vila and Lles promote. Although, as this chapter suggests, those iconoclasts toy with *arielista* forms—such as countering Rodó's appropriation of *The Tempest* with their own reformulations of Shakespeare's *Hamlet* and *Timon of Athens*—they do so only to ridicule and reject the *arielista* enterprise of reform and redemption. Their apostate agendas, therefore, evidence a contested, rather than conflated, landscape of youth indoctrination of the centenary era.

Barbarians at the Gate: Odium, the Poetics
of Crisis, and the Solitary Subject

In the preface to the 1930 edition of *Ante los bárbaros (los Estados*
Unidos y la Guerra): el yanki; he ahí el enemigo, Colombian writer
José María Vargas Vila makes a rather refutable claim. He insists
that *Ante los bárbaros*, originally published as a booklet in Rome in
1900, made him *the* pioneering voice to predict and denounce US
imperialism in Latin America: "not a single one of my contemporaries appeared by my side, nor even close to me in that Initial Campaign of anti-Yankee-ism in America."[3] Even though "every bit of the
anti-Yankee Literature and Politics of the last twenty-five years in
America, comes from the ideas, theories, and passions that make up
this book," he bitterly recalls that his peers "disowned me and then
imitated me."[4] To say that Vargas Vila had an axe to grind would be
an understatement. A dyed-in-the-wool dissident, he was an unbe-
lievably prolific and widely read writer (one who even lived off the
royalties of his many books), yet he was overshadowed by more
canonical writers whose polished aesthetics delivered more palat-
able and calming ideals. However, evident in his categorical insistence that *Ante los bárbaros* "initiated the awakening of a new state
of consciousness in America," is a desire for recognition of his trailblazing, yet largely overlooked role as an anti-imperialist prophet.[5]
Even though the first version of *Ante los bárbaros* and *Ariel* were
both published in 1900, critics and collective memory recall with
alacrity the potency of Rodó's constructive cultural vision, while
Vargas Vila's work remains relegated to obscurity.

But this was not always the case. Rodó and Vargas Vila are among
the literary heavyweights that Cuban writer Miguel Ángel Carbonell
includes in *Hombres de nuestra América* (1915). His assessment positions the two essayists at opposite ends of the literary spectrum.
On the one hand, Carbonell considers Rodó the "prince of American prose, a profound thinker and a refined artist of the contemporary intelligentsia from the Latin Continent. [. . .] He has been able
to keep himself elevated and clean, and his name, on the wings of

fame, has traveled the countries of the race proud and triumphant."[6] In contrast, Vargas Vila is

A terrible iconoclast, he detests myths and beliefs; his lips never pronounce words of mercy, he is a ripper of veils and a scourge of idols. He aspires to emancipate the masses, but he does not want to be a part of them. He longs to redeem, but he is not so conceited to desire the laurel of popularity. He utterly loathes the illiterate masses that bear tyranny, just as he does the vile centurions that exercise it. He detests in equal measure that mob and this octopus.[7]

Given the evident disparities between a seemingly beyond reproach, celebrated *letrado* and an antisocial iconoclast, it is ironic that Carbonell later elects a particularly significant adjective to pinpoint where their respective works converge. Whereas Rodó's "evangelic doctrine dominates and imposes itself. The shadows disappear in the brightness of his powerful and original genius; everything is light around him," Vargas Vila's "evangelic and apocalyptic voice is heard with veneration in all the Continent, with the faith with which believers kneel before a priest that raises the holy wafer between his hands, and anoints the faithful of his church with the oils of his virtues."[8] Despite the sacerdotal description that Carbonell affords him, one would be hard-pressed to conjure a more unyielding nonconformist than Vargas Vila, who, as a sign of his full-fledged iconoclasm, dropped his first names of José and María. Yet, at the same time, the comparison is not entirely without reason, given that the initial chapters of *Ante los bárbaros* are laden with *arielista* language and tropes.

Vargas Vila announces "the hour of the Sower" (*Sembrador*), an optimistic redeemer whose social obligation to the masses and beyond is acutely reminiscent of key parts of Rodó's moral and transcendent project.[9] For example, sowing the seeds of faith and fecundity (two of *Ariel*'s most frequent and recognizable keywords) culminates in the essay's final scene, in which the youngest of Prospero's disciples, Enjolrás, steps onto the street and notices that, "As the masses pass by, I notice that, even though they do not look at the sky, the heavens look down at them. Over their indifferent and dark mass, like a furrowed field, something descends from high above. The vibration of the stars looks like the movement from the hands of a sower."[10] Similarly, Vargas Vila stipulates that he opts for hope over faith ("I have killed the Faith within me, but I have not killed Hope; / she sings in my heart . . . / *I hope*; / I sow the seed in the furrow, and, I await the birth of the Sun, over the remote skies"), which makes his commitment to being a constructive cultivator of Latin American futurity seem resolute.[11] In a categorical statement rather antithetical to his heretical reputation, Vargas Vila affirms that the "sower that devours the grain and does not plant it, mutilates Humanity and dashes the legacy of men."[12]

The *arielista* aura of *Ante los bárbaros*, however, promptly proves unsustainable, as the bulk of the text aggressively diverges from the subtlety and serenity of *Ariel* in tone, content, and expressive forms. The hopeful glimmers in early portions of *Ante los bárbaros* dissipate and in their place appears a resounding roar of dejection and doom. The about-face—from reproducing *arielismo* to upending it—is due in part to the fact that, unlike Rodó, Vargas Vila continued to update his text to incorporate and reflect on subsequent US interventions. In this way, he was able to offer a running testimony not on the fear of what Rodó called *nordomanía*, but its real-time consequences. This chronological collage explains the hybrid, not to mention conflicting, nature of *Ante los bárbaros*, which was expanded and reissued over three decades.

Rodó evokes the sanctity of the classroom and Vargas Vila the intensity of the public square. Replete with unrelenting, embittered critiques of US "filibusterismo" in Latin America—he considers *imperialism* too benevolent of a term—*Ante los bárbaros* sounds the alarm on elapsed and impending catastrophes much louder and more unequivocally than Rodó: "What is the danger of Latin America? / THE YANKEE DANGER."[13] In his nightmarish depiction of US occupations, "Washington stabs Bolívar in the back; and robs his treasures; / the Yankees, devote themselves to dividing up and stripping Latin America."[14] Casting the drama with historicized protagonists instead of polysemic conceptual ones (like Ariel and Caliban) is just one of the techniques that Vargas Vila utilizes to disquiet and denounce. The most effective, evidenced in the following quote, is a typical flourish of accumulation and recapitulation, which he uses to forcefully unmask the repeated and sustained plundering of Latin America by the United States:

> they advertised themselves as sons of Washington, but they were Walker's pirates; / they descended upon those countries like an elephant's foot, and squashed their heart; / so the Republic of Cuba, the Dominican Republic, the Nicaraguan Republic, and the Republic of Panama suffer in their arms; so the Filipino Republic drowned to death in blood; in this way strangled by the friendly hand of the republicans of the North; / in Cuba, conquest disguised as protection; in Manila, the conquest was declared in battle; in Puerto Rico, the possession was a tolerated conquest; in Santo Domingo the occupation was a blatant conquest; in Panama, the intervention was a shameless conquest; always and everywhere, Conquest; / and they call that despicable plundering: Victory.[15]

Vargas Vila's scathing invectives against US interventionism stand out, especially when compared with more rhetorically restrained, not to mention ambiguous and subtle, critiques of US hegemony in the region, like those found in Rodó's *Ariel* or Manuel Ugarte's "Carta abierta al Presidente de los Estados Unidos" (1913). In his widely published letter, Ugarte directly yet politely outlines the anxieties and discord Latin Americans feel under the weight of coercive US commercial practices and political policies. Written to incoming president Woodrow Wilson, under whose administration numerous interventions would occur (in Mexico, Haiti, the Dominican Republic, Cuba, Panama), Ugarte's denunciations are peppered with deferential tones, such as when he asserts that "We love and respect the United States, we admire that great country that should serve as a model for us in many things, we wish to collaborate with it in the work of discovering and enhancing the riches of the continent . . ."[16] Such cordial deference, tactical or otherwise, to the United States would have been unacceptable to Vargas Vila, whose own notoriety as a staunch anti-imperialist would ultimately take a back seat to Ugarte's. Whether read as naïve, timorous, or both, Ugarte's reverential appeal to President Wilson walks a fine rhetorical line between critique and concession, ultimately falling well short of the unmitigated censure like that manifest in *Ante los bárbaros*.

But there is no safe haven in the Colombian's work, and Vargas Vila gives no leeway to Latin Americans, whom he admonishes for their apathy or complicity with the "yankisación" affecting various countries in the region: "they adored Roosevelt; / and, they adored Taft; / and, they adored Elius Rooth [sic], the babbling Saint Peter of those Christs of Conquest, . . . / and, today they adore Wilson, this pedagogue of plunder crowned with smiles."[17] And, in what could be read as a slight to Rodó's often-cited, and frequently exaggerated phrase—"Although I admire them, I do not love them" ("Aunque les admiro, no les amo")—for Vargas Vila, "the admiration of the Yankee, is in Latin America, the most vivid and profound sign of our degradation."[18] In fact, he goes a step beyond Rodó's maxim and insists, "hatred for the Yankee, should be our motto, since, that hate is our duty; an imperative duty."[19]

Even though such emphatic statements leave little room for equivocation, *Ante los bárbaros* is a rather unhinged text, one that constantly erects and subsequently demolishes its own arguments. As Carlos Jáuregui demonstrates in his analysis of Vargas Vila's essay, the reader receives conflicting messages that hinder the text's ability to resonate coherently:

> The Latin America of *Ante los bárbaros* calls for a union that it declares impossible, affiliates itself with a Europe that it considers treacherous, affirms and criticizes Latinity, and uses and denies ethnicity as an essence of identity. *Ante los bárbaros* is a manifesto against the barbarism of one race that is not a race and in favor another one that is not a race either, against the barbarians of the north and, at the same time, criticizing and praising the barbarisms of the south, proclaiming the fallacy of the inferiority of races, but praising English imperialism for being an "imperi-

alism of a race" and for civilizing and producing the "blossoming of the colonies."[20]

Jáuregui opines that, unlike *Ariel, Ante los bárbaros* "fails as a cultural manifesto" because of the pronounced contradictions that reveal "a journey through the emergence and apocalyptic crisis of *arielismo* and its metaphors."[21] When compared with Rodó's dichotomous Ariel and Caliban, which provided an empowering circumvention to positivist prognoses, Vargas Vila's conceptual tropes—the condor of the South and the eagle of the North—lack the optimism and futurity that made *Ariel's* message felt throughout the continent. Whereas Rodó summons Ariel as a spiritual antidote to barbarism, Vargas Vila's symbolic condor is dormant and ultimately impotent, unable, or perhaps unwilling to challenge its potent northern counterpart. Rather than a call to arms or action, *Ante los bárbaros* reads like "a type of death rattle epilogue of *arielista* anti-imperialism."[22]

In the final pages of *Ante los bárbaros*, Vargas Vila evokes the need for a Bolivarian-like movement that would unify the continent against a mutual adversary—and one that would be spearheaded by a redemptive figure Rodó called "el que vendrá," but categorically kneecaps its potentiality:

> the time has come in which we need a Man, or a People, that possessed the superiority, initiative, greatness, and Genius;
> [. . .]
> in the heinous futility of the current moment, there is no such Man, nor People.
> Nobody! Nothing! . . .
> when destiny wishes to punish an epoch, it condemns it to sterility.[23]

As Jáuregui notes, there is no identifiable interlocutor in *Ante los bárbaros*.[24] Despite the glimmers of hope littered throughout the early part of the text, young readers would find little incentive to embrace and execute the kind of benevolent heroic mission that Rodó assigned to them. *Arielismo* certainly fetishized the mystical potentiality of youth, a widespread trend that largely obfuscated alternative iterations of discordant juvenescence. During the same time that coercive articulations of consent imagined the contours of the young subject, other essayists were thinking a resistant subject, an *epistemic subject*, whose aggressive noncompliance and open antagonism to the *letrado*'s moral and social obligations challenged the normative parameters of the *arielista* interpellation.

SOWING THE SEEDS OF DISSENT IN THE AGNOSTIC ORCHARD

According to the prologue of *Huerto agnóstico: cuadernos de un solitario* (1912), one of the many of Vargas Vila's books that have gone largely unnoticed, two young police officers in Panama left behind the following disturbing, accusatory message before taking their own lives: "[T]he reasons for our suicide can be found on page 229 of Vargas Vila's *Ibis*."[25] The incident, whether accurate or invented, prompted plenty of outrage. An Argentine writer even went so far as to make a public appeal to mothers to create an anti-Vargas Vila league aimed at protecting their children from falling under his abhorrently corruptive influence.[26] Rather than try to shift culpability or downplay the panic provoked by such a horrific episode, Vargas Vila exacerbates the scandal by asking and affirming with shocking hubris, "why should I feel Remorse, when I see the flowers that I plant bloom drenched in blood?: to destroy is more glorious than to create."[27]

Embracing his reputation as a firebrand, the matter-of-fact prologue to *Huerto agnóstico*—a title that does not sufficiently capture the unapologetic atheism espoused in its pages—never disputes the critiques of his work as morbid and iconoclastic:

> that the Atheism of my books, naked like a Titan, terrifies souls; [. . .] that the agnosticism of my books, sows desolation in the spirits and, renders them unarmed for any form of *percoric* effort, that is, Sacrifice? [. . .] that [my books] brutally close the horizons of Hope; [. . .] that my books corrupt the Youth. [. . .] that I am a sower of Death, because my theories about Suicide, coming to

fruition in certain minds, has made them seek out the blow from
a revolver . . .;
> that my books are made against God;
> against Religion;
> against the Fatherland;
> against Society;
> against Family;
> against Women . . .
> against all my Idols;
> against all slaveries;
> against all subjugations . . .
> . . .
> you all are right;
> burn my books . . .[28]

Relishing in his confrontational clout—as serious as it is sardonic—
Vargas Vila advises, "this book, like all of my books, is a book of
Negation . . . / I advise weak souls not to even get close to it; it
would be fatal for them."[29] Needless to say, Vargas Vila has a particular reader in mind, and that interpellated subject goes by many
names: "alma de selección," "Hombre Superior," "Hombre Libre," "el
Hombre puro, el Hombre fuerte," "el Hombre Verdadero."[30] Unlike
Rodó's obedient young students, Vargas Vila's superior/free/pure/
strong/true subject inherits the destructive tendencies of Nietzsche
and Max Stirner and prefers solitude to sociability.

Rather than reproduce prevalent ideologies of reform and perfectibility popularized by Prospero's sermon, Vargas Vila assigns a
divergent role for his subject: "no Superior Man, is a Builder; / due
to his Sublime Instinct, he is a Destroyer."[31] Competing subject formations are at the center of this oppositional pedagogy. Against "el
Yo Ideológico" (the Ideological I)—a sense of self overtaken by hegemonic dictums of philosophy, religion, and politics—Vargas Vila
defends "el Yo Fisiológico" (the Physiological I), which he also calls
"el Yo Interior" (the Inner I).[32] Shaped not by ideology but rather by
an instinctual consciousness of egocentricity, "el Yo Interior" brings
to mind Rodó's *reino interior*, but the two should not be conflated.

In *The Politics of Spanish American Modernismo: By Exquisite Design*, Gerard Aching reevaluates the "evasive detachment hypothesis" of the *modernista reino interior* (inner realm), and, through examining Darío's prologues, reframes that figurative imaginary as an empowering space of an individual aesthetic practice with explicit social purposes.[33] As Aching argues, Darío's patent elitism does not preclude social matters, but rather, given its concern with the shifting conditions of literary production, reception, and the poet's role in modernity, it is inextricable from them.[34] In other words, Darío's elitist pose and preferences do not necessarily mean that his persona and work "denote flight." Rather, they constitute an "ambivalent form of engagement."[35] Importantly, Aching's reassessment calls into question the stark dialectic of social confrontation or escapism, as if they were two distinct, steady planes of existence and experience, thereby opening up space for rethinking the nature and aims of solitude at the heart of the *reino interior*.

Perhaps the most explicit articulation of the *reino interior* comes in the form of the parable of the hospitable king in Rodó's *Ariel*. Instead of a begrudging acceptance of the *modernista* artist's unavoidable relationship with social surroundings and conditions, Prospero proposes an exemplary ethics embodied in the generous monarch who welcomes all into his resplendent palace yet seeks refuge to reflect in a secluded room down a long corridor where no one is permitted to enter. This sacred allegorical haven, "the setting of your inner kingdom," is more than an epistemological reprieve from the social obligations assigned to Prospero's students.[36] Indeed, it holds the key to becoming "free men."[37] Yet, that achieved autonomy is both necessary and temporary, as it is inevitably inflected back to transforming the inner dimensions of the *arielista* subject, so that it may subsequently revamp its society.

Solitude is something we usually associate with Rodó the writer, but not with his work. In his biography of Rodó, Víctor Pérez Petit, one of Rodó's closest friends, collaborators, and defenders, recounts the spiritual dejection experienced by turn-of-the-century youth, who were, in his opinion, contaminated by naturalist and decadent literary trends that spread cynical attitudes.[38] *Ariel*, "the shining star that would be the new star of Bethlehem for South American youth," was a regenerative sermon to spur youth in danger of being seduced by creeds of egocentricity into benevolent, forward-looking action.[39] Indeed, both *Ariel* and *Motivos de Proteo* dedicate many pages to encouraging young people to reject positivist pessimisms, look inward, and "develop, to the extent possible, not just one lone aspect but rather the plenitude of your being," all with the aim of transforming themselves, their world, and their successors.[40] It is ironic, then, that despite the "mystical teaching of Latin American youth" that *Ariel* wielded, Rodó was a notorious loner.[41] The most well-known and widely circulated photograph of Rodó, alone in his office surrounded by books, corroborates the fact that he was, in the words of Pérez Petit, a "solitary soul, [...] always self-absorbed."[42] Yet Rodó's seclusion does not preclude his sincere dream of a continental community from reaching and benefitting countless readers.[43]

Although both Rodó and Vargas Vila reflect on the role of solitude in their respective emancipatory visions, *Ariel* never loses sight of the interpellated subject's benevolence and responsibility to others. In contrast, Vargas Vila offers a more extreme iteration of the inner sanctity of *modernista* subjectivity; while solitude is likewise for him a "refuge" from forces that could harm the individual's well-being, that solitude is not, as it is for Prospero, a brief hiatus from the masses, but rather a goal of permanence: "An Isolated Person, a Recluse, is by the sole virtue of remaining away from everyone, a strange and superior being."[44] Just as we witness the failure of *arielista* tropes in *Ante los bárbaros, Huerto agnóstico* goes a step further and enacts a crisis of the interpellated *arielista* subject that pushes it toward a sense of superiority that resides in solitude, not solidarity, embraces resignation over regeneration, prefers self-interest to sacrifice, and seeks abolition instead of edification. Vargas Vila's pedagogy of dissent, then, is concerned primarily with subject formation, or, more accurately, subject *deformation*.

In an ontological mine field monopolized by *arielista* optimism, Vargas Vila delights in molding detractors in a negative fashion: "I de-cretinize (*descretinizo*) the youth, and liberate it from bias."[45] "Desidiotizar" (to de-idiotize) is the endgame for a project that seeks to "deform" and "degrade" whenever and wherever possible.[46] Take, for example, Vargas Vila's succinct reworking of Hamlet's famous soliloquy: "ser un Idiota, o un Sabio; / that is the question."[47] This Shakespearean distortion is suggestive for a number of reasons. First, it could be read as a slight to Rodó, who intertextually appropriated the symbolic capital of Ariel, Caliban, and Prospero from Shakespeare's *The Tempest*—albeit filtered primarily through Renan. In posing a rather stark choice—imbecility or perspicacity—Vargas Vila cuts to the chase in a way that Rodó's lofty rhetoric and elaborate style avoids at all costs. Moreover, in tackling the fraught relationship between being and knowing, Vargas Vila goes beyond a Cartesian consciousness that finds ontological verification in the *act* of thinking, no matter its reliability. We should remember, after all, that Hamlet's dilemma—to endure life's hardships or avoid them through suicide—is spawned primarily by doubt. Even though his impulse is to take his life, the fear and uncertainty surrounding the finality or retribution for the sinful act of suicide cause him to hesitate. In the end, however, Hamlet is mortally wounded by a poisoned blade. But, on his way out, he instructs Horatio, his closest friend, not to drink poison in solidarity, but rather go forth and tell Hamlet's story.

Vargas Vila's reformulation of the Shakespearean soliloquy signals that the question is not existence or death, but rather how religious doxa can warp the subject's decisions about the integrity of its own sovereignty. The subject that looks away from itself for guidance forfeits its interests to external sources. Therefore, distorting Hamlet's predicament kills two birds with one stone; it simultaneously pokes fun at Rodó's dependence on the orienting tropes derived from Shakespeare, as well as subverts the prohibitive religious morality in *Hamlet*. Doubt leaves the door open for susceptibility to dogma, to self-sacrifice. This is why Vargas Vila insists on "the Certainty of *Not Believing*" (la Certidumbre del *No Creer*) as a cornerstone of his project.[48] Certainty derived not from religious faith, but rather from the absurdity of its viability, is a decisive step toward the "abolition of Life."[49] A sovereign conception of life, then, means to "despise Life"—in all of its normative impositions—and having the courage to face death.[50] "Finis Latinorum," a phrase prominently featured in

Antes los bárbaros, along with the final words of *Huerto agnóstico,* "Finis Vitam," suggest that solitude is but a requisite first step in an emancipatory pedagogy that blatantly demystifies and desacralizes the obligatory contours of the *arielista* interpellation.[51] With love, beauty, harmony, burden, and destiny off the table, an alternative centenary subject—misanthropic, solitary, and suicidal—emerges in Latin America. And it appears not in Prospero's prescriptive fictionalized classroom, but necessarily in nonnormative orchards of dissent. These corrupting settings—Vargas Vila's *huerto agnóstico* and Cuban essayist Fernando Lles's malefic *higuera* (fig tree)—make room for select young subjects to be deprogrammed, recalibrated, and let loose.

FERNANDO LLES AND RECALCITRANT NON-BEING

When Fernando Lles y Berdayes published his first book, *La higuera de Timón* (*Timon's Fig Tree*) in 1921, reviews were overwhelmingly unfavorable. Most critics considered the text's pessimism and scandalous imagery dangerous to a tenuous sociopolitical order. One reviewer, a Cuban diplomat named José de la Luz León, labeled Lles "a disturbed, restless, deep, pensive, shapeless, and sad spirit" and lamented that "no light guides us to a calm port, towards no place whatsoever, where our inner fears may be calmed."[52] Other critics, however, averred that as a philosopher Lles surpassed Rodó and belonged in Rubén Darío's *Los raros,* a showcase of famous writers like Verlaine, Poe, and Ibsen.[53] Medardo Vitier, one of the foremost authorities on Cuban intellectual history, not to mention Lles's life-long philosophical sparring partner, even commented in his prologue to *La higuera de Timón* that, "With the exception of some literary works by José Martí, I can affirm that I do not know anything with such force and beauty in contemporary Spanish-language prose," a statement that he was subsequently pressured to recant.[54] Luz's review, which is more concerned with correcting Vitier's excessive praise than with commenting on Lles's essay, prompted Vitier to respond that he had no idea that his endorsement of his friend's debut prose work would be used as a "mortifying preface."[55] In fact,

Vitier acknowledges the accuracy of Luz's estimations: "I know that my prologue has not been accepted as just. More than one distinguished writer has pointed out my excessive praise, my impassioned opinion, and the inexactness of my comparisons."[56] Although Vitier reaches the brink of an apology for his exaggerations, he nevertheless insists on the value of Lles's essay, writing "I still believe that contemporary Spanish prose does not have a handful of pages with more vigor than *La higuera de Timón*."[57]

This episode demonstrates the precarious place that Lles occupies in Cuban literary and philosophical studies. Despite comparisons to three of the *modernista* founding fathers (Martí, Darío, and Rodó), it has been challenging to judge Lles on his own merits, which, when lauded, were prone to substantial backlash. Since Lles "repudiates and condemns . . . any social reform with a gregarious character that restricts or diminishes individual liberties," not to mention that "he always detested hypocrites and fake people," his oppositional stance in part explains the little fanfare he received during his life and since his death.[58] Yet, it is ironic that his work has either been glossed over or situated within an *arielista* tradition that, as I will argue in the following pages, cannibalizes radical subjectivity in the early Cuban Republic and reveals the consumptive logic of literary canonization that masks recalcitrant iterations of individual dissent.

ARIELISMO, NEOCOLONIALITY, AND PATRIA

When the United States co-opted the Cuban War of Independence and rebranded that conflict as the Spanish-American War, essentially recolonizing a decolonizing process thirty years in the making, it shook Latin America's geopolitical and cultural imaginary. In response, Rodó's *Ariel* became one of the most resounding and influential voices against US hegemony in the Western Hemisphere. Rodó's concerns, as it turned out, were justified, as numerous US interventions, some repeated and sustained, would take place in the following few decades throughout Latin America and the Caribbean, the spaces that composed what Greg Grandin termed *Empire's Workshop*.[59]

Just as *Ariel* was a response to events in Cuba in 1898, Cubans also reacted to *Ariel*. Even though Rodó wrote from a small, wealthy country on the verge of an expansive social democracy, thousands of miles away from the nearest US intervention, his message of idealism, agency, reform, and futurity resonated with Cuban writers, intellectuals, and activists trying to navigate the neocolonial aftermath of the Spanish-American War. After the First US Occupation of Cuba from 1899 to 1902, during which time US colonial governors oversaw all political and economic matters on the island, the Platt Amendment of 1903 ensured that Cuba would remain a US neocolony until at least 1934, when it was repealed as a result of the Revolution of 1933. Under the agreement, the United States would only end its first occupation if Cubans agreed to the permanent stipulations of the Platt Amendment, prohibited the island from entering into any treaties with other countries, secured land for a naval station (Guantánamo), validated all future US military acts on the island, and, most importantly, gave the US the right to intervene whenever it saw fit under the pretext of maintaining political stability and protecting Cuban independence and American economic interests, a right that would be frequently evoked in the coming decades.

When Cuba's first president, Tomás Estrada Palma, sought a second term, liberals alleged fraud and violently contested the election results, prompting the Second US Occupation of Cuba from 1906 to 1909. The United States threatened to intervene in 1912 in what became known as La guerrita de las razas (The Little Race War), when the Cuban military, under orders from President José Miguel Gómez, killed between 3,000 and 12,000 Afro-Cubans rebelling against a law that made it illegal to establish political parties on the basis of race. Political unrest and the murder of opposition candidates would provoke the Sugar Intervention from 1917 to 1922. Naturally, there were economic benefits to the United States' tutelary role on the island, as US companies exerted control over industries like transportation, electricity, construction, oil, and sugar. And the resulting systemic corruption created a sort of *cacocracia*, a "thief-ocracy" regulated by bribery and *botelleros* (connected people who got cushy jobs for which they were paid in absentia).[60]

For decades American capitalism and imperialism ensured that the island would be, in Julio Antonio Mella's words, "a country that has never been free," which is why the Cuban Revolution refers to the Republic as the 'Pseudo Republic,' or the Neocolonial, Semicolonial, Dependent, or Obstructed Republic—*la república mediatizada*.[61] In 1918, Cuban poet José Manuel Poveda summed up the bitter discouragement of experiencing repeated cycles of foreign intervention and the accompanying social and administrative disorder that would characterize Cuban life of the Republic, stating, "We are not independent. We are nothing but a colonial factory, obligated to work, and forfeit its harvest and profits, compelled by the whip. [. . .] [A] gust of dissolution has dispersed the creative energies of the national soul. We are the shadow of a nation, the dream of a democracy, yearning for freedom. We do not exist."[62]

With the objective of filling this perceived ontological void, the desire to *hacer patria* (to forge a fatherland) became the primary motif and process of the early Republic, and, as it turns out, one of the rallying cries of the Cuban Revolution decades later: *Patria o muerte*. Rodó was a vital protagonist in that project in the 1900s and 1910s, which became evident when writer Jesús Castellanos inaugurated the 1910 Society of Conferences in Havana by offering lengthy accolades of Rodó's *Motivos de Proteo*, which he called "the new Bible of hope" for Cuba.[63] More often than not, admiration for Rodó, whose enthusiastic praises were often sung in Cuban print culture, reads more like religious devotion than mere appreciation. Take, for example, Raúl Argastabe's article entitled, "At the Feet of Ariel," published in the literary magazine *Letras* in 1914: "We believe that [in Cuba] the furrow will always remain open for the seed of redemption. And we believe that this seed . . . is only in the hands of Ariel who, like in the end of Prospero's speech, gazes down on us from above, disgusted by our miseries, but will soon reach down and plant fertile seeds as soon as Caliban abandons us."[64]

Dissonant factions of the political spectrum conceptualized *patria*—whether as a geopolitical entity, a spiritual affect, or a cultural catalyst—as the ubiquitous remedy to truncate Cuban neocoloniality. I would like to explore an inimical phenomenon: the

development and pedagogy of a counter neocolonial consciousness that resists the framework of patria and its idealistic tropes.
In doing so, I step away from Havana and look to Matanzas, the
hometown of a brilliant, but largely overlooked poet, essayist, and
philosopher named Fernando Lles y Berdayes. Together with his
younger brother Francisco, he published three volumes of poetry,
after which time he dedicated his efforts to cultivating philosophical and sociopolitical essays.[65] In all of his texts published in the
1920s and 30s, such as his 1934 treatise *Individualism, Socialism, and
Communism*, Lles connects the dots between patriotic sentiments,
religiously derived moral codes, political corruption, violence, and
repressive state apparatuses. Lles's project, which negates collective potentiality, centers on a different type of centenary subject—a
radical subject—and its relationship to society and the state, a topic
that would be revisited and redefined in the decades leading up and
after the Cuban Revolution. Given this Marcusean great refusal, it is
curious that literary histories have situated Lles's work overwhelmingly within an *arielista* frame.

In fact, in surveying Cuban literary history it is rare to find a critical assessment that does not explicitly link Lles and Rodó. More
often than not, however, the nature of that connection tends to be
either obfuscated by vague assertions, which subsequent critics
reproduce, or inevitably slanted toward Rodó. For instance, in his
expansive study of *La evolución de la cultura cubana (1608–1927)*
(1928), José Manuel Carbonell offers a rather reductive take on Lles's
connection to Rodó: "His mental affiliation seems to be in Rodó. His
style is harmonious and straightforward."[66] However, for José Antonio Portuondo, the ties that bind Lles to Rodó reside not in ideological affinities, but rather in a shared style of carefully crafted prose:
"In contrast to the disillusioned and bitter group that inaugurated
the Republic, these men of 1910 offer the example of a profound
and intelligent concern for contemporary problems, examined with
essentially idealist criteria and expressed, generally speaking, in a
careful, sculptural style that the Uruguayan José Enrique Rodó was
imposing at the time. This influence is evident, above all, in essayists like Fernando Lles and Emilio Gaspar Rodríguez."[67] Noting Lles's

profound skepticism, which is a defining feature of his work that some critics sidestep or whitewash, Juan J. Remos y Rubio considers Rodó's influence on Lles "purely aesthetic."[68] From Carbonell in 1928, through Portuondo and Remos y Rubio's respective takes in the 1940s and 50s, into the 1970s with Raimundo Lazo's *Historia de la literatura cubana* (1974), and even as recently as the Instituto de Literatura y Lingüística's *Historia de la literatura cubana* (2003), the reading of Lles's work by Cuban critics has tended to pose it as derivative or inseparable from Rodó.[69]

One pioneering exception to this commonplace critical categorization comes from Carlos Loveira, a Cuban writer whose novels *Generales y doctores* (1920) and *Juan Criollo* (1927) exposed the absurd sociopolitical paradoxes of Republican life. An orphan, autodidact, veteran, socialist, and labor activist, Loveira decided to dedicate his *discurso de ingreso* into the Academia Nacional de Artes y Letras in Havana to "Un gran ensayista cubano: Fernando Lles" (1926). Chief among his aims in that speech was offering an appreciation of Lles's work that was not confined to framing it as derivative of Rodó's essays:

> With respect to these literary parallels, I have read that Fernando Lles, like almost all of the essayists in our America, arising out of Rodó's hotbed, has found inspiration for his work in the models of the renowned Uruguayan writer. The notion is erroneous in my opinion. A full, calm, and impartial reading of our compatriot's books is enough to not accept that identity and discredit that comparison. [. . .] To say that Lles owes his initiation in thought and art to Rodó, cannot be anything other than an opinion formed by a superficial impression, when not by a half-opened book.[70]

In a tone both categorical and accusatory, Loveira elaborates on the important, and rather glaring, differences between Lles and Rodó:

> These two authors are antipodes in content and form, in morals and in style. There is an abyss between Lles's vast, piercing, complicated, and agitated ideology, and the purely romantic, spiritual

serenity that prevails in the South American essayist. The work of the latter aspires to erect a renovated ideology through old channels, that does not bother to examine, with very few exceptions, the inner essence of being and of life. The other's work, perhaps touches on this ideology in passing, but only to turn it around, to uncloak its secular failures, its morbid influence, and its false and poisonous conformism.[71]

The specificity of Loveira's assertions did little to dissuade subsequent critics from linking Lles to Rodó. Although a detailed comparative study of all of Lles's and Rodó's essays is beyond the scope of this chapter, I would like to pick up from Loveira's lead and inspect the confluences and departures in Rodó's *Ariel* and Lles's *La higuera de Timón*, two texts whose formal similarities should not, as we will see, be conflated with shared perspectives and objectives.

At first glance, such a comparison is understandable: the texts are roughly the same length, divided into six sections, and employ a narrative figures derived from Shakespearean plays (*The Tempest*, 1610 and *Timon of Athens*, 1623). Moreover, both have a pedagogical purpose and interpellate young subjects through a deceptive "dialogical effect" in which their addressees remain silent.[72] Lastly, they are constructed upon a vast network of intertextual references, many of which derive from Classical sources. Although *La higuera de Timón* shares these formal similarities with Rodó's essay, it vigorously dismantles the intellectual content of the Uruguayan's *arielista* project.

In *La higuera de Timón*, Lles revives the narrative voice of the infamous misanthrope Timon, a citizen of Athens who lived during the Peloponnesian War. Judging by the essay's intertextuality, it is likely that Lles read about Timon of Athens in Spanish translations of Plutarch and Aristophanes. But Plato, Lucian, Seneca, Montaigne, Emerson, and Marx also reference Timon's misanthropy. Despite Timon's classical origins, Shakespeare's *Timon of Athens* became one of the most popular vehicles for disseminating the Athenian's reputation. All of the aforementioned writers tell Timon's story in similar ways. He is a charitable man who hosts lavish banquets and gives money to his friends in need. But, when the money runs out, no one

will reciprocate his generosity, so he denounces the falsity of fair-
weather friends and isolates himself in a cave in the woods. There,
Timon finds an underground treasure of gold and decides to invest
it in the destruction of Athens by dividing it between a cynic and
two prostitutes who promise to spread venereal diseases throughout
the capital. When two senators approach Timon in hopes of convincing him to call off the attack he subsidized, the only solace he
offers is for the Athenians to come hang themselves from a tree he
planted outside his cave.

Lles's *La higuera de Timón* opens with the first-person narrator,
"I, Timon of Athens . . . in these latitudes of the Intertropic," recre-
ating the last scene in Shakespeare's play, that is, the one where he
encourages his fellow Athenians to commit suicide before he chops
down his fig tree.[73] Lles's essay bifurcates into a diatribe against the
neocolonial farce, on the one hand, and a strategy for navigating it,
on the other. Like Nietzsche's Zarathustra, Timon delivers an incisive
denunciation of a grotesque social landscape beneath him, conveyed
by metaphors of eco-toxicity, such as when he decries the "manure
heaps of fraud and lies" that permeate "our swampy democracy," a
clear reference to a particular Cuban neocolonial condition.[74] Unlike
the venerated teacher Prospero, who in *Ariel* delivers a seemingly
benevolent sermon to a select group of students, Timon exhorts a
lone, silent interlocutor, "el pequeño" Antonio, to confront the alien-
ating fact that neocolonial existence is not a world of possibilities to
be enacted or achieved, but rather a stifling cesspool of corruption,
oppression, and disappointment—or, in his words, a "bubbling . . .
trash heap, [. . .] an enormous, germ-filled sewer, utterly fetid and
hideous like a gigantic puss-filled blister."[75]

However, Lles's Timon does not seek to circumvent this toxicity.
Rather, he plants his fig tree there and proclaims it "Timon's Eden,"
where "cursed fruits poison the air by spreading their pestilential
stench."[76] In contrast to the biblical Garden of Eden, Timón's Eden
embraces the connoted downfall of humanity because "the misanthrope knows that there is immense joy in the bottom of the glass
that contains the scum of our pain."[77] This scandalous imagery of
environmental toxicity, and a plethora of related tropes in the text,

challenge the auspicious, serene space of the classroom—the setting for Rodó's spiritualist pedagogy—and illuminate a methodology of desecration that purges moral and nationalist ideals of their sacred character.

In *Ariel*, a book many consider an "American evangel," Prospero tells his students that they have a moral responsibility to renovate Latin American democracies and ways of thinking. The foundation of their "conscience of obligation" is firmly rooted in Christian altruism.[78] Timon clearly offers an antithetical project, a Nietzschean dysangel that disentangles affective manipulations and exposes them as hegemonic mechanisms that mask the actual antagonistic relationship between the subject and the "immense spoliarium" that surrounds it. The Spoliarium, which refers to a dungeon under the Roman Coliseum where mortally wounded gladiators were taken after defeat and relieved of their belongings—is, for Lles, a space in which "war industries settle things with the reason of a machine gun."[79] What Timon calls his "strong pedagogy," his "demolishing enterprise to put everything out in the open," seeks to annihilate "sentimental pedagogies" that market "sublime responsibilities" such as religious morality and patriotic sacrifice, and advocates the absolute sovereignty of the self as the only possibility of autonomy in a country where everything seems corrupted.[80] It is clear that Timon's brand of individualism demystifies Prospero's inflating rhetoric, such as when he prescribes, "Do not aspire to anything that is not living and dying naturally."[81] The desacralization of religious motifs and narratives of resurrection and redemption culminates in a complex and controversial metaphor of the suicide of the epistemic subject.

SUICIDAL METAPHORS AND THE EXTREME AGENCY OF THE EPISTEMIC SUBJECT

The principal symbol of Lles's text, the fig tree, has discrepant implications according to the people who wish to hang themselves from it. On the one hand, Timon offers the branches of his fig tree to an Athenian society that he despises. It is important to note that Lles's hometown of Matanzas was commonly called 'The Athens of Cuba' because it produced so many well-known poets. The metaphorical suicide that Timon facilitates for Athenians/*matanceros* is a gesture of aggression, denunciation, and vengeance. But he also reserves a special branch of his "redeeming fig tree" (*higuera redentora*) for Antonio, his only pupil, to effectuate his own demise: "a leafy and compassionate branch of the secular tree of my orchard, from which you can neatly hang yourself knowing full well that your rest will never again be disturbed."[82] Contrary to the condemnatory nature of the some of the branches, Antonio's hanging is an emancipatory exploit that effaces religious coercion and nationalist ideologies.[83] In *The Future of an Illusion* (1927), Freud argues that the legitimacy of religion rests on its effectiveness at curbing the psychological fear of death by offering a comforting assurance of an eternal afterlife.[84] Reframing the act of suicide as a "momento reparador," a refreshing, restorative, or fortifying moment, depletes the negativity and despair surrounding death, and paves the way for Timon's tree to become an edifying site of a secular consciousness—one that repudiates the redemptive, messianic, and apostolic symbolic capital surrounding José Martí so commonly appropriated by diverse factions through-out Cuban history.[85]

Timon's ominous tree also disempowers ecological tropes that Martí and Rodó used in their respective culturalist projects. Martí, for instance, frequently employed arboreal imagery in his poems and essays to mobilize Latin American unity and liberation. As he writes in "Nuestra América" (1891), "the trees must form ranks to keep the giant with seven-league boots from passing!"[86] Trees, specifi-cally the *ceiba*, would become a recurring motif in Martí's poetry, as well a sacred signifier of Cuban identity and autonomy after the Spanish-American War. For example, in 1898 Spanish military offi-cials surrendered to the United States under a *ceiba* tree in San-tiago, a symbolic act that would be undermined when delegates at the 1928 Pan-American Conference in Havana, who were there to debate the contentious US occupation of Nicaragua, planted a *ceiba* tree as a gesture of Pan-American camaraderie.[87] Timon's threat to chop down his tree subverts the strength and solidarity inscribed in Martí's trees, not to mention Peruvian thinker Manuel González

Prada's insistence that "Let new trees come and give new flowers and new fruit! Old people to the grave, youth to work!"[88] Moreover, his fig tree also opposes the strong aerial symbolism in Rodó's essay. Ariel, the winged spirit, represents a spiritualist empowerment of the future political elite who are responsible for guiding society toward higher, disinterested ideals. The act of hanging oneself from the branches of Timon's fig tree, rooted in the earth, denotes Lles's leitmotif of grounding spiritualist and religious discourses in the empirical reality of the natural world. The rope that restrains the body from ascension further reinforces this idea, as it is made of natural products and anchored to a tree.

In Lles's project, suicide disrupts life-affirming *arielista* rhetoric that propagates the idea that youth has eternal, supernatural qualities and represents the liberating moment when Antonio will shatter the illusion of a transcendent futurity: "your youth should end . . . radiantly, beautifully, and resolved to sink into the profound night of individual nothingness."[89] Antonio's hanging, then, evinces a desired transformation toward "el NO SER," an "opting out," to use Bourdieu's terminology, of what Timon dubs the "morbid contagion" of simulating "vital and ultravital responsibilities"—"that which is willingly and deliberately falsified."[90] Stirner called this moment a "breaking off," a precept echoed in the Emersonian motto of "Act singly."[91] An extreme act of individualist agency, suicide is the metaphorical vehicle deployed to erect an individualist existence devoid of religious narratives and political oppression—or, to use to use Agamben's phrasing, a sovereign act that "realizes itself by taking away its own potentiality not to be."[92] "Non being"—el NO SER—is, above all, a project of sincerity that requires finding the courage that can forge an existence free of "beloved specters" and that is embodied in Timon's catch phrase in the text, *¡Atrévete!* (Dare to be bold!)[93] And this is why in his work Lles resuscitates classical antiheroes, such as Timon the misanthrope, Julian the Apostate, Diogenes the cynic, and Democritus—the laughing philosopher who mocked his contemporaries—and recasts them as transgressive models for young people to emulate, counteracting the blatant hero worship in *Ariel* derived from Carlyle.[94]

In his famous sociological study, Émile Durkheim suggested that more social control, in the form of religion, was an effective deterrent to suicide.[95] Marx, however, saw suicide not as a moral matter, but as a response to authority and capitalist oppression.[96] Lles's life and work support Marx's formulation that suicide is a symptom of larger material and social conditions. For example, as a child during the Cuban War of Independence, he witnessed the devastating effects of Spanish governor-general Valeriano Weyler's *reconcentración* strategy. With the objective of interrupting the flow of resources and other support to the Cuban independence movement, ordinary peasants or *guajiros* were transferred to internment camps located in areas controlled by Spanish troops, such as Matanzas, where hundreds of thousands died of hunger and disease. *Reconcentrados* were essentially concentration camps.[97] The transition from colony to neocolony kept in place similar oligarchical power structures and repressive state mechanisms. The neocolonial chaos that I described earlier reached one of many boiling points in the months leading up to the publishing of Lles's text. The war-era economic boom known as the Dance of the Millions, when the price of sugar was high, benefitted US companies that monopolized the sugar industry on the island and complicit Cuban politicians and businessmen. The Cuban Presidential Palace, now the Museum of the Revolution, is a monument to this lucrative pact, as the structure was completed in 1920 and outfitted by Tiffany's of New York. In October 1920, however, the price of sugar plummeted, ushering in the time of the "Skinny Cows," ravaging Matanzas and returning it to its previous state of economic desolation.

Perhaps more than anything else, the death of Lles's younger brother Francisco helps explain the tone of angst and pessimism in *La higuera de Timón*. On New Year's Day, 1921, the day of hope and new beginnings, Francisco Lles, a poet known for his generous personality, was murdered right in front of his brother Fernando on the corner of América and Tello Lamar in Matanzas. In a letter to Emilio Roig de Leuchsenring, the editor of *Cuba Contemporánea* and *Social*, not to mention the first Historiador de la Ciudad de La Habana, Lles recounts how his brother was shot while trying to stop the gunman from killing the elder Lles. Conflicting accounts of the traumatic episode debate whether or not the younger Lles was targeted for political reasons.[98] Shortly after this event, Lles publishes *La higuera de Timón*, a diachronic testimonial of neocoloniality that he wrote between 1913 and 1921 and that he dedicates to the memory of his brother.[99] It is no surprise that on the heels of this tragedy Lles would advise his pupil, Antonio, against buying into the belief that adolescence is beautiful, transformational, and unconquerable. And there was palpable evidence for such an assertion. The early Cuban Republic was not only a frustrated nationalist era, but also an environment of widespread death and hopelessness. As Louis Pérez points out in his book, *To Die in Cuba: Suicide and Society* (2005), when Lles published his essay in 1921, Cuba had the highest rate of suicides in Latin America, motivated in large part by the financial collapse of the sugar market a few months prior.[100] Suicides were not only frequent but sensationalized, fostering a fascination with the details of such events. Moreover, young people were certainly aware of the precarity of their own existence, as there was an epidemic of infant and teenage mortality in which "nearly half of all deaths (47 percent) were of youth under twenty years old."[101]

Given these apocalyptic contexts, it is no wonder why Lles would de-fetishize nationalist impulses rooted in immanence and instead elaborate a philosophy of radical individualism. For Lles, to talk to Cuban youth about regeneration or transcendence would be disingenuous. It is telling, then, that Lles appropriates the format of *Ariel*, the quintessential youth-centered text in Latin America in the twentieth century, only to subvert its ideological content. Rodó, through the veiled narrative voice of Prospero, delivers what appears to be a constructive, unifying, and harmonious lecture that emphasizes spiritualism, self-development, responsibility, and perfectibility. In contrast to Rodó's moral call to action, Lles derisively dismantles the ideology of *arielismo* by employing metaphors of eco-toxicity and suicide that counter Rodó's representation of youth as a "blessed force."[102] Instead of pretending to glimpse a future ideal on a distant horizon, Timon acknowledges the conspicuous catastrophe and outlines strategies for self-preservation.

CANONIZATION AND ANARCHIST DEPATRIATION

In light of the aforementioned discrepancies, why has Lles been rendered an *arielista*? The impulses and logic of canonicity, which operate according to limited referents, tropes, and forms, certainly play a part. Of course, my objection is not to the inherent reductivity of the enterprise of literary history itself, but rather to the agendas and mentalities that value and canonize literary texts that forward *nationalist* causes. To be sure, canon formation in the early Cuban Republic was inextricably connected to the ideology of *making patria*, and dismissed practices that disrupted that particular national imaginary as not only unpatriotic, but immoral. Two preeminent intellectuals of the 1920s whose work sought to locate the essence of *cubanidad* and mobilize it as a means of cultural revival—Fernando Ortiz and Jorge Mañach—reinforced a religious and political pact by rejecting alternative paradigms, attitudes, and psychologies as nefarious, contrary to the ethics of nation-building.[103] Lles was making a shocking case to the contrary, and theorized an aggressive counter subjectivity. Aesthetically, and in stark contrast to Rodó's highly ornate, polished prose, Lles's texts read like spontaneous, disjointed bursts of individual angst and collective denunciation, a style exemplified in the largely overlooked work of other literary agitators of the time like Vargas Vila and his fellow Colombian Biófilo Panclasta.[104]

A store clerk from Matanzas, Lles was an autodidact and therefore existed on the margins of the established political and economic class to which many Cuban intellectuals belonged.[105] As Rafael Rojas points out, this type of anonymous intellectual, self-taught, encyclopedic, prolific, and rather immobile, was found throughout Cuban towns of the time—a symptom of the so-called "Agonizing Generation," also called the Three Flag Generation, as it was born under Spanish colonialism, and came of age during US neocolonialism, and Cuban independence.[106] War, hunger, disease, political corruption, and violence meant that many Cubans of Lles's generation were unable to acquire a structured education. While autodidacticism certainly does not preclude the existence of philosophical practice in the

Republic, one cannot help but wonder to what extent it contributed to Lles's marginalization in Cuban literature. For Enrique Labrador Ruiz, a Cuban writer who himself had a contentious relationship with the canon, Lles has been "[u]nknown due to bad faith, forgotten for wickedness, silenced for convenience, embalmed by a roving nebula of an inconceivable spirit of cronyism, killed and buried by the four heads of idiots that govern in their way this disgraceful pissant literary republic."[107] Recuperating "that illustrious stranger of Cuban literature" would be a cause that few would join.[108] Despite bitter disagreements, Medardo Vitier never wavered in his praise for Lles: "Fernando Lles is just that, an authentic thinker, and there is nobody, except figures like the Uruguayan Carlos Vaz Ferreira and the Mexicans Vasconcelos and Caso, that can rival or surpass him in our countries, with respect to intelligence."[109] More recently, Rojas follows suit and affirms, "Fernando Lles, who hardly ever left the city of Matanzas, conceived, in the first, dark decades of the Republic, the most lucid philosophical essays ever written in Cuba."[110]

Such acknowledgments signal the importance of salvaging Lles from the pitfalls of a nationalist-driven literary canon. Although my loyalties indeed reside here, I would like to extend this gesture and propose that anarchism, and its circuits of signification, can help explain why Lles was denied the status of philosopher and his work was rarely recognized as literary. For Cuban literary and intellectual authorities, literature was a forum reserved for articulating national values and culture. This idea engenders a logic of double exclusion: since Lles devalued those constitutive elements that made Cuban literature *literature*, his work was not literary, even though, paradoxically, those same authorities classified his work as *arielista* because it so closely resembled Rodó's *Ariel*, the standard of a polished, literary text. Moreover, the complexity of Lles's work precluded him from being labeled an anarchist, since Cuban anarchist literature of the time tended to offer predicable plot points and Manichean themes. This negation is indicative of a trend to fashion radical thought and literature into what I call the 'conservative default,' a canonical maneuver that resituates individual anarchism within the normalizing confines of conservative paradigms and projects, essentially

162 Pedagogies of Dissent

appropriating and redeploying anarchist critique as complicit with the state's interests and methods.

We must keep in mind that Lles, a child of Spanish immigrants, came of age during the height of anarchist activity in Cuba, and his sociopolitical and philosophical leanings were highly informed by anarchist thought. He spent some of his formative years in Asturias, Spain among the Berdayes, his mother's family and well-known anarchists. Upon returning to Matanzas on the eve of the Cuban War of Independence in 1894, Lles, an insatiable reader of Stirner, Proudhon, Bakunin, Kropotkin, Malatesta, Jean Grave, Louise Michel, Marx, and, above all, Nietzsche, would go on to lead an anarchist group for five years.[111] Over the next decade, anarchist strikes and protests were met with violent repression by the Cuban State and its US overseers. The repeated crackdowns on anarchist activities included the seizure of presses and the murder, disappearance, imprisonment, or exile of anarchist leaders, and culminated between 1915 and 1921, which is to say the same years in which Lles wrote *La higuera de Timón*. This personal and historical anarchist context has been neglected, but it is key in reconstructing the obscured nuances of a chaotic neocolonial consciousness. And what better place to look for the contours of a divergent subjectivity than on the margins, in Matanzas, a city implicated but invariably bypassed in order to offer a Havana-centered perspective of Cuban history and experience? After all, the name of the city means "massacre" and it was the first place the United States Navy bombarded in the Spanish-American War, so it was a veritable ground zero for both colonialism and neocolonialism.

Reading Lles's text as both a neocolonial diatribe and an individual anarchist pedagogy suggests that the step-by-step process that Timon outlines for Antonio is a process of *unbecoming*, an unraveling of the constructive rhetoric and tropes of *arielismo* so influential in fueling nationalist discourses in the Cuban Republic. Analogous to other Cuban anarchists, Lles exposes and delegitimizes the traditional building blocks of the ideology of patria: religion, patriotism, and capitalism. However, Lles denies collective revolutionary possibilities and advises Antonio to shed "the ridiculous cloak of optimistic philosophy" and become one of the "exceptions to the rule that march unfailingly towards failure."[112] This subject severed from political engagement brings to mind Žižek's ideas about death, "self-withdrawal," and "the absolute contraction of subjectivity" in *The Ticklish Subject*, except that in Žižek's view, those are prelimi- nary steps to "wiping the slate clean" in order to enable a new revo- lutionary beginning, a new "Truth-Event."[113] In contrast, Lles, whose nihilism was both condemnatory and analeptic, would reject the slate itself as yet another farcical carrot at the end of a stick waiting to wallop any unsuspecting person that follows it.

But there is an irony to Timon's anarchic pedagogy that needs to be addressed: how can the absolute sovereignty of the self, achieved and nourished by negating authority, be a didactic project? In other words, how can one person teach another to be a solitary individual? In Lles's text, the development of the self is not a prerequisite for intervention, but rather a way to avoid participating at all, meaning that he essentially rejects Pierre Bourdieu's idea of interest, which he defines as, "to participate, to admit the game is worth playing and that the stakes created in and through the fact of playing are worth pursuing."[114] Yet, Lles's text is itself an intervention, one that seeks to shape Antonio into an individual in the image of a figure of authority, which aligns Timon with Prospero's paternalism, even though they propose disparate objectives. Like Frantz Fanon, Lles invokes vio- lence as a means to effectuate a cathartic de-subjectivation, but, unlike the Martinican philosopher, perhaps only to subsequently enact a prescriptive re-subjectivation of his "distressed confidant" (*atribulado confidente*).[115]

One way of thinking through the problematics and efficacy of Lles's pedagogy of dissent is to consider the imagined interlocutor of the text, el pequeño Antonio, the subject "suckled in error, bred for terror" who never utters a word during Timon's bitter mono- logue.[116] Given Lles's fondness for resuscitating and referencing clas- sical figures, could Antonio be a reconfiguration of Mark Antony, the Roman politician and military commander? According to Plutarch, who was one of Lles's sources for Timon, Mark Antony, to whom he refers as Antonius, felt such an affinity with Timon's misanthropy that he built a solitary refuge on the Isle of Pharos and called it the Timonium, where, after losing the Battle of Actium, he later committed suicide.[117] Timon the misanthrope inspired a disgruntled Mark Antony to isolate himself after defeat, and Lles's Timon echoes this gesture of resignation as a strategy for navigating a circular neocolonial condition. In this way, Lles's oppositional aesthetic writes back against Rodó's *Ariel* by employing a similar narrative, intertextual structure, and classical tropes. Those formal similarities may account for why Antonio has been interpreted as representing the Cuban intelligentsia, much like Prospero's students in *Ariel*.

But what if Antonio was based on someone Lles knew? This might be one of the few moments in Lles's oeuvre when an intertextual reading proves counterproductive. Instead of wading through and weighing multilayered or conflictive possibilities that require Lles's implied reader to fill in the links of a deferred signifying chain, it is possible that "el pequeño Antonio" could have been Antonio Berdayes, Lles's cousin on his mother's side, who was ten years old and lived in nearby Limonar when Lles published *La higuera de Timón*. A labor leader of *henequeneros* (workers who made rope out of agave), Antonio Berdayes became an active saboteur and supporter of the 26th of July Movement, the guerrilla force spearheaded by Fidel Castro. In 1957, a year after the Granma landed in eastern Cuba, Fulgencio Batista's military officials arrested, interrogated, tortured, and killed Berdayes, only to later decapitate and dynamite his corpse to make it look like he died while trying to plant a bomb. This appalling event turned Berdayes into a martyr of the Revolution in its early stages, an honor that quickly dissipated. Although today there are a few schools and neighborhood Committees for the Defense of the Revolution in Matanzas named after Antonio Berdayes, he is glaringly absent from Revolutionary history.[118] His erasure is symptomatic of the Revolution's effacements and recastings, most infamously in the case of Camilo Cienfuegos, possibly murdered for his dissent and later canonized, and Che Guevara, who was packed off to fight wars in Latin America. Berdayes's labor background perhaps accounts for his absence, as the labor movement, although largely supportive of the Revolution, was marginalized, then eliminated after 1959.

Although Lles's critiques of the Pseudo-Republic align with Castro's, it is understandable why the Cuban Revolution would not recuperate him as an ideological precursor. In the first place, Lles's texts were largely inaccessible, due to a hyperintellectualism performed through a complex intertextual network. For example, *La higuera de Timón* barely surpasses one hundred pages in length, yet contains several hundred references that showcase a prodigious knowledge of classical philosophy, world literature and religion, and the history of math, science, and geography. More to the point, however, is the fact that Lles's doctrine "sowed revolt" (as Émile Armand would say), but not to induce or participate in collective reforms.[119] From his earliest polemical writings denouncing Christianity in a student newspaper in 1908 until his final exercise in political theory entitled *Nazism, Fascism, Plutocracy, Oligarchy, Marxism, and Democracy,* one of three unedited manuscripts he was working on when he died, Lles showed himself to be an ardent nonconformist, perpetually unconvinced by what one of his close friends called "mere songs of praise of the greatness of a purpose or of the nobleness of an intention."[120] He renounced both sides of the political spectrum that vied for power. Right-wing political leaders who desperately sought, but never received, his endorsement, wrote him off as an obstinate radical. Revolutionaries of the Generation of 30 dismissed him as a complicit conservative whose unwillingness to wholeheartedly advocate for their cause equaled support for the status quo. Implicit in Lles's resistance to any nationalist or collective framework is a decolonizing epistemology that ridicules what Jean Grave called "the absurdity of patriotism," which is manifest when Timon repeatedly and sarcastically replicates the chant, "¡Viva la patria!"[121]

By discouraging youth from engaging in reformative sociopolitical endeavors for fear that they would reproduce new hierarchies of oppression, Lles's work was clearly antithetical to the aims of the Cuban Revolution, a movement with a fraught relationship to anarchism and intent on erasing non-communists who initially backed the Revolution. Not only that, communists were marginal in early Revolutionary coalitions, later integrated or cast out, on a case-by-case basis.[122] Just as the Cuban Republic dismissed Lles for being too divisive, the Revolution buried him for the same reason. But Antonio Berdayes's relative absence in Revolutionary history is more difficult to reconcile. In his speech-turned-manifesto *History Will Absolve Me* (1953), Castro claims, "to be Cuban implies a duty, and to not fulfill it is a crime and treason. We are proud of the history of our *patria*; [. . .] We have been taught very early to revere the glorious example of our heroes and martyrs [. . .] and that to die for the *patria* is to live. We have learned all this and will not forget it . . ."[123] This was precisely the affective ideology that Lles warned his young cousin about in *La higuera de Timón*. In their respective responses to the same neocolonial process, set some thirty years apart, both Castro and Lles divest death of its negative implications. For Castro, *patria* is the incentive and recompense for a revolutionary sacrifice. Lles, on the other hand, disrupts and deterritorializes the sacrificial logic of *patria* by humanizing the subject vis-à-vis a dehumanizing metaphorical act that exposes the inherent violence and repression in any formulation of nationhood or nationness.

This brief intervention into forgotten or skewed manifestations of resistance elicits divergent significations surrounding death as a decolonizing act. Whereas there is a sense of personal agency in Lles's formulation of metaphorical suicide, Berdayes's martyrdom confirms Timon's fear that his pupil would not heed his advice and end up on the "cross of sterile sacrifice," which, since Berdayes was literally blown to bits on an electric post, turned out to be an eerily prophetic concern.[124] Revisiting and interrogating why Lles's dissent has been reframed as complicit with an *arielista* project, and how Berdayes has been largely erased from revolutionary memory, illustrate the complex trajectory of making and unmaking the ideology of *patria* in neocolonial and revolutionary Cuba. In conflicting ways, both Lles and Berdayes exemplify that unpacking radical subjectivity in Cuba is not necessarily a choice between *Patria o muerte*, but rather, in both cases, *Patria es muerte*.

CHAPTER 4

Rodó Revered, Reviled, and Revamped

Neoarielismo *in the Twenty-First Century*

THE PASSING OF what some may assume is Rodó's last stand—the centenary of his death (2017)—brings yet another opportunity to address, and perhaps affirm, nagging doubts about the relevance of Rodó's work and his obsolescence in contemporary Latin American literary, sociocultural, and political landscapes. As opposed to the critical vigor aroused by the one-hundred-year anniversary of the publication of *Ariel* (2000), the centenary of Rodó's death has passed largely unnoticed, which in some ways solidified, as Carlos Fuentes suggested twenty years ago, the idea that Rodó was the "irritating, insufferable, admirable, stimulating, disappointing" uncle in the family portrait of Latin American literature.[1] Straddling a liminality between lukewarm reverence and benign neglect, *Ariel* no longer seems the lightning rod for adulations and accusations that it once was, perhaps the inevitable result of over a century of meticulously litigating its every nook and cranny. But before we resign ourselves to such critical fatigue and move to place yet another of the many nails that have been hammered into Rodó's coffin over the years, it is worth pausing to appreciate the multitude of ways in which *arielismo* continues to be recycled and repurposed in the twenty-first century. This book has argued that since its inception—however loosely pinpointed—*arielismo* has been a malleable paradigm, a flexible set of ideas and ideals, as persistent as they are imprecise, ripe for appropriation and reformulation by seemingly any faction. Despite the contemporary exhaustion with all things Rodó, a variety of *neo-arielista* perspectives and projects in a new century make clear that his relevance extends far beyond customary dichotomies and milestones and that, furthermore, Rodó's resonance remains central to contemporary Latin American debates. This concluding chapter of *Centenary Subjects* will chart an abbreviated history of *arielismo* and pay special attention to its impact and longevity in *neoarielista* perspectives and movements in the current century.

Dialectics, Detractors, and Defenders

In the theatrical opening scene of Rodó's narrativized essay an "old and venerated teacher" whom his "young disciples" call Prospero, delivers the final address of the term in a classroom. Prospero—whose mature voice Rodó assumes when he was barely thirty years old—invokes a nearby statue of Ariel as the inspiration for his pedagogical monologue in which he encourages his young audience—who remain silent during his discourse—to embark on a transcendent historical mission. Throughout Prospero's lecture, Ariel functions as a symbol of Latin American spiritual and cultural agency, while Caliban represents the dehumanizing effects of materialism and utilitarianism, phenomena that Rodó associates with the United States. The Ariel/Caliban dialectic embedded in the text is not strictly a reformulation of Shakespeare's *The Tempest*, but rather an unequivocal adaptation of Ernest Renan's *Caliban* (1878), a text that promoted politically disenfranchising the masses in the wake of the Paris Commune. In a similar way, Prospero's message of personal development has elitist implications. The target audience of *Ariel* is imagined (and, in turn, imagines itself) as exceptional agents who, by recognizing "legitimate inequalities," can assume a directive role in steering their societies away from the egalitarian excesses of democratic systems like that of the United States.[2] Rodó's elitism is also manifest in a rich metaphorical style that intertextually incorporates ideas derived from European intellectuals. Furthermore, the fact that Rodó completely sidesteps the issue of race so as to frame Latin Americans as part of a cultural genealogy that dates back to classical civilization, is another indication of the divisive legacy implicit in *Ariel*'s professed spirit of serenity and synthesis.

At the same time, Prospero's lesson/sermon outlined empowering ideals that focused on the inner life of young men and encouraged them to develop all facets of their personalities in the spirit of Ancient Greece and Christian morality. *Ariel* effectively marketed the idea that the Latin American spiritual regeneration could curb and counter restrictive materialist drives and interpretations of reality espoused by positivism and dispersed by what he called *nordomanía*, or fascination with and emulation of the United States.[3] Proponents of the neospiritualist or neoidealistic movement—of which *arielismo* was very much a part—sought to reclaim the metaphysical and spiritual facets of reality that positivism negated. Neospiritualists maintained that life cannot be relegated to deterministic paradigms rooted entirely in the natural sciences. Therefore, positivism's dogmatic adherence to materialism excluded other essential, even if unquantifiable, facets of human existence, such as intuition, religiosity, love, beauty, affect, imagination, creativity, an appreciation for the aesthetic dimension of humanity, a validation of enthusiasm over indifference, and, above all, developing a personality comprised of a harmonious reconciliation of extremes. Yet, although Prospero consistently argues against dichotomies, *Ariel*, and in turn *arielismo*, has been overwhelmingly read according to them. This is especially true of the conceptual protagonists of Ariel and Caliban—which Rubén Darío and Paul Groussac anticipated by several years—that readers have taken as stand-ins for, respectively, Latin America and the United States.[4]

As the centennial of Rodó's birth passed in 1971, Emir Rodríguez Monegal complained that, "Rodó continues to be poorly read (*mal leído*)."[5] Those misreadings, especially of *Ariel* as an anti-American text, even predate its publication, and continue to the present day.[6] Before *Ariel* reached the hands of the reading public in 1900, a publicity promotion appeared in the Uruguayan newspaper *El Día* (1899), classifying Rodó's text as an anti-American study.[7] Rodó took to the pages of *El Día* on January 23, 1900 to clarify that "It is not true that the principal theme of the new work is, as some have said, the influence of Anglo-Saxon civilization in Latin nations. The book offers only an unintentional opinion about North American civilization, and it tries to characterize in it what can and should serve as a model and what should not be the object of imitation."[8] In other words, Rodó envisioned his essay as a nonpolemical work about the spirit, not an anti-American manifesto. According to Enrique Anderson Imbert,

> Unfortunately, some readers reduced *Ariel* to a scheme that discredits its purpose: for these readers Ariel versus Caliban symbolizes Hispanic-America versus Anglo-America, spirit versus technics. Reducing the book to such a scheme does not make it appear to be a call for mental, spiritual, and physical effort, but rather a school for conformists. [. . .] The United States theme is only an accident, an illustration for a thesis on the spirit. To contrast the two Americas and to launch a political manifesto were so far from Rodó's intention that *Ariel* was not an anti-imperialist work. He makes allusion only to moral imperialism not so much exercised by the United States as by the desire of imitation on the part of Spanish America.[9]

The truth is that one would not be hard pressed to find much more incisive denunciations of the United States from a Latin American perspective than what Rodó offers in *Ariel*, where Prospero declares, "even though I don't love them, I admire them."[10] Rodó tried to put a fine point on the issue by arguing that the materialism of US culture was a *symptom* of utilitarianism, not the *definition* of it, but this did little to downplay what quickly became the defining feature of *Ariel*. In fact, there may be as many compliments of the United States as there are condemnations. For example, while Prospero praises its access to public education, as well as its strong principles of liberty, unity, energy, individualism, and the glorification of work, he also highlights how that country's infatuation with materialism, utilitarianism, and equality frustrate the pursuit of higher ideals. This does not mean, however, that the United States is devoid of the spirit, since, as Prospero points out, "They have known how to save, in the shipwreck of all ideals, the highest ideal, keeping alive the tradition of religious sentiment."[11]

While the nature and extent of Rodó's admonishments of the United States constitute one of the most constant and contested aspects of *arielismo*, his intentions and legacy have likewise been subject to ardent detractors and defenders over the years. Indeed, a list of critiques surrounding his dated and problematic worldview is easy to assemble: *Ariel*'s divisive class implications, paternalistic vision of democracy, its neglect of ethnic and gender diversity, not to mention its grandiose aesthetic seemingly have little to impart today. And these have been the same critiques that have dogged *Ariel* and *arielismo* from its inception. While students were inspired to transcend the material challenges and limitations they faced, they, as well as other entities, took issue with *Ariel*'s problematic handling of the aforementioned phenomena. For instance, in his undergraduate thesis in philosophy at the Universidad Nacional Mayor de San Marcos (1905), José de la Riva Agüero, grandson of Peru's first president, noted a disparity between Rodó's message and the *mestizo* masses. "If," he writes, "Rodó's sincerity was not clear in each one of his pages, it could be suspected that *Ariel* hides a secret intention, a cruel joke [. . .] To propose ancient Greece as a model for a race contaminated by the hybrid racial-mixing with Indians and Blacks; to speak about recreation and an open game of fantasy to a race that if it succumbs it will be due to a frightening frivolity; to celebrate Classical leisure before a race that is dying of laziness!"[12]

This incompatibility, or irony, was not lost on Peruvian Marxist thinker José Carlos Mariátegui, who like other radicals would lose the taste for Rodó during the 1920s and 1930s due to their increasingly militant stances with respect to the metaphors of identity that *Ariel* promoted.[13] In an article on revolutionary socialism in

Latin American in 1929—just months after publishing his influential *Siete ensayos de interpretación de la realidad peruana*—Mariátegui singled out Rodó's vision as anachronistic, writing "It is ridiculous to continue to talk about the contrast between a materialist Saxon America and an idealist Latin America, between a blond Rome and a pale Greece. All these are topics irremissibly discredited. The myth of Rodó no longer works—it has never worked—in a useful and fundamental way on anyone's soul. Let's adamantly reject all those caricatures of ideologies and places and let's figure things out by engaging in a serious and frank way with reality."[14]

Subsequent rebukes, which considered *Ariel*'s metaphorical protagonists incompatible with their circumstances, intensified over the following decades, including from Rodó's compatriots. In an essay titled "Ariel y Calibán americanos" (1930), Uruguayan poet Juan Zorrilla de San Martín, whose *Tabaré* (1888) is that country's national poem (his face also adorns the twenty peso note), rejects Rodó's appropriation of Ariel as an "unstable" and ineffective symbol for Latin American unity, preferring instead Caliban as an emblem of progress.[15] Another poet, Peruvian Luis Humberto Delgado would make a similar claim, averring that Ariel is an ill-suited metaphor for Latin America. In *El suplicio de Ariel* (1935), Delgado states, rather pessimistically, that "*ARIEL*'s lamp wastes its glow in the darkness. The flame of that light remains lit in a creed that the governments of American republics do not understand."[16] For his part, and anticipating a similar move by Roberto Fernández Retamar years later, Argentine writer Aníbal Ponce in *Humanismo burgués y humanismo proletario* (1938) refashions the symbolic roles of the Shakespearean players in Rodó's text. In Ponce's formulation, Prospero is a despot who enslaves Ariel, while Caliban represents the rebellion of the proletariat.[17]

But the most scathing attack on Rodó's significance would come from Peruvian politician Luis Alberto Sánchez. In *Balance y liquidación del novecientos: ¿Tuvimos maestros en nuestra América?* (1941), Sánchez, a politician of the Peruvian Aprista Party who served as vice president, senator, and briefly as the prime minister of Peru, argues that while the *arielistas* purported idealism and regeneration, they feared any real reforms that might unsettle the intellectual and social oligarchy for which the text was written.[18] Sánchez would again critique Rodó in *¿Existe América Latina?* (1945), where he aligns the Uruguayan with the primary proponents of anti-*mestizaje* ideas such as Carlos Octavio Bunge, César Zumeta, and Alcides Arguedas. "During a period of Latin American history," Sánchez writes, "the thesis of the degeneration of the mixed-race people thrived. Those were the days of Rodó and the *arielistas*. By pretending to create a Greece—or a France—impossible in our racially-mixed lands, they lost sight of reality and converted what could not be more than a literary dream into a sociological doctrine.[19] Bunge's *Nuestra América* (1903), an essay that sources an array of pseudo-scientific evolutionary and zoological perspectives to warn against what he sees as the ill effects of racial hybridization, could not be more ideologically and aesthetically different from Rodó's work. Furthermore, Sánchez also maintain that *Ariel* directly informed Venezuelan writer César Zumeta's *El continente enfermo*, even though it was published a year before Rodó's essay. Carlos Real de Azúa, a trailblazing scholar of Rodó's work, calls out Sánchez's obsession to "establish Rodó's paternity over a group—which he himself despised—of his *"arielistas."* "Moreover," Real de Azúa contends, "in a move that is unacceptable, he has endeavored to find in Rodó the source of their worst traits."[20]

Rodó's legacy was susceptible not only to inaccuracies and exaggerations, but also paradoxical appropriations and reformulations. In the wake of the Bolivian Revolution of 1952, for example, Fernando Díez de Medina echoes Rodó's obsolescence in *Sariri: una réplica al "Ariel" de Rodó* (1954):

South Americans of today, brought up in the dramatic perplexities of two world wars [. . .] in the threshold of perhaps a third ask themselves: Is *Arielismo* an idealistic utopia or an instrument of collective edification? Are the master's ideas still applicable in the current world rife with passion and confusion? The idealized democracy that the Uruguayan thinker preached, does it coincide with the tumult and backwardness of our racially mixed America?

[. . .] [T]he symbolic synthesis of Caliban and Ariel is too simplistic [. . . ;] *'Arielismo'* is too much of a literary product. [. . .] Rodó's aesthetic and didactical idealism is not for us what it was for our parents [. . . and] it lacks social significance. [. . .] More properly tuned tools than *Ariel's* very thin stylus are needed in order to build a strong American present. [. . .] Rodó's words are not useful in these convulsive years.[21]

Carlos Jáuregui adeptly shows how despite those categorical rejections, Díez de Medina in fact reconstructs a kind of replica of the symbolic protagonists and power dynamics in Rodó's essay. Drawing on mythical figures from indigenous folklore, Díez de Medina replaces Ariel with Thunupa, Caliban with Makuri, and Prospero with Sariri. Whereas Thunupa stands in for the state, liberal democracy, and the pedagogical mission of a directive minority, Makuri symbolizes the rebelling masses and class conflict. For his part, Sariri endorses Thunupa's humanitarian and paternalist stance of educating working-class and indigenous Bolivians so as to incorporate them into a national framework. Jáuregui's analysis reveals that although *Sariri* pretends to be an "indigenist redefinition of *arielismo*," it recreates *Ariel's* top-down worldview that centers on the man of letters who disciplines the masses.[22]

Rodó's work was a seemingly inescapable reference for both reactionaries and revolutionaries alike as they negotiated the sociopolitical and economic power dynamics of Pan-Americanism and communism during the 1960s and 1970s. For instance, weeks after his inauguration, President Kennedy gave a speech at a White House reception for Latin American diplomats and members of Congress (March 13, 1961) in which he outlined a new chapter in Pan-Americanism—an Alliance for Progress—that proclaimed the ideals of hemispheric cooperation, economic development, and freedom. In an ironic twist, Kennedy encouraged nations of the Americas to "work to eliminate tyranny"—which he explicitly associated with Cuba—and, at the same time, "transform the American Continent into a vast crucible of revolutionary ideas and efforts" that would significantly change the social landscapes of their countries.[23] Just one month later, however, the Bay of Pigs Invasion would stand in stark contrast to the collaborative Pan-Americanism that Kennedy purported. Four months after the debacle, a Special Meeting of the Inter-American Economic and Social Council of the Organization of American States convened in Punta del Este, Uruguay in August 1961 to sign the "Charter of Punta del Este, Establishing an Alliance for Progress Within the Framework of Operation Pan America." Economic integration and development were the centerpieces of the "Alliance of Progress," which afforded primary roles to the Inter-American Development Bank and the International Monetary Fund, two entities that continue to be at the center of issues of (under)development in the region.

As the leader of the Cuban delegation, Che Guevara took the stage to rebuke the imperialist veneer of the "Alliance for Progress," but not before thanking the Uruguayan chairmen for gifting him a copy of Rodó's complete works. However, Guevara explains:

> I am not beginning these remarks with a quotation from that great American for two reasons. The first is that I went back after many years to *Ariel*, looking for a passage that would represent at the present time the ideas of a man who is more than Uruguayan, a man who is our American, an American from south of the Rio Grande; but throughout his *Ariel* Rodó speaks of the violent struggle and opposition of the Latin American countries against the nation that fifty years ago was also interfering in our economy and in our political freedom, and it is not proper to mention this, since the host is involved.[24]

Guevara's reluctance to marshal Rodó's words against the Organization of American States could have indeed stemmed from being respectful to one's host. On the other hand, it is also permissible to assume that the Uruguayan's tepid admonishments of the United States decades prior, while germane, were not robust enough to sufficiently communicate the Cuban Revolution's opposition to the Alliance's actual intentions of marginalization, sabotage, and regime change of the island nation. This explains why Guevara opted instead to cite Martí's anti-imperialist potency in his speech, "On Growth and Imperialism." Ultimately, Cuba was the lone member country to not sign the Charter, and, subsequently in 1962, it was expelled from the Organization of American States, whose anti-communist platform grew more vigorous in the leadup to the Cuban Missile Crisis.[25]

This brief, but decisive, moment in the history of the Americas illustrates Rodó's diminished viability for revolutionary projects in the 1960s. The fact that Guevara had not read *Ariel* in "many years" and did not have at the ready a celebrated phrase from Rodó's essay only reinforces the primary complaints that the Uruguayan's work has repeatedly incurred over the decades: its outdatedness and lack of audacity. Despite the timeless and transcendent aura that gets attributed to the *arielista* projection, leftist intellectuals, such as Argentine intellectual Jorge Abelardo Ramos, considered Rodó's work timid and frozen in time. In his monumental *Historia de la nación latinoamericana* (1968), Ramos examines the long historical trajectory of Latin America's semi-colonial condition, embodied in nationalist mindsets that frustrate regional unity and that follow cues from Europe and the United States.[26] In Ramos's view, Rodó is the "preacher of the status quo" whose embellished writing style made sure not to hurt anyone's feelings and whose spiritual agenda was so banal that it quickly became a conservative doctrine.[27] Not only that, he believes that Rodó's meager criticisms of the United States could easily be construed as flattering.[28] In short, "There was no fury in *Ariel*," which positioned it as out of step with the aesthetics of rage and ideologies of insurrection propagated by third world, tricontinental, and decolonization movements of the era.[29]

Moreover, Rodó's spiritual focus, which simultaneously critiqued and circumvented material realities, revealed a disconnect in the supposed universality of his optimistic message. In Ramos's view, "[Rodó] proposes a return to Greece, even though he omits pointing out the paths for Indians, *mestizos*, laborers, and servants in Latin America to meditate about a superior culture in their plantations, farms, or reedbeds."[30] For that reason, *Ariel*'s ideals—no matter how lofty or aloof—could not be effectively operationalized because they are extraneous to the exigencies of those excluded, either explicitly or implicitly, from Rodó's bourgeois worldview. This impasse prompted perhaps the most famous corrective issued with respect to *Ariel's* ideological baggage, which would also, ironically, reanimate Rodó's presence in the Latin American imaginary: Roberto Fernández Retamar's *Calibán* (1971). Writing from within the Cuban Revolution, Fernández Retamar—as Martinican writer Aimé Césaire had done before him in *Une Tempête* (1969)—reformulated the metaphorical protagonists of Shakespeare's *The Tempest* with a postcolonial twist.[31] Both Césaire and Fernández Retamar redeemed Caliban as representative of the racialized peoples of the region who defy their colonizers (i.e., Prospero), rather than barbarians who need to be civilized and controlled. With a gesture that flipped one of the region's primary scripts, Fernández Retamar asserts:

> Our symbol then is not Ariel, as Rodó thought, but rather Caliban. This is something that we, the *mestizo* inhabitants of these same isles where Caliban lived, see with particular clarity: Prospero invaded the islands, killed our ancestors, enslaved Caliban, and taught him his language to make himself understood. What else can Caliban do but use that same language—today he has no other—to curse him, to wish that the "red plague" would fall on him? I know no other metaphor more expressive of our cultural situation, of our reality. [. . .] what is our history, what is our culture, if not the history and culture of Caliban?"[32]

From this perspective, Rodó's impulse to transcend, both textually and ideologically, the historical legacies of genocide, slavery, strife, and imperialism in Latin America could be construed as an attempt to eschew or downplay the possibility of marginalized actors enacting their own agendas of empowerment. For this reason, Fernández Retamar reclaims Caliban's literary deformity (projected somatically) as metaphorically representative of the colonized, exploited peoples of the region, which allows a modified collective imaginary based on revolutionary ideals and anti-imperialist actions to emerge in the mirror of Latin American identity. Even though, as Fernández Retamar argues, Rodó got the symbol wrong, he did successfully identify the United States as the primary menace facing Latin America.

Rodó and *Ariel* remained a preferred punching bag in another influential book that aimed to rectify what it considered a distorted, widespread narrative that inculpates the United States for Latin America's underdevelopment. In *Del buen salvaje al buen revolucionario* (1976)—which soon after appeared in English as *The Latin Americans: Their Love-Hate Relationship with the United States*— Venezuelan journalist Carlos Rangel acknowledges US imperialism in the region, but disputes the idea that all of Latin America's sociopolitical and economic problems can be chalked up to the interference of that foreign adversary.[33] In his view, Latin Americans of all political persuasions propagate this "victimization" myth in order to extenuate their own failures and justify their resentment for their collective fears and shortcomings. For Rangel, *Ariel* has played a leading role in fomenting this false image of reality by disseminating an overly simplified and inaccurate breach between the mystic spiritualism of the South and the vulgar materialism of the North.[34] This dichotomy, Rangel suggests, sets up an infinite line of signification that makes any action taken by the United States reactionary, and all efforts to combat them in Latin America revolutionary. Therefore, for Rangel, *Ariel* is a "superficial and pompous book," unreadable today, whose influence on the Latin American psyche derives from a misreading.[35] Rangel explains, "If someone really takes the time to re-read it carefully, they will quietly return the volume to its place, with some shame, for what it reveals not about North Americans (which is practically nothing) but rather about ourselves."[36] Despite his disagreement with various aspects of radical movements in the Americas, Rangel applauds the fact that in recent years those factions have thrown Rodó and his book in the dustbin of history. "Marxism in Latin America," Rangel writes, "takes on now the same functions that Rodó's manifesto fulfilled at the beginning of the century, and it does so infinitely better, with reference to a potent and totalizing cosmovision, embodied not in a mythical Athens, nor in an exhausted 'Latinity,' but rather in a center of power that is a true and contemporary rival of the United States."[37]

Rangel's criticisms received a swift response from one of Rodó's most astute commentators and ardent defenders, Uruguayan literary critic Arturo Ardao. In "Del mito Ariel al mito Anti-Ariel" (1977), Ardao maintains that Rangel and other critics of Rodó contort *Ariel* to fit their agendas and rely primarily on the Ariel/Caliban dialectic to justify their biases.[38] An ample chorus of scholars—overwhelmingly from Uruguay—have been vigilant in trying to safeguard Rodó's reputation against misrepresentations. The second subtitle of Hugo Torrano's *Rodó: acción y libertad* (1973), for instance, is transparent about those intentions: *restauración de su imagen* (restoration of his image).[39] Such endeavors continue in contemporary scholarship, as evidenced in Gustavo San Román's research, which seeks in part to "rescue some unjust evaluations" of Rodó's work and defend his reputation against academic "attacks and criticisms."[40] As this brief overview of the critical reception of *Ariel* indicates, there is a long history of apologists and defamers of Rodó's reputation, a debate into which I do not enter in this book. Instead of vying to defend or destroy Rodó's legacy, I am intrigued by what it obscures, which has been the focus of the previous chapters of this book. While, as Mario Benedetti underscores, it is easy to retrospectively point out where and how Rodó got some things wrong—he was, after all, a luminary with limitations—it is important to remember that he "opened the first breach" for so many topics with which Latin Americans continue to grapple.[41] Even as early as 1945, Medardo Vitier recognized that "if there should be a return to Rodó, I do not believe that it would be to adopt the solution he offered . . . , but rather to reconsider the problem."[42] This is precisely what appropriations of Rodó have done in a new century. Although berated and bruised, *arielismo*—as a pervasive cynosure of anxieties, justifications, censures, and chimeras from all directions—has been repurposed in ways both predictable and novel in the twenty-first century.

RODÓ RENEWED: NEOARIELISMO

In her 2000 edition of *Ariel*, Belén Castro Morales makes the case that Rodó's message—even if not the symbols he used to illustrate it, which have sparked such controversy over the last one hundred years—continues to be viable when confronting the "thousand forms of violence, corruption, exploitation, unjust inequalities, domination, and demagogy" that exist in today's world.[43] In other words, Rodó still has something to impart as a remedy (or at the very least source of inspiration) for seemingly anything unpleasant, negative, or dangerous, be it geopolitics, education, culture, or the human condition writ large. Whereas since the 1920s Latin American leftists lambasted Rodó's shortcomings, *neoarielismo* in the twenty-first century is largely aligned with progressive interests and causes. At the same time, beginning with Cuban student activist Julio Antonio Mella, founder of the first international Cuban Communist Party (1923)—for whom, according to Fernández Retamar, Rodó had a "decisive influence"—and Peruvian Víctor Raúl Haya de la Torre's anti-imperialist Alianza Popular Revolucionaria Americana (APRA) founded in Mexico (1924), *Ariel* has been frequently cited as an originary force of radical agendas.[44] Surpassing mere rhetorics of autonomy, the utopic ideals that Prospero espouses in his serene sermon took on immediacy and bellicose connotations in guerrilla resistance fronts, including Augusto Sandino's armed campaign against US marine forces in Nicaragua in the 1920s and '30s, Fidel Castro (who drew inspiration from Rodó's work while was a student activist at the University of Havana) and the Cuban Revolution he led, as well as left-wing urban guerrilla groups like the Montoneros (Argentina) and the Tupamaros (Uruguay) of the 1960s and 1970s.[45]

In light of *Ariel*'s prominence in radical movements, perhaps it should not surprise us that the so-called Pink Tide (*marea rosa*)—when a plethora of left-leaning heads of state were elected in South America in the 2000s—has been framed as a natural culmination (or contemporary iteration) of the *arielista* trajectory. In *El arielismo: de Rodó a García Monge* (2008), Costa Rican philosopher Arnoldo Mora writes, "The prevailing geopolitical reality in the first decade of the twentieth century returns *arielista* ideas and beliefs to their full actuality, although in a new version adapted to the current context. *Arielismo* is more than just a glorious page of Our America's ideological and cultural history. Today it is more vigorous and relevant than ever."[46] In fact, former Venezuelan president Hugo Chávez's defiant rejections of US imperialism and the Washington Consensus have elicited more than a few comparisons to *arielismo*. While Chávez's Bolivarian stances on political liberation, cultural agency, spiritual superiority, and regional alliances are reminiscent of those Rodó outlines in *Ariel*, his militaristic credentials, confrontational rhetoric, and socialist platform that serves, and indeed recenters, the very masses that Rodó's elitism sidelined, signal an obvious departure from *Ariel*'s pacifying tones and subtle objections to US hegemony. One need only recall the litany of insults that Chávez directed at former US president George W. Bush—calling him ignorant, immoral, psychologically ill, a liar, a donkey, a coward, a murderer, a drunk, and, from the podium of the United Nations in New York City in September of 2006, the devil—to appreciate the belligerent features of Chávez's so-called *arielismo*, which, as it turns out, some have linked to other insurgent groups like the Fuerzas Armadas Revolucionarias de Colombia (FARC) and the Ejército Zapatista de Liberación Nacional in Chiapas, Mexico.

Those manifestations of "armed *arielismo*" or "arielismo con metralleta" (machine-gun Arielism)—which contrast significantly with Rodó's calls for moderation—have also been compared to contemporary international struggles like the Libyan Revolution of 2011.[47] *Arielismo* has always been constituted by such capacious accommodations, but generally in ways restricted to Hispanic or Lusophone contexts.[48] Therefore, that one of the predominant Latin Americanist paradigms would be expanded to include diverse protests and liberationist projects around the globe demonstrates the extent to which its functionality as a coalescing prism transcends the region for which it was conceived. In fact, the *arielismo* that inspired Latin American university reform movements in the early 1900s has also been linked to the Arab Spring of 2010 in Tunisia, Egypt, and other countries in the Middle East, throughout Europe—evident in *los indignados* ("the outraged") in Spain and student riots in London in 2012—as well as in the numerous Occupy movements throughout the world.[49] Interestingly, although leftist actors have long denounced Rodó as a representative of reactionary class structures, his work was also a crucial source for those very progressive projects and popular, anti-imperialist mobilizations, especially as they pertain to student activism.

An intriguing instantiation of this can be found in the Chilean Student Movement, comprised of coalitions of student groups such as the Federación de Estudiantes de la Universidad de Chile [FECh], Federación de Estudiantes de la Universidad Católica de Chile [FEUC], Federación de Estudiantes de la Universidad de Santiago de Chile [FEUSACH], and others. The Chilean Student Movement took shape in 2006 and picked up steam in 2011 and 2012, when news outlets around the world covered the sometimes violent encounters between protestors and police, as well as the subsequent election of some of the movement's most notable young leaders to public office under the Bachelet administration.[50] Those who comprised its ranks took issue with the specialized logics of capitalism and utilitarianism—the very critiques Rodó outlined over a century before. Moreover, the massive outpouring of secondary and university students denounced neoliberal education policies regarding access and affordability. Among the numerous placards that dotted marches in 2011 organized by the broad coalition of students—"Public Education for Sale," "End Education for Profit," "5 Years Studying, 15 Paying"—was a series of signs that read "Neoarielistxs Indignadxs" (Outraged Neo-Arielists).

According to one of those participants, the use of the slogan was "half serious and half in jest," with some underlying and unanswered questions being "what is *neoarielismo*? And better yet, what does it have to do with the student movement? [. . .] There is not a natural link between *neoarielismo* and the student movement, just as there was not one between *arielismo* and university reform. What one does find are possibilities."[51] Those *neoarielistx* agendas, as the spelling indicates, bring a sense of actuality in the form of gender and queer inclusivity to what may otherwise be an anachronistic formula. While *arielismo* is not the pillar of those activists' platform, the terminology some within the movement have adapted offers a requisite nod to its genealogy, but ultimately resemanticizes it to fit their own needs.

Neoarielismo has emerged in recent years as a go-to for scrutinizing the neoliberal logic that views education in terms of economic
value, which translates into the crisis, or crises, that the humanities
continue to confront. In *Las armas de las letras: ensayos neoarielistas* (2008), Grínor Rojo, a Chilean writer and professor, issues
an urgent appeal to restore Rodó's views on reclaiming humanism
in the face of an expanding global technocracy.[52] Slashed funding,
sharp reductions in university majors in the humanities, and general skepticism about that discipline's practical and financial value,
drive *Las armas de las letras* to refute neoliberalism—"an improved
and perfected grandchild of yesterday's positivism"—and "return to
aesthetics its credentials as a powerful agent in and for social and
political practice."[53] The humanities, Rojo opines, fosters critical and
creative capacities that run counter to paradigms that quantify individual existence and worth in strictly economic terms.

At the same time, *neoarielismo* resurfaces as a lens through
which to understand the hemispheric dialectics of the politics of
representation. In his review of Jean Franco's book, *The Decline and
Fall of the Lettered City* (2002), Rojo takes issue with the perva-
siveness of what he considers "la cultura de la incultura" ("the culture of a lack of culture"), which is to say, the prevalence of popular
images of poverty, drugs, sex, and violence being taken as representative of Latin American culture.[54] Rojo laments the precarity of
high culture as marginalized actors infringe on the privileged spaces
of representation, which, according to Javier Sanjinés, explains the

> rejection of subaltern studies, postcolonial theory, and
> multiculturalism on the part of certain intellectual sectors of Latin
> America. They consider them a type of colonization of thought
> by theories elaborated in the North American academy, from the
> perspective of what is often referred to as *area studies*. [. . .] these
> intellectuals accuse postcolonial studies and subaltern studies of a
> kind of "neoarielismo," in which the configuration of Latin Amer-
> ica of its societies and cultures, is given in an eccentric and anom-
> alous manner.[55]

"In this sense," Sanjinés continues, "the neoarielista position, still dominant in the cultural and academic strata in Latin America, reproduces the anxiety constitutive of the original arielismo of Rodó and other modernists who . . . manifest a proud anti-Americanism, together with a contempt or fear of the masses and democracy."[56] Similarly, in *Latinamericanism after 9/11* (2011), John Beverley—another founding member of the Latin American Subaltern Studies Group in 1992, comprised primarily of Latin Americanist scholars from Latin America who work at universities in the United States—sees *neoarielismo* as part of a

> neoconservative turn in Latin American criticism [which] could be seen as an attempt by a middle- and upper-middle-class, university-educated, and essentially white, criollo-Ladino intelligentsia to recapture the space of cultural and hermeneutic authority from two forces that are also themselves in contention with each other: the first being the hegemony of neoliberalism and what are seen as the negative consequences of the uncontrolled or unmediated force of the market and commercialized mass culture; and the second, social movements and political formations based in identity politics of "populisms" of various sorts, which involve new political and cultural actors no longer necessarily beholden to the political or strategic leadership of a university-educated, and ethnically mainly European or criollo-mestizo intelligentsia.[57]

Neoarielismo registers the anxieties of what was never intended as a populist paradigm. Interestingly, just as Latin American writers living in New York City at the turn of the twentieth century took issue with what they considered Rodó's inaccurate portrayal of US culture, this century shows Latin American intellectuals opposing reductive or distorted representations of their own countries and cultures from the United States.[58]

In *La reinvención de Ariel. Reflexiones neoarielistas sobre posmodernidad y humanismo crítico en América Latina* (2013), Mexican literary critic Víctor Barrera Enderle revisits Rodó not to reinstate a hegemonic intellectual class, as we see in Rojo's uneasiness surrounding new forms of collective agency. Rather, Barrera Enderle advocates a "critical humanism," a mode of constant questioning that stands in opposition to abstract or utopic humanistic inquiries of yore.[59] The contemporary incarnation of the *neoarielista* subject—independent from normativities—would be "a subject that can think and act, and make diverse circumstances that surround it concrete, without letting itself be tempted by the siren song of power. *Ariel* asks youth to instruct themselves; Caliban asks it to take action and make its voice heard. *Neoarielismo* would be a way of combining both proposals in an attempt to create new spaces for dialogue and criticism."[60] As evidenced in this excerpt, returning in order to reinvent, seems to end up reinscribing the same message of synthesis that Rodó articulated over a century ago. Such inevitable circularity—to reclaim Rodó in order to revitalize his message only to recycle its constitutive features—signals the pressing issues of the day—globalization, climate change, violence, public policy based on partisanship rather than disinterested debate—but hesitates to outline specific remedies or courses of action to pursue. Specificity, however, was never *Ariel* or *arielismo*'s strong suit. Instead, their equivocal, suggestive strategies have long been, and continue to be sources of agency and contention for reactionaries, radicals, and the rest.

The ethereal nature of the spiritual ideals at the center of the *arielismo* is also propitious for a millennial generation who, generally speaking, have never known a world without Internet and whose lives have been shaped virtually. This is the constituency that Diego Canessa targets in his *El Ariel digital* (2019), for whom he aims to bring Rodó's message into the present and reactivate its animating potential. The professed intention of *El Ariel digital* is to:

> bring our intangible cultural heritage to the twenty-first century and tell the twenty million Latin American students of today that this is your cultural heritage, without which you will not be able to get through this moment of systemic discontinuity that the planet

is living right now. Because you do not have ethical, geographic, or conceptual references. It is of great importance to [. . .] tell young people that this was the beginning of Latin American historical consciousness.[61]

By presenting Rodó as *the* architect of "Latin American historical consciousness," instead of Bolívar or Martí, for example, Canessa evidences just how pervasive the *arielista* eclipse that I have analyzed in this book continues to be. Of course, his goal is to put Rodó on a new generation's radar as a mandatory source to fuel the ideals of their own collective mission, such as figuring out how to effectively respond to the crises in Central America, Mexico, and Venezuela. In this sense, *arielismo* is an eternally renewable resource with limitless possibilities. Such generalized returns to Rodó as a wellspring of guidance in a new century reinforce his paradoxical influence on Latin American culture, politics, philosophy, and literature—pervasive yet ephemeral, both emancipatory and normative—which continues to be marshaled for all sorts of projects, but most of all as an inevitable touchstone of Latin American identity, its relationship to the United States, class politics, youth culture, inner life, materialism, humanistic education, and optimistic ambitions for the future.

Coda

Evanescent Veneers of Interpellative Essayism

WHILE THIS BOOK began by interrogating the constitutive characteristics, commonalities, shades, shifts, and paradoxes of *arielismo* as a formal movement or general perspective, its principal objective has been to bring into sharper relief the fraught racial formations, epistemological strains, and anarchistic divergences that tend to get erased or subsumed by the canonical shadow of *Ariel*'s prestige. This meant revisiting foundational assessments of Rodó's treatise, and the well-worn debates surrounding its significance, in order to foreground specific inflections of one of the most decisive yet overlooked essayistic archives in Latin America. As I have shown throughout this book, the *arielista* archive—when read closely and contextually—displays internal frictions and failures in the conceptualization and control of the constituencies it targets. Therefore, by exploring the normalized and eccentric nuances of *arielista* interpellations and imaginings of centenary subjects—heroic young agents tasked with an ambitious historical mission at an opportune yet inauspicious moment in Latin American history—this book has sought to demystify *youth* as a reified category, and highlight the mixed signals that politicians, pedagogues, and philosophers crafted with respect to their bodies, minds, and spirits in an era of changing sociopolitical conditions and charged hemispherical conflicts. Ultimately, *Centenary Subjects* revises *arielismo*'s potentiality and casts unprecedented light on the discounted problematics that configure the *arielista* archive.

Reframing, as I propose, *arielismo* through the analytic of centenary subjects allows us to discern with more clarity the constraints at play in the prophetic visions and pedagogic designs that Latin American intellectuals deployed to encourage young people, and by extension the countries they were by and large destined to lead, to be modern or become modernized. Those intellectuals and students spanned the political spectrum, but they believed in the power of the written word to energize, reform, rise above, resist, as well as, in many instances, regulate. While in the previous pages I paid special attention to the internal fault lines and external obstacles that frustrated the enactment of those projects, my investigation also corroborates what we already knew about *arielismo*'s impact: that its interpellative potency ricocheted hemispherically and globally, inspiring students to undertake a comprehensive program of self-development, integrate new ways of knowing and being, collectively organize (and establish groups and magazines named after *Ariel*), and revolutionize their environments, all with a burst of enthusiasm hitherto unseen. One of the primary merits of *arielismo*—its widespread reach—has also, ironically, been a hinderance to ascertaining its particularities. In other words, *arielismo* became reduced to a repetitive script whose enunciation, not its details or divergences, solidified an abstract understanding of what I have shown to be a diverse repertoire of essayistic praxis. This is why I have delineated a cartography of *arielismo* in the Americas, a vast intellectual, print, and political landscape that attests to the circulation, consolidation, and, in some cases, negation of *arielista* repertoires, stretching from the Southern Cone, to the Andes, through Central America, the Caribbean, Mexico, the United States, Europe, and beyond. *Arielismo* is the connective tissue that binds that mosaic of endeavors into a capacious paradigm that, in many respects, fixed the essay genre in early twentieth-century Latin America predominantly as an offshoot of Rodó's work.

Yet, by the same token, questioning *arielismo*'s congruous character, and reframing its manifold components (that tend to get effaced or conflated) as centenary subjects, flips conventional scripts on a generation of essayists, thereby bringing new modes of analysis to their work, both in tandem with Rodó's influence and, especially and importantly, notwithstanding it. I would like to emphasize that my reassessment and reconfiguring of the *arielista* archive should not be misconstrued as diminishing or discounting Rodó's well-earned place as a pillar of Latin American literature and intellectual history. Asking Rodó to step aside, but not completely out of the frame, permits overdue, renewed scrutiny of a range of dense, and at times insufferable texts that rarely get the benefit of a careful read due to their real or perceived association with the Uruguayan *modernista* writer. This explains why they are habitually chalked up in a dilatable way as *arielismo*. However, as I argue, those essays are instrumental for understanding a key era in the region's history (especially in terms of confronting an emergent US empire). My examination, therefore, attempts to make them less esoteric, while at the same time showcasing their complex inner workings. Moreover, with a lone exception, none of the primary essays that I focus on in this book have been translated into English, which accounts for their relative absence in some fields of study and their concomitant critical discussions. For that reason, *Centenary Subjects* opens up new inquiry into those texts and situates them at the intersection of literary and cultural studies and political and philosophical histories of the Americas in comparative, hemispheric, and transatlantic frameworks, in hopes that its findings concerning youth subjectivation, imperialism, racial formation, epistemology, spiritualism, education, and radical thought will illuminate the precise contours of *arielismo*'s deep-seated and spectral presence in Latin America's imaginary.

NOTES

Unless otherwise noted, all translations are my own. In addition, I
provide the original Spanish quotes,
some lengthy, when deemed
pertinent.

1. Rodó, too, had to contend with
his own "eclipse," or lack of interest in his work, but, as some scholars maintain, the pendulum swung
back the other way and he enjoyed
"una actualización sin eclipse."
Emilio Oribe, *Rodó: estudio crítico
y antología* (Buenos Aires: Losada,
1971), 7.

2. After its publication in 1900, *Ariel*
became one of the most popular
books in Latin America. However, despite assertions to the
contrary, *Ariel* was not an immediate bestseller, especially in the
way we understand that term today. See Víctor Pérez Petit, *Rodó: su
vida, su obra* (Montevideo: Latina,
1918), 227; Roberto González Echevarría, *The Voice of the Masters:
Writing and Authority in Modern*

Latin American Literature (Austin:
University of Texas Press, 1985), 17;
Orlando Gómez-Gil, *Mensaje y vigencia de José Enrique Rodó* (Miami:
Ediciones Universal, 1992), 57. This
was due largely to understandable
geographical and communicative
obstacles of the time. In fact, Rodó's
essay was not widely read in Latin
America during the first years after
its publication. Carlos Real de Azúa,
*Medio siglo de Ariel: su significación
y trascendencia literario-filosófica*
(Montevideo: Academia Nacional
de Letras, 2001), 53. Despite a slow
start, however, Rodó's impressive
self-marketing campaign—he maintained personal correspondence
with numerous intellectual figures
throughout the hemisphere and
sent them, and the literary reviews
in which they collaborated, copies of his work—generated reviews
of *Ariel* (most notably by Clarín)
and new editions. After the first
and second Uruguayan editions

of the essay, subsequent editions were published in Santo Domingo (1901), Cuba (1905), Mexico (1907 and 1908), and Spain (1908). Real de Azúa, *Medio siglo de Ariel*, 55–56. After Rodó's death in Italy in 1917, Hugo Barbagelata and Francis de Miomandre included a French translation of *Ariel* in *Pages choisies* (1918), a collection of Rodó's work published in Paris by Librairie Félix Alcan. And in the early 1920s, *Ariel* was translated into English and Portuguese. For a more complete publication history of *Ariel* after 1911, see Real de Azúa, *Medio siglo de Ariel*, 56–58.

3. José Enrique Rodó, *Ariel* (Madrid: Cátedra, 2000), 141.

4. Fernando Aínsa, "El centenario de *Ariel*: una lectura para 2000," in *Arielismo y globalización*, ed. Leopoldo Zea and Hernán Taboada (Ciudad de México: Fondo de Cultura Económica, 2002), 89.

5. Pedro Henríquez Ureña, *Historia cultural y literaria de la América Hispánica* (Madrid: Verbum, 2012), 222.

6. Víctor Barrera Enderle, *La reinvención de Ariel. Reflexiones neoarielistas sobre posmodernidad y humanismo crítico en América Latina* (Monterrey: Conarte, 2013), 25.

7. Luis Alberto Sánchez, *Balance y liquidación del novecientos: ¿Tuvimos maestros en nuestra América?* (Lima: Universidad Nacional Mayor de San Marcos, 1968), 105; Eduardo Devés Valdés, *El pensamiento latinoamericano en el siglo XX*, tomo 1: *Del Ariel de Rodó a la CEPAL (1900-1950)* (Buenos Aires: Biblios, 2000),

29; Diego Alonso, *José Enrique Rodó: una retórica para la democracia* (Montevideo: Trilce, 2009), 94, 98. Other scholars describe *Ariel* as an "ethical and intellectual breviary for Latin American youth," a "manifesto for Latin America's cultural and spiritual emancipation," an American and modernista manifesto, and a "political manifesto." Orlando Gómez-Gil, *Historia crítica de la literatura hispanoamericana: desde los orígenes hasta el momento actual* (New York: Holt, Rinehart and Winston, 1968) 453; José Antonio Aguilar Rivera, "La dialéctica de la redención," *Nexos en línea*. February 1, 2012, *https://www.nexos.com. mx/?p=14683*; José Miguel Oviedo, *Historia de la literatura hispanoamericana*, tomo 2 (Madrid: Alianza, 2001), 326; Jaime Pensado, "Student Activism: Utopian Dreams," *ReVista: Harvard Review of Latin America* (Fall 2012), *https://archive. revista.drclas.harvard.edu/pages/ book/universities-fall-2012*.

8. José Miguel Oviedo, for example, avers that *arielismo* does not constitute a school or precise form of Americanist thought, since its ideological and chronological features are vague. Oviedo, *Breve historia del ensayo hispanoamericano* (Madrid: Alianza, 1990), 54.

9. Carlos Real de Azúa, *Historia visible e historia esotérica: personajes y claves del debate latinoamericano* (Montevideo: Arca, 1975), 127. While some scholars pinpoint 1915 as the moment when Rodó's influence started to decline,

others claim that *arielismo* was a phenomenon that lasted into the 1930s, which manifests the chronological uncertainty that scholars have about the imprint of Rodó's ideas. See, for example, Medardo Vitier, *Apuntaciones literarias* (La Habana: Editorial Minerva, 1935), 117; and Amílcar Antonio Barreto, "Enlightened Tolerance or Cultural Capitulation? Contesting Notions of American Identity," in *Colonial Crucible: Empire in the Making of the Modern American State*, ed. Alfred McCoy and Francisco Scarano (Madison: University of Wisconsin Press, 2009), 148.

10. Note the inseparability of *arielismo* and Rodó's *Ariel* in the *Diccionario de Filosofía Latinoamericana*: "*Arielismo* expresses an idealistic vision of Latin American culture as a model of aristocracy and spiritual elevation in contrast to U.S. culture as an example of sensualism and materialist vulgarity. Rodó's *arielismo* is based on an elitist idea: a select minority of the best should guide society by following a disinterested ideal, which fosters greater Latin American unity." Héctor Guillermo Alfaro Gómez, "Arielismo," in *Diccionario de Filosofía Latinoamericana*, ed. Horacio Cerutti-Guldberg, Mario Magallón Anaya, Isaías Palacios Contreras, María del Rayo Ramírez Fierro, and Sandra Escutia Díaz (México: Universidad Autónoma del Estado de México, 2000), 44.

11. Real de Azúa, *Historia visible*, 133; Alfonso García Morales, "Un capítulo del "arielismo": Rodó en México," in *La crítica literaria española frente a la literatura latinoamericana*, ed. Leonor Fleming and María Teresa Bosque Latra (México: UNAM, 1993), 95.

12. Alan McPherson, "Anti-Americanism in Latin America," in *Anti-Americanism: History, Causes, and Themes*, ed. Brendon O'Connor (Oxford: Greenwood World Publishing, 2007), 84; Devés Valdés, *El pensamiento latinoamericano*, 35.

13. Real de Azúa, *Historia visible*, 144; Belén Castro Morales, "Utopía y naufragio del intelectual arielista: representaciones espaciales en José Enrique Rodó," in *José Enrique Rodó y su tiempo: cien años de Ariel*, ed. Ottmar Ette and Titus Heydenreich (Madrid: Iberoamericana/Vervuert, 2000), 99.

14. José Miguel Oviedo, "The Modern Essay in Spanish America," in *The Cambridge History of Latin American Literature*, vol. 2, ed. Roberto González Echevarría and Enrique Pupo-Walker (Cambridge: Cambridge University Press, 1996), 371. See also Romeo Pérez Antón, "Arielismo ¿impulso o freno para América Latina?" *Prisma* 17 (December 2001): 36. In addition, there are those who consider the label "*arielismo*" a negative byproduct of Rodó's essay, that is, as "a pervading trend that consists of a Latin American moral or spiritual superiority, rejecting measures of modern development, and consistently blaming the United States for all the ills of Latin America." Joaquín Roy,

"José Enrique Rodó," in *Encyclopedia of the Essay*, ed. Tracy Chevalier (Chicago and London: Fitzroy Dearborn Publishers, 1997), 1501. For an examination of the concept of ideological efficacy in Rodó's work, see Bruno Bosteels, "'Así habló Próspero': La eficacia de la ideología en el modernismo hispanoamericano," *Torre de Papel* 7, no. 3 (1997): 95–100.

15. Enrique Krauze, "Mirándolos a ellos. Actitudes mexicanas frente a Estados Unidos," *Letras libres* 9, no. 102 (June 2007): 43: "Los jóvenes en Hispanoamérica despertaron al siglo XX leyendo el *Ariel*. [. . .] Ediciones . . . aparecieron en todo el continente, al grado de que en el Perú varios jóvenes intelectuales formaron grupos "arielistas." Parte de la obra de Vasconcelos en los años veinte—*La raza cósmica*, profecía de Iberoamérica como crisol de razas y culturas, el verdadero *melting pot*—puede verse como una variación sobre el tema de Rodó. Ninguno de esos escritores desconocía el eco bolivariano en el "arielismo", el ideal de una nación de naciones unida por "altos valores del espíritu." El "arielismo" que predicaron fue, en suma, la primera ideología alternativa generada en nuestros países, frente (contra) el liberalismo clásico y sus sucedáneos directos (el positivismo y el evolucionismo). Con el tiempo, se constituyó en un antecedente o un complemento (cercano o remoto, tácito o abierto) de los grandes y apasionados "ismos" del siglo XX en América Latina: anarquismo, socialismo, indigenismo, nacionalismo, iberoamericanismo, hispanismo, populismo, fascismo, comunismo."

16. While a list of all writers, intellectuals, and politicians classified as *arielistas* would be long and span many years, the following essayists frequently make the cut: Víctor Andrés Belaunde, José de la Riva Agüero (Peru), Max Henríquez Ureña (Dominican Republic), Pedro Emilio Coll, Manuel Díaz Rodríguez, César Zumeta (Venezuela), Emilio Gaspar Rodríguez, Fernando Lles y Berdayes (Cuba), Justo Sierra (Mexico), Baldomero Sanín Cano, Miguel Jiménez López, Calixto Torres (Colombia), Joaquín García Monge, Carlos Gagini, Roberto Brenes Mesén (Costa Rica), Alcides Arguedas, Daniel Sánchez Bustamante (Bolivia), Francisco Contreras (Chile), Gonzalo Zaldumbide, Alfredo Espinosa Tamayo, Alejandro Andrade Coello (Ecuador).

17. Gonzalo Montero Yávar, "Democratic Arielismo, Utopian Imaginaries and the Transnational Cultural Practices in the Chilean Group 'Los Diez' (1914–1924)," *Confluencia: revista de hispánica de cultura y literatura* 31, no. 2 (Spring 2016): 138–52; and Mark van Aken, "The Radicalization of the Uruguayan Student Movement," *The Americas* 33, no. 1 (July 1976): 109–29.

18. For example, Martin Stabb denies that there is an *arielista* literary style or that anti-Americanist

sentiment in early twentieth century Latin America owes its origins to Rodó's work. Martin Stabb, *América Latina en busca de una identidad: modelos del ensayo ideológico hispanoamericano, 1890–1960*, trans. Mario Giacchino (Caracas: Monte Ávila Editores, 1969), 64.

19. Oribe, *Rodó*, 21.

20. Georg Lukács, "On the Nature and Form of the Essay," in *Soul and Form*, trans. Anna Bostock (London: Merlin Press, 1974), 7.

21. Theodor Adorno, "The Essay as Form," in *Notes to Literature*, vol. 1, trans. Sherry Weber Nicholsen (New York: Columbia University Press, 1991), 3.

22. As Carla Giaudrone points out, the centenary was also an auspicious moment for commemorative commissions, as mechanisms of the State, to remind (or revise) cultural nationalist symbols, monuments, narratives, and genealogies, and made extensive use of print culture to do so. Carla Giaudrone, "El gaucho en el ámbito iconográfico del Centenario uruguayo (1925–1930)," *Revista Hispánica Moderna* 61, no. 2 (December 2008): 150. For an extensive treatment of centennial cultural initiatives in Argentina, see Fernando Degiovanni, *Los textos de la patria: nacionalismo, políticas culturales y canon en Argentina* (Rosario: Beatriz Viterbo, 2007).

23. Rodó, "El centenario de Chile," in *El mirador de Próspero*, vol. 1 (Madrid: Editorial América, 1915), 165: "Más arriba del centenario de Chile,

del de la Argentina, del de Méjico, yo siento y percibo el centenario de la América Española. En espíritu y verdad de la historia, hay un solo centenario hispanoamericano."

24. In the case of Uruguay, for example, the centenary tends to be described as the period between 1910 and 1930. Thus, even the date was a contested issue, whether it should be the twenty-fifth of August (when, in 1825, the Congreso de la Florida, comprised of representatives from *cabildos* from Provincia Oriental, declared their independence from Brazil), or the eighteenth of July (when the first Uruguayan constitution was written in 1830).

25. To follow Diana Sorensen's analysis of the decade of the 1960s in Latin America, both the centenary and *arielismo* could be considered "rhetorical categories" in their own right. Diana Sorensen, *A Turbulent Decade Remembered: Scenes from the Latin American Sixties* (Stanford, CA: Stanford University Press, 2007).

26. Alain Badiou, *The Century*, tran. Alberto Toscano (Cambridge, UK: Polity Press, 2007), 3.

27. Michel Foucault, "The Subject and Power," *Critical Inquiry* 8, no. 4 (Summer 1982): 781.

28. See Lewandowski, who traces these shifts in Foucault's thinking on the "privatized techne of the self" within his formulations of power. Joseph Lewandowski, "Rethinking Power and Subjectivity after Foucault," *symplokē* 3, no. 2 (July 1995): 221–43.

29. Mario Benedetti writes that "Still today [*Ariel*] has to be one of the most widely read and cited books in classrooms, university programs, and socio-political investigations in Latin America." Mario Benedetti, *Genio y figura de José Enrique Rodó* (Buenos Aires: Editorial Universitaria de Buenos Aires, 1966), 46.

30. Rodolfo Mezzera, "Discurso del doctor Rodolfo Mezzera, Ministro de Instrucción Pública," *Homenaje a José Enrique Rodó. Ariel: Revista del Centro Estudiantil Ariel* 1, no. 8–9 (February–May 1920): 172: "Ese llamado a la juventud de América, que tuvo la virtud de sacudirla y despertarla, es un monumento imperecedero [. . .] porque es el primer gesto realizado en pro de la solidaridad de América, es la primera manifestación de que completada y ampliada, parece haberse concretado ya en nuestros anhelos, en nuestros pensamientos, en nuestras orientaciones definitivas de la política internacional y hasta en los íntimos goces de nuestra afectividad y de nuestro sentimiento. ¿Quién se atrevería a negar que las páginas inmortales de "Ariel" han sido, en realidad, las estrofas de un verdadero himno de América? ¿Quién ignora que desde hace veinte años cada uno de sus párrafos ha sido repetido como un evangelio y enseñado, de generación en generación, como el más alto ideal a que puede aspirar americanismo, la elevación moral del continente? Esta faz de la vida de Rodó,—quizá la

más eficaz y realizadora—tiene que ser destacada a pleno sol, porque de ella deriva uno de los acontecimientos más trascendentales que registra la historia de los últimos años: la verdadera comunión espiritual de América."

31. José G. Antuña, "José E. Rodó," *Homenaje a José Enrique Rodo. Ariel: Revista del Centro Estudiantil Ariel* 1, no. 8–9 (February–May 1920): 142.

32. Juan Vicente Ramírez, "Discurso del señor Juan Vicente Ramírez, Presidente de la Delegación de estudianos paraguayos," *Homenaje a José Enrique Rodó. Ariel: Revista del Centro Estudiantil Ariel* 1, no. 8-9 (February–May 1920): 214: "De pronto, resonó en América la voz potente y armoniosa de Rodó, de este gran taumaturgo del pensamiento, de este raro brujo de las almas enfermas, y empezaron a difundirse sus elocuentes discursos sobre las superiores energías del espíritu. Desde entonces, las nuevas generaciones de mi patria no apartaron el oído . . ."

33. For instance, in his speech Juan Antonio Buero proclaims, "I speak to the youth of America, to that brilliant youth, you in body and in spirit, that today has gathered its representatives in this city of the Plata, which is its city, and I say to them: Cultivate faith in yourselves like the most precious florescencia of your spirits; always conserve your sublime aspirations, even if they be impossible; perennially vivify your generous enthusiasms in

the Fountain of Youth! Those are your chimeras, and youth is reality. 'Love that treasure and force,' Rodó said, 'ensure that the lofty feeling of its possession remains ardent and effective in all of you.'" Juan Antonio Buero, "Sesión de Enseñaza Secundaria," in *Evolución. Relación oficial del Primer Congreso Internacional de Estudiantes Americanos* 3, no. 21–24 (March–June 1908): 217. The Primer Congreso was extensively chronicled in *Evolución*, the monthly magazine published by the Asociación de los Estudiantes in Montevideo (founded in 1905). Buero—who would later represent the Uruguayan delegation at the Versailles Conference (1919), and subsequently at the League of Nations (1928–1935)—was the co-editor of the publication. *Evolución*'s principal editor, Baltasar Brum, became the President of Uruguay (1919–1923), and, in defiant opposition to President Gabriel Terra's dictatorship in 1933, died of a self-inflicted gunshot wound to the head, which he administered in the middle of a street in Montevideo. For further details, see Raúl Jacob, *El Uruguay de Terra, 1931–1938: una crónica del terrismo* (Montevideo: Ediciones de la Banda Oriental, 1983); Gustavo Gallinal, *El Uruguay hacia la dictadura* (Montevideo, Editorial Nueva América, 1938); and António Costa Pinto, *Latin American Dictatorships in the Era of Fascism: The Corporatist Wave* (New York: Routledge, 2020), 62–67.

34. A fourth meeting slotted for Santiago de Chile in 1914 was canceled due to the First World War and a lack of funding. Hugo Baigini, "Redes estudiantiles en el Cono Sur (1900–1925)," *Revista Universum* 17 (2002): 282.

35. Mina Alejandra Navarro, "La hora americana," *OSAL* 13, no. 31 (April 2012): 264–65.

36. Hugo Barbagelata, *Una centuria literaria: poetas y prosistas uruguayos, 1800–1900* (Paris: Biblioteca Latino-Americana, 1924), 421.

37. Ángel Rama, *La ciudad letrada* (Hanover, NH: Edicions del Norte, 1984), 110.

38. Juan Carlos González-Espitia, *On the Dark Side of the Archive: Nation and Literature in Spanish America at the Turn of the Century* (Lewisburg, PA: Bucknell University Press, 2010).

39. For analyses of homoerotic and homophobic elements in Rodó's work, see Sylvia Molloy, "The Politics of Posing," in *Hispanisms and Homosexualities*, ed. Sylvia Molloy and Robert McKee Irwin (Durham, NC: Duke University Press, 1998): 141–60; Oscar Montero, "Hellenism and Homophobia in José Enrique Rodó," *Revista de Estudios Hispánicos* 31, no. 1 (1997): 25–39; and Oscar Montero, "Modernismo and Homophobia: Darío and Rodó," in *Sex and Sexuality in Latin America*, ed. Daniel Balderston and Donna J. Guy (New York: New York University Press, 1997): 101–17.

40. Carlos Alonso, *The Spanish American Regional Novel: Modernity and*

Autochthony (New York: Cambridge University Press, 1990), 7.

41. Julio Ramos, *Divergent Modernities: Culture and Politics in Nineteenth-Century Latin America*, tran. John D. Blanco (Durham, NC: Duke University Press, 2001), 226.

42. Nicola Miller, *Reinventing Modernity: Intellectuals Imagine the Future, 1900–1930* (New York: Palgrave Macmillan, 2008), 3.

43. See, respectively, Charles Hatfield, *The Limits of Identity: Politics and Poetics in Latin America* (Austin: University of Texas Press, 2015); Mariano Siskind, *Cosmopolitan Desires: Global Modernity and World Literature in Latin America* (Evanston: Northwestern University Press, 2014); and Fernando Degiovanni, *Vernacular Latin Americanisms: War, the Market, and the Making of a Discipline* (Pittsburgh, PA: University of Pittsburgh Press, 2018).

44. Nancy Ochoa Antich, "El pensamiento de Rodó y su influencia en Ecuador," in *Lecturas contemporáneas de José Enrique Rodó*, ed. José Ramiro Podetti (Montevideo: Sociedad Rodoniana, 2018), 320–21.

45. Miller, for example, locates the influence of *arielismo* in "Vasconcelos's theory of the cosmic race; in Argentine Socialist Manuel Ugarte's development of a political (rather than cultural) anti-imperialism; in the University Reform of 1918 and in the subsequent political radicalization of the student community that led to the foundation of the American Popular Revolutionary Alliance (APRA) and the Cuban Communist Party. And it is probably true that many thundering Latin American political leaders of recent decades have unknowingly derived nourishment from Rodó's slim volume of 1900, which, one suspects, few have ever heard of and fewer have read." Miller, *Reinventing Modernity*, 26.

CHAPTER 1

1. Castro Morales, "Un proyecto intelectual en la encrucijada de la modernidad," in *Ariel*, by José Enrique Rodó (Madrid: Anaya y Mario Muchnik, 1995), 161.

2. José F. Buscaglia-Salgado, "Race and the Constitutive Inequality of the Modern/Colonial Condition," in *Critical Terms in Caribbean and Latin American Thought*, ed. Yolanda Martínez-San Miguel, Ben Sifuentes-Jáuregui, and Marisa Belausteguigoitia (New York: Palgrave Macmillan 2016), 117.

3. In fact, as Marilyn Miller points out, Vasconcelos would make an abrupt "about-face" shortly after his seminal race treatise, essentially writing it off as a fatuous whim. Marilyn Miller, *Rise and Fall of the Cosmic Race: The Cult of Mestizaje in Latin America* (Austin: University of Texas Press, 2004), 40. In contrast, Juliet Hooker's hemispheric

re-reading of Vasconcelos's work (including texts other than *The Cosmic Race*) emphasizes the radical aims and complex nature of the Mexican philosopher's treatments of race, racist tropes, and *mestizaje*, especially in relation to the United States. Juliet Hooker, *Theorizing Race in the Americas: Douglass, Sarmiento, Du Bois, and Vasconcelos* (New York: Oxford University Press, 2017), 155–94.

4. Verdesio's work demonstrates how indigeneity still provokes a sort of dismissive, racialized backlash in which white settlers are romanticized as national heroes, which helps impugn contemporary Charrúa re-emergence in Uruguay, a "country without Indians." Gustavo Verdesio, "Un fantasma recorre el Uruguay: la reemergencia charrúa en un 'país sin indios,'" *Cuadernos de literatura* 18, no. 36 (July–December 2014): 86–107.

5. Matthew Frye Jacobson, *Whiteness of a Different Color: European Immigrants and the Alchemy of Race* (Cambridge, MA: Harvard University Press, 1999), 6-7.

6. Ruth Frankenberg, introduction to *Displacing Whiteness: Essays in Social and Cultural Criticism*, ed. Ruth Frankenberg (Durham, NC: Duke University Press, 1997), 16.

7. Michael Omi and Howard Winant, *Racial Formation in the United States: From the 1960s to the 1990s* (New York: Routledge, 1994), 56. As Ruth Hill demonstrates, Omi and Winant's concept of racial project also functions as a generative analytic for bringing into sharper focus the supposed racial absences in Latin American intellectual history prior to the centenary era. See Ruth Hill, "Entre lo transatlántico y lo hemisférico: Los proyectos raciales de Andrés Bello." *Revista Iberoamericana* 75, no. 228 (July–September 2009): 719–35.

8. Anke Birkenmaier, *The Specter of Races: Latin American Anthropology and Literature Between the Wars* (Charlottesville: University of Virginia Press, 2016).

9. Lorgia García-Peña, *The Borders of Dominicanidad: Race, Nation, and Archives of Contradiction* (Durham, NC: Duke University Press, 2016), 14–15.

10. For more extensive treatments of white supremacy in nineteenth-century Latin America, see Hill, "Primeval Whiteness: White Supremacists, (Latin) American History, and the Trans-American Challenge to Critical Race Studies," in *Teaching and Studying the Americas: Cultural Influences from Colonialism to the Present*, ed. Michael Emerson, Caroline Levander, and Anthony Pinn (New York: Palgrave Macmillan, 2010), 109–38; and "Ariana Crosses the Atlantic: An Archaeology of Aryanism in the 19th Century River Plate." *Hispanic Issues On Line* 12 (2013): 92–110.

11. Pérez Petit, *Rodó*, 122: "Esta ruda contienda arrojó nuestros ánimos, el de Rodó y el mío, en la mayor de las tribulaciones. Queríamos y anhelábamos la libertad de Cuba,

último pueblo de América que permanecía sujeto al yugo de España no obstante sus viriles luchas por la independencia y la actuación gloriosa de los Martí y los Maceo. Pero, deseábamos, al par, que esa libertad fuera conquistada, como había sido conquistada la de toda Sud-América, por los hijos de la nación sujuzgada y, a lo sumo, con el concurso de pueblos hermanos. Un nuevo Bolívar nos hubiera llenado de orgullo. Pero, lo que no admitíamos de ningún modo, era la intervención de Norte América. Cierto que propiciaba la independencia de Cuba; pero no lo agradecíamos el servicio. ¿Qué tenía que ver esa nación extraña en la contienda de los pueblos de otra raza? ¿Qué tenía que inmiscuirse en algo que para nosotros era "un asunto de familia"? En esa lucha estábamos por España. Cuba libre, sí; pero no por el favor o el interés de Norte América."

12. Pérez Petit, *Rodó*, 122.

13. Rodó, *Ariel*, 196.

14. From the initial pages of Rodó's essay it becomes clear that the introspective agency that Prospero advocates aims to produce a "conquista de las almas." Rodó, *Ariel*, 230.

15. Rodó, *Ariel*, 151.

16. Leopoldo Alas [Clarín], "Reseña sobre *Ariel*," *Revista Literaria, Los Lunes de El Imparcial* (April 23, 1900): 4: "lo que Rodó pide a los americanos latinos es que sean siempre . . . lo que son; es decir, *españoles*, hijos de la vida clásica y de la vida cristiana."

17. For an analysis of the ways in which conflicting opinions surrounding Hispanist sympathies took shape throughout the Americas at the end of the nineteenth century, see McDaniel, "La *Revista de Cayo Hueso* (1897) como arbitraje del anticolonialismo en Cuba: intervenciones crítico-literarias entre Nueva York, la Florida y Perú," *La Habana Elegante* 56 (Fall-Winter 2014), *www. habanaelegante.com/Fall_Winter_ 2014/Invitation_McDaniel.html*.

18. Pérez Petit, *Rodó*, 122.

19. Bonifacio Byrne, "Mi bandera," in *Lira y espada* (La Habana: El Fígaro, 1901), 174.

20. Translation by Manuel A. Tellechea, in *Herencia: The Anthology of Hispanic Literature of the United States*, ed. Nicolás Kanellos (Oxford, UK: Oxford University Press, 2002), 559.

21. Byrne, "Mi bandera," 175.

22. Rachel Price, *The Object of the Atlantic: Concrete Aesthetics in Cuba, Brazil, and Spain, 1868–1968* (Evanston, IL: Northwestern University Press, 2014), 140.

23. In regards to the nefarious presence of US overseers on the island: "By not establishing with precision the unbreachable limits of Cuban sovereignty, a mirrored conditionality was created in the country's domestic life. On the one hand, this imposed self-limitation and even surreptitious submission to signs and suggestions emanating from Washington and, on the other, it gave different factions the option of going to the American Protector (or threatening to) to

resolve internal disputes. This was a double perversion, based on the threat of invoking an international treaty." Steven Palmer, José Antonio Piqueras, and Amparo Sánchez Cobos, Introduction to *State of Ambiguity: Civic Life and Culture in Cuba's First Republic*, ed. Steven Palmer, José Antonio Piqueras, and Amparo Sánchez Cobos (Durham, NC: Duke University Press, 2014), 10.

24. Dylon Lamar Robbins, "War, Modernity, and Motion in the Edison Films of 1898," *Journal of Latin American Cultural Studies* 26, no. 3 (July 2017): 359.

25. Charles Musser, *Edison Motion Pictures, 1890–1900: An Annotated Filmography* (Germona: Giornate del Cinema Muto, 1997), 482.

26. In a 1901 report filed by Major Edgar S. Dudley, a Judge-Advocate for the Division of Cuba, he writes "The evacuation of Havana, January 1, 1899, was a mere matter of formality. The political control of the island had been with the United States from the date of signing the protocol." Edgar S. Dudley, "Report of Civil Affairs Considered in Office of the Judge-Advocate of the Department, Calendar Year 1900," in *Annual Reports of the War Department for the Fiscal Year Ended June 30, 1900*, part 11: Report of the Military Governor of Cuba on Civil Affairs, vol. 1, part 3 (Washington: Government Printing Office, 1901): 426.

27. Musser, *Edison Motion Pictures*, 478.

28. Robbins, "War, Modernity, and Motion," 361.

29. Quiroga's book "writes the text of the present in a way that allows the older text to come to the fore. Its method is not displacement but rather dismantling—both the privilege of the past and the timelessness of the present." José Quiroga, *Cuban Palimpsests* (Minneapolis: University of Minnesota Press, 2005), ix.

30. Louis A. Pérez, *On Becoming Cuban: Identity, Nationality, and Culture* (Chapel Hill: University of North Carolina Press, 1999), 89. However, as David Sartorius maintains, Afro-Cubans' allegiances to Cuban nationalism or Spanish colonialism were not as clear-cut, as they negotiated a multiplicity of strategic positionings. David Sartorius, *Ever Faithful: Race, Loyalty, and the Ends of Empire in Spanish Cuba* (Durham, NC: Duke University Press, 2013), x–xi.

31. Pérez, *On Becoming Cuban*, 94.

32. Pérez, *On Becoming Cuban*, 94.

33. Lillian Guerra, *The Myth of José Martí: Conflicting Nationalisms in Early Twentieth-Century Cuba* (Chapel Hill: University of North Carolina Press, 2006), 4.

34. Rafael Rojas, *Essays in Cuban Intellectual History* (New York: Palgrave Macmillan, 2008), 25.

35. Miguel Ángel Carbonell, *Hombres de nuestra América* (La Habana: La Prueba, 1915), 237: "conquistadores del siglo."

36. Orville H. Platt, "The Pacification of Cuba," *The Independent* 53 (June 27, 1901): 1467.

37. Manuel Márquez Sterling, *Alrededor de nuestra psicología* (Habana: Avisador Comercial, 1905), 56.

38. Márquez Sterling, *Alrededor de nuestra psicología*, 55: "El peligro de Cuba no consiste en que puedan conquistarla; el peligro fundamental estriba en que el cubano, sin haber constituido [un] bloque, y poniéndose a distancia de constituirlo, es conquistable."

39. Maceo: "Rights are not begged for, they are won with the blade of a machete." Quoted in Georgina Leyva Pagán, *Historia de una gesta libertadora, 1952–1958* (La Habana: Editorial de Ciencias Sociales, 2009), 36. Silvio Castro Fernández, *La masacre de los Independientes de Color en 1912* (La Habana: Ciencias Sociales, 2002), 10: "La libertad no se pide, la libertad no se mendiga, se conquista."

40. According to Félix Lizaso, "The post-Republic cultural movement finds, after several years of indecision, a decisive force in Rodó's doctrine. The curtain had been raised, with the Republic, on a scene on which there was only the echo of voices from the previous period. Those men who emerged still lacked orientation. The new direction was precise and Rodó's work helped set that course in a decisive way. It is a coincidence that with the first figures of that period spread the idealist movement that *Ariel* espoused in America." Félix Lizaso, *Ensayistas contemporáneos, 1900–1920* (La Habana, Editorial Trópico, 1938), 176.

41. *Opiniones sobre la obra de Emilio Gaspar Rodríguez* (Habana: Montalvo y Cardenas, 1928), 38.

42. José Vasconcelos, "Cuba, guía de la estirpe," *El Fígaro* 42, no. 13–15 (1925): 80.

43. Vasconcelos, "Cuba, guía de la estirpe," 80: "Vosotros en cambio, además de mantener la herencia conquistada por vuestros héroes, habeis realizado un triunfo social, un triunfo étnico del que no hay ejemplo en muchos pueblos latinoamericanos. Habéis duplicado, triplicado el número de habitantes, mientras otros países de nuestra raza despueblan a causa de los malos gobiernos, y ese aumento de vuestra población ha sido obtenido sin sustitución, sin desplazamiento de la sangre autóctona y con aumento de la sangre afín. Y en estos instantes sois acaso más iberoamericanos que en los días de la Independencia. Vuestra población multiplicada sigue siendo española, sigue siendo cubana y es ahora más rica y posee una cultura superior a la de la época heróica de la Independencia. Después de veinte años de vida independiente, Cuba es más cubana. Pocos países de América podrían afirmar lo mismo. Qué importa que vuestras empresas estén manejadas desde Wall Street."

44. Fernando Ortiz, *La reconquista de América: reflexiones sobre el panhispanismo* (París: Paul Ollendorf, 1911), 70-79.

45. Ortiz, *La reconquista de América*, 101.

46. Germán Labrador Méndez, "Dynamiting *Don Quijote*: Literature, Colonial Memory and the Crisis of the National Subject in the Monumental Poetics of the Cervantine Tercentenary (Spain 1915–1921)," *Journal of Iberian and Latin American Studies* 19, no. 3 (December 2013): 185–97. For a discussion of the *Quijote* during the Cuban Revolution, see Alejandro Loeza, "Del idealismo al carnaval: el *Quijote* en Cuba," in *Comentarios a Cervantes: actas selectas del VIII Congreso Internacional de la Asociación de Cervantistas*, ed. Emilio Martínez Mata and María Fernández Ferreiro (Asturias: Fundación María Cristina Masaveu Peterson, 2014): 702–13.

47. José Antonio Baujín, *Del donoso y grande escrutinio del cervantismo en Cuba* (La Habana: Letras Cubanas, 2005).

48. Esteban Borrero Echeverría, *Alrededor del Quijote* (La Habana: Moderna Poesía, 1905), viii. Cuban intellectuals echoed that affective connection in numerous ways. For instance, Néstor Carbonell opined that Don Quijote was "the greatest of the Spanish conquistadors, because he is the only one who has known how to preserve for Spain, even after its demise, the conquests achieved centuries ago." Néstor Carbonell, "Mario Muñoz Bustamante," in *Prosas oratorias* (La Habana: Editorial Guáimaro, 1926), 31. For his part, Alberto Lamar Schweyer maintains that Cubans should not forget the "big errors that Spain

committed against us," but rather forgive and seek a "sentimental reconciliation with the colonizing nation." Alberto Lamar Schweyer, "Latinoamericanismo," *El Fígaro* 40, no. 10-11 (1923): 143.

49. Ortiz, *La reconquista de América*, 97.

50. Ortiz makes clear, however, that Cubans do not hold grievances toward Spaniards in Cuba: "Not one Spaniard was bothered for their colonial politics; not one Spanish society had to disband. The historical Spanish Casino that said sweet nothings to the intransigences of the fundamentalists, carried on dauntlessly. The Spanish Bank improved its unofficial false position. Not one important Spanish daily newspaper suspended for an hour its activities; only one changed its old political name from the *Union Constitutional* to *The Spanish Union*. The official organ of the maritime posting did not alter its title page and continued to be titled *Diario de la Marina*." Ortiz, *La reconquista de América*, 110, 203.

51. Jesús Castellanos, "Los dos peligros de América: a propósito de dos libros nuevos," in *Los optimistas* (La Habana: Avisador Comercial, 1914), 227: "El espíritu español tiene que despedirse de América como el espíritu inglés se despidió hace un siglo de las trece colonias. Venga, sí, en buen hora, el sano turbión de los trabajadores españoles, pero venga a americanizarse, a cubanizarse, no a españolizarse."

52. Ortiz, *La reconqusta de América*, 109, 79; Castellanos, "Los dos peligros de

América," 226. Spanish immigrants to Cuba in the years after 1898 were often negatively portrayed, stemming from their frequent involvement in labor activism. See Amparo Sánchez Cobos, *Sembrando ideales: anarquistas españoles en Cuba, 1902–1925* (Sevilla: Consejo Superior de Investigaciones cientificas, 2008); Frank Fernández, *Cuban Anarchism: The History of a Movement*, trans. Charles Bufe (Tucson, AZ: See Sharp Press, 2001). We can see such anxieties in an article published in the magazine *Cuba en Europa* entitled "Quienes deben emigrar a Cuba" (Barcelona, 1915). According to its author, Dr. Fernando Escobar, the island needs Spanish workers who will roll up their sleeves, get to work, and, most importantly, not complain about and organize around issues of working conditions and rights. Fernando Escobar, "Quienes deben emigrar a Cuba," *Cuba en Europa* 6, no. 128 (1915): 1–2.

53. Ortiz, *La reconquista de América*, 108.

54. Ortiz, *Entre cubanos... (psicología tropical)* (París: Paul Ollendorf, 1913), 2.

55. Ortiz, *Entre cubanos*, 48, 20. Ortiz even chalks up a loss by University of Havana's football game against students from Louisiana to the fact that "we always lose, we have squandered the institutions of our Republic, because we lack discipline and constant energy, which is the secret to all triumphs and successes" (48).

56. Ortiz elaborates, "Culture . . . culture from abroad, from across the seas, where self-sufficient countries live the life of ideas, those who can boast about their generosity, those who life the torch of progress above the crowd of ignorant nationalities." Ortiz, *Entre cubanos*, 57, 68–69.

57. Ortiz, "La inmigración desde el punto de vista criminológico," in *Archivos de psiquiatría y criminología aplicadas a las ciencias afines*, vol. 6, ed. José Ingenieros (Buenos Aires: Talleres Gráficos de la Penitenciaría Nacional, 1907): 332–40.

58. José Sixto Solá, "El pesimismo cubano," *Cuba Contemporánea* 1, no. 4 (December 1913): 24, 56.

59. Sixto Solá, "El pesimismo cubano," (285): "Nuestra población es, pues, cada vez mayor y cada vez más homogénea; ese aumento de población está constituído principalmente por nacimientos de cubanos e inmigraciones de españoles, y sabido es que el negro, en contacto con el español, se disuelve. Y tanto el aumento de población como la mayor proporcionalidad de la blanca, son factores importantísimos de adelanto."

60. José Antonio Saco frequently expressed the idea that "The colonization of Cuba is both necessary and urgent in order to give the white population a moral and numeric predominance over the excessively large population of color; it is necessary and urgent, so as to counterpose it in eastern Cuba against the one million two hundred thousand Haitians and Jamaicans that, from the

coasts of their islands, look closely at Cuba's empty shores and deserts; it is necessary and urgent, in order to neutralize to a certain extent the terrible influence of the thirteen million blacks that surround us—millions growing by the day and that could swallow us up in the not too distant future, if we remain idle; in short, it is necessary and urgent in order break the dangerous lever pulled by enemy hands, as it could put Cuba in a very bitter trance, thereby covering it grief, and flooding it with blood." Cited in Ortiz, *José Antonio Saco y sus ideas cubanas* (La Habana: El Universo, 1929), 74.

61. Birkenmaier, *The Specter of Races*, 22.

62. For a thorough analysis of Ortiz's seminal, not to mention evolving thoughts on race, see Birkenmaier, *The Specter of Races*, 19–46; Rojas, *Essays in Cuban Intellectual History*, 35–40.

63. Rodó, "La filosofía del Quijote y el descubrimiento de América," in *El camino de Paros (meditaciones y andanzas)* (Valencia: Cervantes, 1918), 28–31. As was customary, Pérez Petit followed suit, opining, "They want to separate us Latins, South Americans, we who have character, and still revere ideas, from idealism so as to channel us into the herd comprised of exclusive utilitarianism, — we are the ones that still cannot see pass by, without an emotional feeling, the knight of La Mancha on the amber, dusty routes in search of a grievance to avenge or a wrong to rectify!" Pérez Petit, *Rodó*, 193.

64. Rodó, "La filosofía del Quijote," 30.

65. Rufino Blanco-Fombona, "Carta abierta," in *Ensayos históricos* (Caracas: Ayacucho, 1981), 211.

66. Blanco-Fombona, "Carta abierta," 214.

67. Blanco-Fombona, "Carta abierta," 218: "El que plagie a un Rodríguez no plagia a nadie"; "Plagiar a ese microcéfalo vale como asegurar que el Orinoco necesita para engrosar su cauce el agua de un albañal."

68. Blanco Fombona, "Carta abierta," 214, 210. It is no wonder, then, why Peter Earle and Robert Mead classify Blanco-Fombona as "one of the biggest polemicists of the continent and a great cultivator of the diatribe . . . [who] flaunts the violence, vigor, and passionate accent of a prosist that converts his plume into a sword he always uses to attack or defend." Peter Earle and Robert Mead, *Historia del ensayo hispanoamericano* (México: Ediciones de Andrea, 1973), 66–67.

69. Blanco-Fombona, "Carta abierta," 215.

70. Federico García Godoy, "*Los conquistadores* por Emilio Gaspar Rodríguez," in *Obras casi completas*, tomo 3: *Notas críticas*, ed. Andrés Blanco Díaz (Santo Domingo: Centenario, 2017), 455–56.

71. Enrique Gay Calbó, "Bibliografía: Emilio Gaspar Rodríguez," *Cuba Contemporánea* 15, no. 43 (March 1927): 269–70.

72. Gay Calbó writes, "It is still fresh the polemic that arose about whether or not the notable and

embattled Venezuelan writer Rufino Blanco-Fombona took ideas and paragraphs from this book for his "essay of interpretation" entitled *El Conquistador español del siblo XVI*. Both authors accuse each other. And I think that in both the predilection for that type of study was already well defined long ago. Emilio Gaspar Rodríguez published *El retablo de Maese Pedro* in 1916. Rufino Blanco-Fombona already had an honorable and substantial *oeuvre* behind him, as a guarantee of the seriousness of his methods. Did one copy from the other? Was it just a coincidence? I have not read *El Conquistador español del siglo XVI*, which according to Blanco-Fombona—and it is logical—was written before the Spring of 1922 when it appeared. And around that time some copies of *Los Conquistadores* arrived in Spain." Gay Calbó, "Bibliografía," 269–70.

73. Francisco García Calderón, *Latin America: Its Rise and Progress*, trans. Bernard Miall (New York: Scribner, 1913), 45.

74. Manuel Ugarte, *El porvenir de la América latina* (Valencia: Prometeo, 1920), 48.

75. Lamar Schweyer, "Emilio Gaspar Rodríguez," *El Fígaro* 39, no. 3 (1922): 44: "rama vigorosa de aquel gran árbol que se llamó José Enrique Rodó, árbol a cuya sombre florece hoy el pensamiento y el sentir americanos. Aunque rara vez deja entrever su admiración por Rodó, el autor de "Los Conquistadores"

es fiel discípulo del gran pensador uruguayo. En la forma, en la exposición, en la misma visión que tiene de las cosas, se nota la influencia bien ejercida del inmenso escritor que se inmortalizó en "Motivos de Proteo." Más propio que discípulo, es llamarle imitador, sin que ello reste mérito a su obra ni rebaje su talento. Imitar implica seguir rumbos ya trazados por otro y no marchar por un camino trillado; el discípulo sigue al maestro y el imitador trata de superarlo."

76. Indeed, the idea that Rodríguez was an essayist "in the manner of Rodó" was commonplace, such as when Lizaso argues that his work "can be considered of quintessential *arielismo*." Gilberto González y Contreras, "Un notable ensayista cubano," *América* 3, no. 1 (July 1939): 14–15; Lizaso, *Ensayistas contemporáneos*, 176–77.

77. Josefina Suárez and Pío E. Serrano, "El *Quijote* en Cuba. Introducción," *El Quijote en América* (Centro Virtual Cervantes), https://cvc.cervantes.es/literatura/quijote_america/cuba/introduccion.htm.

78. Emilio Gaspar Rodríguez, *Los conquistadores: héroes y sofistas* (Nuremberg: J. Rosenfeld, 1919), 29.

79. Blanco-Fombona, *El conquistador español del siglo XVI*, in *Ensayos históricos*, ed. Rafael Ramón Castellanos (Caracas: Ayacucho, 1981), 3.

80. Blanco-Fombona, *El conquistador español del siglo XVI*, 123: "Eran bien españoles."

81. Blanco-Fombona, *El conquistador español del siglo XVI*, 115: "Eran, de

veras, los conquistadores campeones de la fe. El espíritu religioso de España estaba en ellos. Los movía el mismo sentimiento que impuso la unión por la fe, en la guerra contra el moro. A los torpes incentivos de la conquista de América se aliaba no pocas veces al ideal religioso más puro y desinteresado. Este sentimiento de sincera piedad ennoblece las degollaciones, las violaciones, los saqueos, las más bajas actividades del instinto puestas en juego por la bestia humana."

82. Blanco-Fombona, *El conquistador español del siglo XVI*, 137: "Salvan, para la civilización caucásica y latina, aquel mundo que yacía en manos de razas amarillas, la mayor parte bárbaras. Esa ha sido la trascendencia civilizadora de su acción y de la acción ulterior de España." In a previous article, Blanco-Fombona made clear that Latin Americans owe their "four drops of white blood" to Spain. Blanco-Fombona, "La España materna," in *La lámpara de Aladino: notículas* (Madrid: Renacimiento, 1915), 228. It is also important to note how revisionist slants permeate contemporary conceptions of bloody historical episodes, such as when King Juan Carlos of Spain claimed in 2001 that "Ours was never a language of imposition, but rather of encounter; nobody was ever forced to speak Spanish: the most diverse array of peoples made Cervantes's language their own, by their own free will." "El idioma de Cervantes

nunca fue una lengua de imposición, sino de encuentro," *ABC. es* (April 24, 2001), *https://www.abc. es/cultura/abci-idioma-cervantes- nunca-lengua-imposicion-sino- encuentro-200104240300-26646_ noticia.html*.

83. Blanco-Fombona, *El conquistador español del siglo XVI*, 151: "el lote de los que se dejan vencer."

84. Blanco-Fombona, *El conquistador español del siglo XVI*, 152: "la raza blanca les infunde su espíritu [a los indígenas] [. . .] En muchas de estas sociedades el elemento superior, el caucásico, no ha sido renovado todavía en cantidad suficiente para absorberlos por completo a todos. Tarde o temprano ocurrirá. En algunos países ya ha ocurrido."

85. Emilio Roig de Leuchsenring, "Mario Muñoz Bustamante," *Social 6*, no. 2 (February 1921): 37.

86. Néstor Carbonell, "Mario Muñoz Bustamante," 31.

87. Sigmund Freud, "Remembering, Repeating, and Working-Through," in *Beyond the Pleasure Principle and Other Writings*, trans. John Reddick (New York: Penguin, 2003), 37.

88. Blanco-Fombona, *El conquistador español del siglo XVI*, 4.

89. Gisela Aguirre, *José Ingenieros* (Buenos Aires: Planeta, 1999), 9.

90. In the assessment of one prominent Cuban intellectual of the era, "José Ingenieros was not the first intellectual figure of our America. The Peruvian Francisco García Calderón was deeper and more insightful than him when it comes to

assessing social phenomena. And José Vasconcelos is dramatically more intense. [. . .] And perhaps Vas [sic] Ferreira and Antonio Caso's ethical conceptions are more intense than his, but none of those mentioned has contributed to the American intellect a vaster scientific documentation nor have they presented a more ample intellectual front than the author of *La simulación en la lucha por la vida* and *El hombre mediocre.*" Alberto Lamar Schweyer, "José Ingenieros y su aporte al pensamiento americano," *Social* 10, no. 12 (December 1925): 13.

91. Jorge Salessi, *Médicos, maleantes y maricas: higiene, criminología y homosexualidad en la construcción de la nación argentina (Buenos Aires, 1871–1914)* (Buenos Aires: Beatriz Viterbo, 1995), 149.

92. By 1914, forty percent of Argentina's population was foreign born. See Tulio Halperín Donghi, "¿Para qué la inmigración? Ideología y política inmigratoria y aceleración del proceso modernizador: el caso argentino (1810-1914)," *Jahrbuch für Geschichte Lateinamerikas. Anuario de Historia de America Latina* 13, no. 1 (December 1976): 481.

93. As Patricia Funes explains, "the festivities of the Centennial were held with full pomp and pageantry, but in a State of Siege [*Estado de Sitio*]. This restriction of individual liberties was the State's answer to the social conflict engendered by the labor movement. Anarchist and socialist sectors had unleashed a series of

protests the year before, which were harshly suppressed. Moreover, the deadly attack on the chief of police (Ramón Lorenzo Falcón) and his secretary (Juan Lartigau) in November of 1909, in conjunction with the threat of boycotting the centennial celebrations, motivated the government to not only curtail liberties, but also to enact the Law of Social Defense. [. . .] Immigrant and maximalist tend to be one identity and the word 'solvent' (*disolvente*), a frequent motto." Patricia Funes, "Literatura y nación en tiempos del Centenario. Argentina y Uruguay (1910-1930)," in *Los uruguayos del del Centenario: nación, ciudadanía, religión y educación (1910-1930)*, ed. Gerardo Caetano (Montevideo: Ediciones Santillana, 2000), 250.

94. Degiovanni, *Los textos de la patria.*

95. Salessi, *Médicos, maleantes y maricas*, 135.

96. Salessi, *Médicos, maleantes y maricas*, 147: "Al parecer, especialmente durante la primera década del siglo veinte, Ingenieros desviaba la atención de su origen inmigrante y siciliano y copiaba, exagerándolos, tics y reacciones defensivas de la clase a la que quería y no conseguía acceder."

97. *Vanguardia* 15, no. 996 (1909): 2: Santa Fe, 30—Se ha comprobado plenamente la noticia sobre la tentativa de envenenamiento de las aguas. Así corre al menos la voz, sobre la cual guarda la policía un prudente silencio. Se habla de un complot tramado por veinte sicilianos

(¿salvados del terremoto de Sicilia?) que procuraban aprovechar la confusión que el hecho producirá para saquear la ciudad. Cuatro de ellos se dice que fueron sorprendidos dentro del terreno, cuando iban a echar el veneno a los filtros.

Se ha ordenado la disecación de los filtros, la que se efectuó hoy."

98. Jennifer Guglielmo, introduction to *Are Italians White? How Race is Made in America*, ed. Jennier Guglielmo and Salvatore Salerno (New York: Routledge, 2003), 9.

99. José Ingenieros, "La justicia de Bertoldo," in *Crónicas de viaje (1905-1906)* (Buenos Aires: L. J. Rosso, 1919), 49.

100. William Z. Ripley, *The Races of Europe: A Sociological Study* (New York: D. Appleton, 1915), 121.

101. Ripley, *The Races of Europe*, 114.

102. See Jacobson, *Whiteness of a Different Color*, 56-62. Also, Peter Vellon shows how southern Italians in Louisiana at the turn of the twentieth century were viewed as "a link connecting the white and black races." In addition, Vellon points out that Italian language newspapers in the United States (1880s–1920s) railed against African savagery, perhaps as a way of distancing the connection that was frequently portrayed. Peter Vellon, "Between White Men and Negroes," in *Anti-Italianism: Essays on a Prejudice*, ed. William J. Connell and Fred Gardaphé (New York: Palgrave Macmillan, 2010): 27; Vellon, *A Great Conspiracy Against Our Race: Italian Immigrant Newspapers*

and the Construction of Whiteness in the Early Twentieth Century (New York: New York University Press, 2014), 39.

103. Guglielmo, "Introduction," 11. Jacobson also examines how this happened in the courts: "In the case of Rollins v. Alabama (1922), for instance, an Alabama Circuit Court of Appeals reversed the conviction of one Jim Rollins, a black man convicted of the crime of miscegenation, on the grounds that the state had produced "no competent evidence to show that the woman in question, Edith Labue, was a white woman." Labue was a Sicilian immigrant, a fact that, this court held, "can in no sense be taken as conclusive that she was therefore a white woman, or that she was not a negro or a descendant of a negro." Although it is important to underscore that this court did not find that a Sicilian was necessarily nonwhite, its finding that a Sicilian was inconclusively white does speak volumes about whiteness in 1920s Alabama." Jacobson, *Whiteness of a Different Color*, 4.

104. In Argentina, we could look to the Cocoliche character, which emerged from Buenos Aires theater in the mid-1880s. The Cocoliche was an immigrant from southern Italy who spoke a broken mix of Italian and Spanish and was one of the popular vehicles for mocking Italian immigrants. In addition, as Rusich points out, there was a spectrum for representation of Italian

immigrants in the Argentine novel, which goes from Eugenio Cambaceres, who reserved the brunt of his negative portrayals for Italians from the south, to Roberto Payró, who offered more favorable depictions. Luciano Rusich, *El inmigrante italiano en la novela argentina del 80* (Madrid: Playor,1974), 93–224.

105. Carlos Néstor Maciel, *La italianización de la Argentina: tras la huella de nuestros antepasados* (Buenos Aires: J. Menéndez e hijo, 1924), 119, 128, 149, 197.

106. Maciel clarifies that he does not reject "the best Italian elements," but cautions that in Naples and Sicily there are "inferior categories of population." Maciel, *La italianización*, 194, 61.

107. Maciel, *La italianización*, 180–81.

108. Maciel, *La italianización*, 197.

109. Maciel, *La italianización*, 35, 219.

110. Maciel, *La italianización*, 175, 210.

111. Molloy, "The Politics of Posing," 152.

112. José Ingenieros, "Las razas inferiores," in *Crónicas de viaje (1905-1906)* (Buenos Aires: L. J. Rosso, 1919), 166.

113. Ingenieros, "Las razas inferiores," 163. "Es un craso error, sin embargo, que nos falsea la interpretación del papel histórico de la raza negra en la formación del pueblo y el carácter americanos. Los negros importados a las colonias eran, con toda probabilidad, semejantes a los que pueblan San Vicente: una oprobiosa escoria de la especie humana. Juzgando severamente, es fuerza confesar que la esclavitud—como

función protectiva y como organización del trabajo—debió mantenerse en beneficio de estos desgraciados, de la misma manera que el derecho civil establece la tutela para todos los incapaces y con la misma generosidad con que se asila en colonias a los alienados y se protege a los animales. Su esclavitud sería la sanción política y legal de una realidad puramente biológica." Indeed, Ingenieros would reiterate time and again the idea that, "the abolition of slavery has been a misfortune for those black people. Any system of production founded in the work of slaves gave them the benefit of ensuring their existence. [. . .] The capitalist has no interest at all in ensuring the individual existence of wage-earning black workers; he does not lose anything if they die, he just hires others. And he hires them for a lower salary when the supply and misery of the applicants are at their greatest. That is why slavery represented for these blacks a relative happiness, just as it did for the domestic animals that humans subjected. "However," he continues, "from the distant library and in the warmth of feelings as absurd as they are generous, there is no lack of philosophers that purport to support these inferior races by clamoring against slavery" (241).

114. Ingenieros, "Las razas inferiores," 164: "Los hombres de razas de color no deberían ser, política y jurídicamente, nuestros iguales; son ineptos para el ejercicio de la capacidad civil

y no debieran considerarse "personas", en el concepto jurídico."
115. Ingenieros, "Las razas inferiores,"
163: "Los hombres de las razas blancas, aun en sus grupos étnicos más inferiores, distan un abismo de estos seres, que parecen más próximos de los monos antropoides que de los blancos civilizados."
116. Ingenieros, "Las razas inferiores," 163-169. "Lamentar la desaparición de las razas inadaptables a la civilización blanca, equivale a renunciar los beneficios de la selección natural. Los ganaderos se desviven por seleccionar y refinar sus razas, prefiriendo las cabezas de ganado fino y estableciendo enormes diferencias de precio entre unas y otras." [. . .] "El sociólogo que observa las razas humanas con el cerebro y no con el corazón, está obligado, por lo menos, a pensar lo mismo que el criador en materia de razas equinas o lanares." For his part, Ingenieros's mentor, José María Ramos Mejía, animalized immigrants in *Las multitudes argentinas* (1899), where he writes, "Any local brain (*craneota inmediato*) is more intelligent than an immigrant just off the boat. The immigrant is somewhat shapeless, I would say *cellular*, in the sense of its complete removal from anything that has to do with measured achievements in mental organization. The immigrant is a slow brain, like that of an ox at whose side he has lived; myopic in mental sharpness, and has a clumsy and obtuse ear for picking

up the spontaneous and facile acquisition of images that are transmitted through the cerebral senses. What obscurity of perception, what obtuseness to transmit the most elemental sensation through that skin that resembles an elephant's in its difficulties as a physiological conductor!" José María Ramos Mejía, *Las multitudes argentinas* (Buenos Aires: Félix LaJouane, 1899), 290.
117. Ingenieros, "Las razas inferiores," 166. "Cuanto se haga en pro de las razas inferiores es anticientífico; a lo sumo se les podría proteger para que se extingan agradablemente, facilitando la adaptación provisional de los que por excepción puedan hacerlo. Es necesario ser piadosos con estas piltrafas de carne humana; conviene tratarlos bien, por lo menos como a las tortugas seculares del Jardín Zoológico de Londres o a los avestruces adiestrados que pasean en el de Amberes. No contaría con nuestro voto el severo tribunal misissipense que, en el pueblo poéticamente llamado Magnolia, acaba de condenar a diez años de trabajos forzados a una mujer blanca llamada Teresa Perkins, por haberse casado con un negro. Pero sería absurdo tender a su conservación indefinida, así como favorecer la cruza de negros y blancos. La propia experiencia de los argentinos está revelando cuan nefasta ha sido la influencia del mulataje en la argamasa de nuestra población, actuando como levadura de nuestras más funestas fermentaciones de multitudes . . ."

118. For example, according to Ingenieros, "The superiority of the white race is an accepted fact, even by those who deny the existence of strife among the different races. Natural selection, inviolable in the long run for man and the all other species alike, tends to extinguish races of color, each time that they find themselves face to face with the white race in regions in which the latter inhabit." Ingenieros, *Sociología argentina*, 36.

119. Ingenieros, *Sociología argentina* (Buenos Aires: L. J. Rosso, 1918), 423. "el único remedio para obviar a los males de las naciones sudamericanas: asimilar la cultura y el trabajo de las naciones europeas más civilizadas: regenerando la primitiva sangre hispano-indígena con una abundante transfusión de sangre nueva, de raza blanca."

120. Even in "La inmigración desde el punto de vista criminológico" (1906), which appeared in *Archivos de psiquiatría y criminología* (1907), which Ingenieros edited, Fernando Ortiz affirms that "White immigration is the one that must be favored." Ortiz, "La inmigración desde el punto de vista criminológico." Ortiz leans toward "immigrants from Northern European counties, like Norway, Germany, Ireland, Poland, etc., with a preference for those from Spain, Portugal, Italy, and the Balkans." "And," he continues, "it is strange to observe how even within each one of those countries that there are fewer criminals in the Northern regions than in the Southern ones. So, from Spain immigration from Cantabria, Galicia, Catalonia, and Andalusia should be given preference; and from Italy, immigrants from Piedmont, Lombardy, Emilia-Romagna, Veneto, Liguria, etc., over those from Campania, Apulia, Calabria, and Sicily." Ortiz, "La inmigración desde el punto de vista criminológico," 333–34.

121. Ingenieros, *Sociología argentina*, 256: "La cuestión de razas es absurda cuando se plantea entre pueblos que son ramas diversas de la misma raza blanca; pero es fundamental frente a ciertas razas de color, absolutamente inferiores e inadaptables."

122. Theodore Allen, *The Invention of the White Race*, vol. 1: *Racial Oppression and Social Control* (London: Verso, 1994), 22.

123. Ingenieros, *Sociología argentina*, 433–34: "Hay un hecho uniformemente admitido por la etnografía: las razas blancas han mostrado en los últimos veinte o treinta siglos una superioridad para la organización social del trabajo y de la cultura; sus núcleos especiales son llamados naciones civilizadas. Los dioses y los héroes de la *Ilíada* pertenecían a la raza blanca, lo mismo que los estadistas, los filósofos y los poetas de Grecia y de Roma; blancos eran los llamados bárbaros que repoblaron el mundo romano; blancos los pueblos cristianos y heréticos del medioevo europeo; blancos los que promovieron

el Renacimiento de las ciencias, las letras y las artes, que inició una era nueva en la historia de la humanidad." The salsa classic, "Si Dios fuera negro" (If God were Black), composed by Puerto Rican musician Roberto Angleró, pokes fun at such hegemonic appraisals of whiteness. "If God were Black," so goes the chorus, "everything would change. Our race would be the one calling the shots." If that were the case, the verses reason, then presidents, governors, lawyers, doctors, lilies, chalk, Snow White, Mona Lisa, the day, the sun, the morning, cotton, the Pope, ministers, angels, and Jesus Christ would also be Black.

124. Charles Hale, "Political Ideas and Ideologies in Latin America, 1870–1930," in *Ideas and Ideologies in Twentieth Century Latin America*, ed. Leslie Betrell (Cambridge: Cambridge University Press, 1996), 117. Like *El hombre mediocre, Hacia una moral sin dogmas*, which targets "the youth that listen to me," derives from his lecture notes in the university. Ingenieros, *Hacia una moral sin dogmas: lecciones sobre Emerson y el eticismo* (Buenos Aires: L. J. Rosso, 1917), 9.

125. Ingenieros, *El hombre mediocre* (Buenos Aires: L. J. Rosso, 1917), 11–16.

126. Ingenieros, *El hombre mediocre*, 12.

127. Alfred J. López, introduction to *Postcolonial Whiteness*, ed. Alfred J. López (Albany: SUNY Press, 2005), 1.

128. Paula Moya, *The Social Imperative: Race, Close Reading, and Contemporary Literary Criticism* (Stanford, CA: Stanford University Press, 2015), 37. This simultaneity is not unlike that which Susan Buck-Morss examined. She convincingly argues that Hegel developed his master/slave dialectic, which was subsequently taken as constitutive of Western consciousness, not divorced from but rather directly influenced by the real-world revolt of the Haitian Revolution. Susan Buck-Morss, *Hegel, Haiti, and Universal History* (Pittsburgh, PA: University of Pittsburgh Press, 2009).

129. María Josefina Saldaña-Portillo, *Indian Given: Racial Geographies across Mexico and the United States* (Durham, NC: Duke University Press, 2016), 18.

130. Ann Twinam, *Purchasing Whiteness: Pardos, Mulattos, and the Quest for Social Mobility in the Spanish Indies* (Stanford, CA: Stanford University Press, 2015), 63.

131. Emir Rodríguez Monegal, "América/utopía: García Calderón, el discípulo favorito de Rodó," *Cuadernos Hispanoamericanos* 417 (March 1985): 166.

132. García Calderón, *Latin America*, 15. It is telling that the translator of *Les démocraties latines de l'Amérique*, Bernard Miall, translates *le métissage* (mestizaje) as "the color problem." Of course, this translation gives mestizaje a negative connotation, one that accurately reflects García Calderón's views on

race in Latin America. Implicit in that translation, of course, is the assumption that the United States is a white country, not "restless," despite ample evidence to the contrary erased in national mythology. I have made some adjustments to Miall's translations based on the original French text.

133. Garcí Calderón, *Latin America*, 16.
134. García Calderón, *Latin America*, 351.
135. For a discussion of how other Latin American writers and statesmen, contemporaries of García Calderón, venerated whiteness during the early twentieth century, see George Reid Andrews, *Afro-Latin America, 1800–2000* (Oxford, UK: Oxford University Press, 2004,) 119–24.
136. García Calderón, *Latin America*, 354–62.
137. García Calderón, *Latin America*, 355.
138. Santiago Castro-Gómez, "(Post) Coloniality for Dummies: Latin American Perspectives on Modernity, Coloniality, and the Geopolitics of Knowledge," in *Coloniality at Large: Latin America and the Postcolonial Debate*, ed. Mabel Moraña, Enrique Dussel, and Carlos Jáuregui (Durham, NC: Duke University Press, 2008), 277.
139. García Calderón, *Latin America*, 355. *Assombrir* can also mean to "cast a shade over," suggesting a more apocalyptic influence of blackness, which undoubtedly fits in with García Calderón's racializing critiques.
140. García Calderón, *Latin America*, 355–56.
141. García Calderón, *Latin America*, 358–59.
142. García Calderón, *Latin America*, 359.

143. "The principle of the method is, that facts which increase or diminish together, and disappear together, are either cause and effect, or effects of a common cause." John Stuart Mill, *A System of Logic, Ratiocinative and Inductive, Being a Connected View of the Principles of Evidence, and the Methods of Scientific Investigation*, vol. 2 (London: Longmans, Green, and Co., 1865), 284.
144. García Calderón, *Latin America*, 357. Carlos Octavio Bunge offered the same observation a decade earlier in *Nuestra América: ensayo de psicología social* (Buenos Aires: Casa Vaccaro, 1918).
145. García Calderón, *Latin America*, 358.
146. García Calderón reiterates this idea at various times in his essay: "Haiti is still a barbarous democracy. It is not easy to turn a colony of negro slaves into an orderly and prosperous republic merely by virtue of political charters of foreign origin; and it has not been proved that parliamentarism, municipal life, and the classic division of powers, the creation of the East, form an adequate system of government for negroes and mulattos. Haiti possesses immense natural wealth, yet the taxes are crushing, the railways go bankrupt, labourers emigrate, and agriculture and industry are dwindling . . .; all because the indolence of the race does not permit it to take advantage of the fertility of the soil nor to govern itself." García Calderón, *Latin America*, 231.
147. James Martel, *The Misinterpellated Subject* (Durham, NC: Duke University Press, 2017).

148. For details, see Marlene Daut, *Tropics of Haiti: Race and the Literary History of the Haitian Revolution in the Atlantic World, 1789–1865* (Liverpool: Liverpool University Press, 2015); and Laurent Dubois, *Haiti: The Aftershocks of History* (New York: Picador, 2013).

149. Arlene Torres and Norman E. Whitten, Introduction to *Blackness in Latin America and the Caribbean*, ed. Arlene Torres and Norman E. Whitten, vol. 2 (Bloomington: Indiana University Press, 1998), 12. For detailed treatments of the multifarious ways in which the specter of Haitian blackness fueled fears in the Caribbean in the nineteenth century, see Sibylle Fischer, *Modernity Disavowed: Haiti and the Cultures of Slavery in the Age of Revolution* (Durham, NC: Duke University Press, 2004); Ada Ferrer, *Freedom's Mirror: Cuba and Haiti in the Age of Revolution* (New York: Cambridge University Press, 2014); Jorge Camacho, *Miedo negro, poder blanco en la Cuba colonial* (Madrid: Iberoamericana, 2015).

150. Eduardo Bonilla-Silva, *Racism without Racists: Color-Blind Racism and the Persistence of Racial Inequality in America* (Lanham, MD: Rowman & Littlefield, 2014), 230. García Calderón, *Latin America*, 362.

151. Aníbal Quijano, "Colonialidad y modernidad/racionalidad," in *Los conquistados: 1492 y la población indígena de las Américas*, ed. Robin Blackburn and Heraclio Bonilla (Bogotá: Tercer Mundo, 1992), 438.

152. In this sense, *Les démocraties latines de l'Amérique* anticipates a series of Latin American meditations centering on that paradox, from José Carlos Mariátegui's *Siete ensayos de interpretación de la realidad peruana* (1928) to Eduardo Galeano's *Las venas abiertas de América Latina* (1971), as well as documentary films, such as Stephanie Black's *Life and Debt* (2001) and Oliver Stone's *South of the Border* (2009), which underscore how the policies and practices of the International Monetary Fund (IMF) and the World Bank consistently saddle the region with insurmountable debt, thereby making economic dependency more acute.

153. García Calderón, *Latin America*, 379–82.

154. Slavoj Žižek, "*Homo Sacer* as the Object of the Discourse of the University," *Lacan.com* (September 25, 2003), https://www.lacan.com/hsacer.htm.

155. Michael Hardt and Antonio Negri, *Empire* (Cambridge: Harvard University Press, 2000), 284.

156. Hardt and Negri, *Empire*, 309.

157. Walter Mignolo, *The Idea of Latin America* (Malden: Blackwell, 2005), 58.

158. Mignolo, *The Idea of Latin America*, 57.

159. Mignolo, *The Idea of Latin America*, 67.

160. For a chronological summary of Latin American appropriations of this idea in the mid-nineteenth century, see Aims McGuinness, "Searching for 'Latin America': Race and Sovereignty in the Americas in the 1850s," in *Race and Nation in Modern Latin America*, eds. Nancy P. Appelbaum, Anne S. Macpherson,

and Alejandra Rossemblat (Chapel Hill: University of North Carolina Press, 2003), 88.

161. Alonso, "The *criollista* novel," in *The Cambridge History of Latin American Literature*, vol. 2, ed. Roberto González Echevarría and Enrique Pupo-Walker (Cambridge: Cambridge University Press, 1996), 199.

162. See Bill Ashcroft, Gareth Griffiths, and Helen Tiffin, *The Empire Writes Back: Theory and Practice in Post-Colonial Literatures* (London: Routledge, 2002); Sylvia Molloy, "Postcolonial Latin America and the Magic Realist Imperative: A Report to an Academy," in *Nation, Language, and the Ethics of Translation*, ed. Sandra Bermann and Michael Wood (Princeton: Princeton University Press, 2005): 370–79.

163. Francisco Ortega, "Postcolonialism and Latin American writing, 1492–1850," in *The Cambridge History of Postcolonial Literature*, vol. 1, ed. Ato Quayson (Cambridge: Cambridge University Press, 2011), 289.

164. Esther Aillón Soria, "La política cultural de Francia en la génesis y difusión del concepto *l'Amérique latine*, 1860–1930," in *Construcción de las identidades latinoamericanas: ensayos de historia intelectual (siglos XIX y XX)*, ed. Aimer Granados and Carlos Marichal (México: Colegio de México, 2004), 72.

165. García Calderón, *Latin America*, 391–400.

166. García Calderón, *Latin America*, 15.

167. The table of contents also highlights this distinction. The chapter dedicated to Haiti, the Dominican Republic, and Central America is entitled "Anarchy of the Tropics" and the one concerning Paraguay reads "Perpetual Dictatorship."

168. Paul Farmer, *AIDS and Accusation: Haiti and the Geography of Blame* (Berkeley: University of California Press, 2006), 4.

169. In fact, Farmer pushes back against this idea and proposes that the route of infection arrived in Haiti via the United States. In addition, Farmer asserts, "the map of HIV in the New World reflects to an important degree the geography of U.S. colonialism," as the most economically dependent nations in the region are also those with the highest number of AIDS cases. Farmer, *Geography of Blame*, 1–7; 260–61.

170. García Calderón, *Latin America*, 358.

171. García Calderón, *Latin America*, 298.

172. García Calderón, *Latin America*, 305.

173. Halford Mackinder, "The Geographic Pivot of History," *The Geographic Journal* 4, no. 23 (April 1904): 421–37.

174. García Calderón, *Latin America*, 292.

175. García Calderón, *Latin America*, 292.

176. García Calderón, *Latin America*, 323.

177. "Rooted in medieval fears of Genghis Khan and Mongolian invasions of Europe, the yellow peril combines racist terror of alien cultures, sexual anxieties, and the belief that the West will be overpowered and

enveloped by the irresistible, dark, occult forces of the East." Gina Marchetti, *Romance and the "Yellow Peril": Race, Sex, and Discursive Strategies in Hollywood Fiction* (Berkeley: University of California Press, 1993), 2.

178. García Calderón, *Latin America*, 398.

179. J. F. V. Keiger, *Raymond Poincaré* (Cambridge, UK: Cambridge University Press, 1997), 16–17.

180. García Calderón, *Latin America*, 387.

181. García Calderón, *Latin America*, 396.

182. García Calderón, *Latin America*, 396.

183. García Calderón, *Latin America*, 394.

184. G. J. Meyer, *A World Undone: The Story of the Great War, 1914–1918* (New York: Bantam Dell, 2006), 566. After his travels in South America, Clemenceau returned to politics and became one of the most important historical figures in France. A few years later, during another stint as prime minister from 1917 to 1920, Clemenceau brokered, in conjunction with British prime minister David Lloyd George and US President Woodrow Wilson, the Treaty of Versailles, the 1919 peace accord that officially consolidated peace after World War I. In the treaty, Clemenceau stipulated that Germany not only withdraw all forces and resources from Belgium and occupied parts of France, but also drastically dismantle their weaponry and pay retributions to the allied forces for territorial occupation (including Poincaré's homeland of Lorraine) and resources, both human and material (see articles 231–247). Clemenceau's demands, and therefore those of France, were to be publicly accepted by the Germans in a most symbolic venue. At Clemenceau's request, the Treaty of Versailles was signed in the Hall of Mirrors, the very place where in January 1871 Wilhelm I announced himself as the Emperor of the German Empire. See John Röhl, *Young Wilhelm: The Kaiser's Early Life, 1859–1888* (Cambridge: Cambridge University Press, 1993), 174.

185. "Only the federation of all the Latin republics under the pressure of Europe—that is to say, of England, France, and Italy, who have important markets in America—might save the nations of the Pacific." García Calderón, *Latin America*, 392.

186. Mabel Moraña, Enrique Dussel, and Carlos Jáuregui, Introduction to *Coloniality at Large: Latin America and the Postcolonial Debate*, ed. Mabel Moraña, Enrique Dussel, and Carlos Jáuregui (Durham, NC: Duke University Press, 2008), 9.

187. Moraña, Dussel, and Jáuregui, "Colonialism and its Replicants," 3; Ramón Grosfoguel, "Developmentalism, Modernity, and Dependency Theory in Latin America," in *Coloniality at Large: Latin America and the Postcolonial Debate*, ed. Mabel Moraña, Enrique Dussel, and Carlos Jáuregui (Durham, NC: Duke University Press, 2008), 321.

188. Enrique Dussel, *1492: El encu-brimiento del otro: hacia el origen del "mito de la modernidad": Con-ferencias de Frankfurt, Octubre de 1992* (Bogotá: Ediciones Antropos, 1992), 22.

189. Raymond Poincaré, Preface to *Latin America: Its Rise and Progress*, by Francisco García Calderón, tran. Bernard Miall (New York: Scrib-ner's, 1913), 14.

190. Keiger, *Raymond Poincaré*, 49–50, 344.

191. Aillón Soria, "La política cultural de Francia," 90.

192. Grosfoguel, "Developmentalism, Modernity, and Dependency The-ory," 329.

193. Nelson Maldonado-Torres, "Secu-larism and Religion in the Modern/Colonial World-System: From Sec-ular Postcoloniality to Postsecular Transmodernity," in *Coloniality at Large: Latin America and the Post-colonial Debate*, ed. Mabel Moraña, Enrique Dussel, and Carlos Jáuregui (Durham: Duke University Press, 2008), 373.

194. García Calderón, *Latin America*, 394.

CHAPTER 2

1. Alain Badiou, *The True Life*, trans. Susan Spitzer (Cambridge, UK: Pol-ity, 2017), 7–8.

2. Walter Benjamin, *Early Writings (1910–1917)*, trans. Howard Eiland (Cambridge, MA: Harvard Univer-sity Press, 2011), 198.

3. Benjamin, *Early Writings*, 205.

4. Benjamin, *Early Writings*, 204, 136.

5. The pursuit of truth, however, is not predicated on the suppression of the sacred, since, according to Benjamin, "The youth that professes faith in itself *signifies* religion, which does not yet exist." *Early Writings*, 117, 169.

6. Andrés Bello, "Modo de estudiar la historia," in *Obras completas* 19 (Caracas: Ministerio de Educación, 1957), 251; Rojas, "El lenguaje de la juventud: En diálogo con *Ariel* de José Enrique Rodó," *Nueva Socie-dad* 238 (March–April 2012): 28. See also "Discurso pronunciado

en la instalación de la Universi-dad de Chile el día 17 de septiem-bre de 1843," as well as other per-tinent texts and speeches, in Bello, *La eterna juventud de Andrés Bello*, ed. Alfonso Calderón (Santiago de Chile: Ministerio de Educación Pública, 1984).

7. Rodó, *Ariel*, 139: "Ariel, genio del aire, representa, en el simbolismo de la obra de Shakespeare, la parte noble y alada del espíritu. Ariel es el imperio de la razón y el sentimiento sobre los bajos estímulos de la irra-cionalidad; es el entusiasmo gene-roso, el móvil alto y desinteresado en la acción, la espiritualidad de la cultura, la vivacidad y la gracia de la inteligencia, —el término ideal a que asciende la selección humana, rec-tificando en el hombre superior los tenaces vestigios de Calibán, sím-bolo de sensualidad y de torpeza, con el cincel perseverante de la vida."

8. Rodó, *Ariel*, 187.

9. Alberto Methol Ferré, *Las corrientes religiosas* (Montevideo: *Nuestra Tierra* 35, 1969), 44.

10. Methol Ferré, *Las corrientes religiosas*, 45. Rodó sought to rescue the spirit of Christianity as a belief system that encourages ideals, fosters superior moral conduct, and acts as a restraint against utilitarianism. See Rodó, *Ariel*, 168, 190, 209.

11. Carlos Arturo Torres, *Los ídolos del foro: ensayo sobre las supersticiones políticas* (Madrid: Editorial América, 1916), 181.

12. Aníbal González, "Modernist Prose," in *The Cambridge History of Latin American Literature*, vol. 2, ed. Roberto González Echevarría and Enrique Pupo-Walker. (Cambridge: Cambridge University Press, 1996), 94.

13. García Calderón, "Apreciación de Francisco García Calderón," in *Los ídolos del foro: ensayo sobre las supersticiones políticas*, by Carlos Arturo Torres (Madrid: Editorial América. 1916), 12–13.

14. Torres, *Los ídolos del foro*, 17.

15. Torres, *Los ídolos del foro*, 277.

16. Torres, *Los ídolos del foro*, 21-22.

17. Torres, *Los ídolos del foro*, 53.

18. Torres, *Los ídolos del foro*, 191.

19. Eduardo Posada Carbó, "Las guerras civiles del siglo XIX en la América Hispánica," in *Memoria de un país en guerra: los Mil Días: 1899–1902*, ed. Gonzalo Sánchez and Mario Aguilera. (Bogotá: Planeta Colombiana, 2001), 62.

20. Jaime Jaramillo Uribe, *El pensamiento colombiano en el siglo XIX*

(Bogotá: Editorial Temis, 1964), 448.

21. These run the gamut: "The suggestiveness of a sonorous word, the prestige of a misunderstood formula, the brilliance of the colors of a flag, the idolatry of a blindly-accepted tradition, all primitive forms of that grand law of imitation [that] have led men and parties, full of generous enthusiasm, but rash, to sterile immolation, to collective sacrifice, to national annihilation in the bloody hysteria of our revolutions." Torres, *Los ídolos del foro*, 19.

22. Torres, *Los ídolos del foro*, 35.

23. Torres, *Los ídolos del foro*, 17-18.

24. "A concept that could be true in its epoch and therefore was vigorously affirmed in human conscience, endures, with lethal cataleptic force, with superior action of presence to the demolitions of time and the corrective imposition of new ideas, when the perspectives that made it possible have already varied in a definitive way and the circumstances that propelled it as necessary and legitimate have disappeared." Torres, *Los ídolos del foro*, 17.

25. Torres, *Los ídolos del foro*, 275.

26. According to González Echevarría's reading, the "ornate building [of the *reino interior* embodied in the parable of the hospitable king] containing the still air whence, nevertheless, the voice of the master issues in unbroken vibrations, is a contrary figure; rather than the lightness of spirit or the softness of voice, the building evokes the weight and substantiality of stone; instead of a free, generous exchange, it represents

a defensive posture, an exclusion. No dialogic exchange here, but rather an enclosure in which the building, like a shell, hardens into shape around a vacuum." González Echevarría, *The Voice of the Masters*, 25–27. Diego Alonso looks at Rodó's political ideas and actions as a member of parliament in order to argue against the idea that he endorsed divisive policies with respect to class, and, moreover, that *Ariel*'s pedagogical vision equated a one-sided "ideological imposition," or the "función ideologizante" which Ángel Rama identified as a constitutive facet of *modernista* intellectuals' social roles. Alonso, *José Enrique Rodó*, 101–8; Rama, *La ciudad letrada*, 110.

27. Torres, *Ídola fori*, 30.

28. Torres, *Los ídolos del foro*, 280.

29. Rodó, "Rumbos nuevos," in *El mirador de Próspero* (Valencia: Editorial Cervantes, 1919), 46: "La iniciación positivista dejó en nosotros, para lo especulativo como para lo de la práctica y la acción, su potente sentido de relatividad; la justa consideración de las realidades terrenas; la vigilancia e insistencia del espíritu crítico; la desconfianza para las afirmaciones absolutas; el respeto de las condiciones de tiempo y de lugar; la cuidadosa adaptación de los medios a los fines; el reconocimiento del valor y del hecho mínimo y del esfuerzo lento y paciente en cualquier género de obra; el desdén de la intención ilusa, del arrebato estéril, de la vana anticipación."

30. Rodó, "Rumbos nuevos, 45.

31. Torres, *Los ídolos del foro*, 26.

32. Torres, *Los ídolos del foro*, 76, 278.

33. Torres, *Los ídolos del foro*, 103.

34. Torres, *Los ídolos del foro*, 111–12.

35. Torres, *Los ídolos del foro*, 27–28.

36. Torres, *Los ídolos del foro*, 301–2.

37. Torres, *Los ídolos del foro*, 30.

38. Torres, *Los ídolos del foro*, 267.

39. Torres, *Los ídolos del foro*, 203: "ese fluído extraño que llamamos pensamiento, inteligencia, entendimiento, razón, alma, espíritu, potencia cerebral, virtud, belleza, saber, porque posee mil nombres, bien que sea una sola su esencia."

40. Wendy Brown, *Regulating Aversion: Tolerance in the Age of Identity and Empire* (Princeton, NJ: Princeton University Press, 2008), 25.

41. For extensive analysis regarding Torres's nonpolemical, serene reputation, see Rubén Sierra Mejía, *Carlos Arturo Torres* (Bogotá: Editorial Nomos, 1989) and Carlos Gabriel Salazar Cáceres, *Carlos Arturo Torres Peña: vida, época, pensamiento* (Boyacá, Colombia: Editorial Talleres Gráficos Ltda., 1997).

42. Brown, *Regulating Aversion*, 89.

43. Brown, *Regulating Aversion*, 25.

44. Rodó, "Rumbos nuevos," 48.

45. Torres, *Los ídolos del foro*, 188.

46. For Rodó, there are two types of instinct; a dangerous instinct that manifests itself in the imitative tendencies of the masses and an ideal instinct that permits a select minority of the "legitimate human superiorities" to transcend mediocre influences. Rodó, *Ariel*, 26.

47. Torres, *Los ídolos del foro*, 132: "el impulso de las multitudes representa cuanto hay de más inconsciente e irrazonado en las acciones humanas; . . . querer allegar un átomo de razón a esas impulsiones instintivas sería tanto como pretender discutir con el terremoto o convencer al ciclón . . ."

48. Torres, *Los ídolos del foro*, 133.

49. Torres, *Los ídolos del foro*, 135.

50. Torres, *Los ídolos del foro*, 134.

51. Thomas Carlyle, *Heroes and Hero Worship* (London: Chapman and Hall, 1869), 4.

52. Brown, *Regulating Aversion*, 26.

53. Torres, *Los ídolos del foro*, 132, 302.

54. Torres, *Los ídolos del foro*, 17.

55. Rodó, *Liberalismo y jacobinismo* (Montevideo: Librería y papelería "La Anticuaria" de A. Ossi, 1906), 84. "En arte, como en moral, como en cualquier género de ideas, la ausencia de la intuición de los matices es el límite propio del espíritu de la muchedumbre. [. . .] Allí donde el criterio cultivado percibirá veinte matices de sentimientos y de ideas, para elegir entre ellos aquel en que esté el punto de la equidad y la verdad, el criterio vulgar no percibirá más que dos matices extremos: el del *sí* y el del *no*, el de la afirmación absoluta y el de la negación absoluta, para arrojar de un lado todo el peso de la fe ciega y del otro lado todo el peso del odio iracundo."

56. García Calderón, "Apreciación," 5-7.

57. Samuel Guy Inman, *Problems in Pan Americanism* (New York: George H. Doran Company, 1921), 333.

58. Francisco Contreras, "El problema de América Latina," *El Fígaro* 11, no. 5 (1926): 14.

59. Oviedo, *Historia*, 116. Critics view Ugarte's relationship with *arielismo* in a variety of conflicting ways. For example, some critics classify Ugarte as an *arielista* but do not make any explicit connection between Ugarte and Rodó. See Arturo Roig, *Teoría y crítica del pensamiento latinoamericano* (México. Fondo de Cultura Económica, 1981), 58; Carlos Altamirano, *Historia de los intelectuales en América Latina: los avatares de la "ciudad letrada" en el siglo XX* (Buenos Aires: Katz Editores, 2008), 10; Juan Moreiro, "Los pensadores de fin de siglo. El periodismo y la crítica," in *Manual de la literatura hispanoamericana*, tomo 3: Modernismo, ed. Felipe B. Pedraza Jiménez (Pamplona: Cénlit Ediciones, 2008), 565; Krauze, *Redeemers: Ideas and Power in Latin America*, trans. Hank Heifetz and Natasha Wimmer (New York: Harper Collins, 2011), 39; Jussi Pakkasvirta, *Un continente, una nación?: intelectuales latinoamericanos, comunidad política y las revistas culturales en Costa Rica y el Perú (1919-1930)* (San José: Universidad de Costa Rica, 2005), 84. Other critics take a more neutral position and argue that *Ariel* influenced or inspired Ugarte's essays. See Jean Franco, *An Introduction to Spanish-American Literature* (Cambridge, UK: Cambridge University Press, 1994), 162; Alfaro Gómez, "Arielismo," 45; Miguel Ángel

Barrios, *El latinoamericanismo en el pensamiento político de Manuel Ugarte* (Buenos Aires: Biblos, 2007), 37. Jason Borge argues that Ugarte's essays try to "disentangle imperial conflicts from the realm of *arielista* essentialism, and . . . implicat[e] Latin American elites as complicit in its crimes codified by the Roosevelt Corollary." Jason Borge, *Latin American Writers and the Rise of Hollywood Cinema* (New York: Routledge, 2008), 4. Other critics downplay Rodó's influence on Ugarte and reject altogether the *arielista* label that others attribute to him. See Stabb, *América Latina en busca de una identidad*, 168; Carlos Beorlegui, *Historia del pensamiento filosófico latinoamericano: una búsqueda incesante de la identidad.* (Bilbao: Universidad de Deusto, 2004), 87.

60. Ugarte received an anonymous letter in 1912, which in part reads: "Do us the favor of taking your disruptive doctrines elsewhere. Don't come around here promoting a bad-mannered and crude revolutionary character. We don't want revolutionaries. We need farmers, industrialists, and men useful in any way to our country, but not disruptive and socially demoralizing influences. Mr. Ugarte, please do us the favor of departing the country or else you'll make us cut your guts out when you least expect it. We're telling you this for your own good." Ugarte, *El epistolario de Manuel Ugarte, 1896–1951*, ed. Graciela Swiderski (Buenos Aires: El Archivo, 1999), 33.

61. Ugarte, *Mi campaña hispanoamericana* (Barcelona: Cervantes, 1922), 76.

62. Ugarte, *El porvenir de la América Latina*, 173.

63. Degiovanni, *Vernacular Latin Americanisms*, 20–21.

64. The first edition of *El porvenir de la América Latina* was published in 1911 by Sempere in Valencia. However, Prometeo, also located in Valencia, republished a slightly modified version in 1920 under the title, *El porvenir de la América española.*

65. Ugarte, "La juventud sudamericana," in *Crónicas del bulevar* (Paris: Garnier, 1903), 73.

66. Ugarte, "La juventud sudamericana," 74–78.

67. Ugarte, *Enfermedades sociales* (Barcelona: Casa Editorial Sopena, 1907), 166.

68. Ugarte, "La juventud sudamericana," 83.

69. Ugarte, "La juventud sud-americana," 82–83.

70. Ugarte, *Las ideas del siglo* (Buenos Aires: Editorial Partido Socialista de la Argentina, 1904), 8.

71. Ugarte, *Las ideas*, 5.

72. Ugarte, *Enfermedades sociales*, 184: "Imponer dogmas científicos, religiosos, o sociales es *entrar matando*, es preparar a los pueblos para la fe y no para el libre examen" (original emphasis).

73. Ugarte, *Enfermedades sociales*, 40.

74. Ugarte, *Enfermedades sociales*, 147. For his part, José Ingenieros echoed a similar sentiment: "All knowledge should be considered provisional and integrable: the truth—understood as the agreement

between ways of thinking and the data derived from experience at a given moment—is in continuous development, due to the innumerable phenomena that reality incessantly presents to our senses, allowing our imagination to elaborate hypotheses that are increasingly less imperfect." Ingenieros, *Sociología argentina*, 13–14.

75. Ugarte, *Enfermedades sociales*, 181: "Nacemos a la vida intelectual ceñidos por un pasado, que, desde luego, no es imposible sacudir, pero que esteriliza nuestros primeros ímpetus, obligándonos a gastar las mejores energías en una tarea de deseducación."

76. Ugarte, *El porvenir de la América Latina*, 23.

77. Ugarte, *El porvenir de la América Latina*, 166.

78. Ugarte, *El porvenir de la América Latina*, 24.

79. Ugarte, *El porvenir de la América Latina*, 273.

80. Ugarte, *El porvenir de la América Latina*, 273: "La masa enorme de creencias, acatamientos, tradiciones, idealismos, ceremonias y jerarquías que hemos convidado en llamar religión."

81. Helio Gallardo, *500 años. Fenomenología del mestizo: violencia y resistencia* (San José de Costa Rica: Departamento Ecuménico de Investigaciones, 1993), 12.

82. Freud, *The Future of an Illusion*, tran. James Strachey (New York: W. W. Norton and Company, 1975), 38; Ugarte, *El porvenir de la América Latina*, 274–75.

83. Karl Marx and Friedrich Engels, *The German Ideology* including *Theses*

on *Feuerbach* and *Introduction to the Critique of Political Economy* (Amherst, NY: Prometheus Books, 1998), 570.

84. Peter Berger, *The Sacred Canopy: Elements of a Sociological Theory of Religion* (Garden City, NY: Doubleday, 1967), 133.

85. Robert Wuthnow, *Rediscovering the Sacred: Perspectives on Religion in Contemporary Society* (Grand Rapids, MI: William B. Eerdmans, 1992), 90.

86. Ugarte, *El porvenir de la América Latina*, 275–76.

87. Ugarte, *Enfermedades sociales*, 186.

88. Berger, *The Sacred Canopy*, 35.

89. Ugarte, *El porvenir de la América Latina*, 279.

90. Ugarte, *El porvenir de la América Latina*, 277.

91. "It is very probable for a country that dedicates one day a week to prayer is a country of duty and responsibility, and therefore a solid country." Ugarte, *El porvenir de la América Latina*, 279.

92. Ugarte, *El porvenir de la América Latina*, 283: "entre los errores de la doctrina y los de los que la defienden, hay que confesar que no cabe por ahora en el Sur una moral que no tenga por base la que fue cuna de nuestra civilización."

93. Ugarte, *El porvenir de la América Latina*, 124.

94. For more details regarding Habermas's engagements with religion and civil society, see Jürgen Habermas, *Postmetaphysical Thinking: Philosophical Essays*, tran. William Mark Hohengarten (Cambridge: MIT Press, 1992); and Philippe

Portier, "Religion and Democracy in the Thought of Jürgen Habermas," *Society* 48, no. 5 (September–October 2011): 426–32.

95. Ugarte, *El porvenir de la América Latina*, 285.

96. Žižek, "On Ecology," in *Examined Life*, directed by Astra Taylor (Montreal: Zeitgeist Films, 2009). DVD.

97. Žižek, *First as Tragedy, Then as Farce* (London and New York: Verso, 2009), 37.

98. Žižek, *First as Tragedy*, 18.

99. Friedrich Nietzsche, *Human, All Too Human. A Book for Free Spirits*, trans. R. J. Hollingdale (Cambridge, UK: Cambridge University Press, 2005), 22–23.

100. Nietzsche, *The Gay Science*, trans. Walter Kaufman (New York: Vintage, 1974), 275; *Human, All Too Human*, 22.

101. Ugarte, *El porvenir de la América Latina*, 254.

102. Herbert Marcuse, *One-Dimensional Man: Studies in the Ideology of Advanced Industrial Society* (Boston: Beacon Press, 1964), 17.

103. Francisco Romero, *Sobre la filosofía en América* (Buenos Aires: Raigal, 1952), 72.

104. John Haddox, "Latin American Personalist: Antonio Caso," *The Personalist Forum* 8, no. 1 (Spring 1992): 110.

105. "Carlos Vaz Ferreira," *Claridad* 196 (December 14, 1929), in *Recortes de prensa sobre Carlos Vaz Ferreira*, vol. 5 (Anáforas. Universidad de la República de Uruguay. Facultad de Información y Comunicación), 119. https://anaforas.fic.edu.uy/jspui/handle/123456789/43145.

106. For extensive details about Vaz Ferreira's life and work, see Arturo Ardao, *Introducción a Vaz Ferreira* (Montevideo: Barreiro y Ramos, 1961).

107. "El gran día de la Repúbica Oriental del Uruguay," *América Central* (August 26, 1916), in *Cuaderno de Recortes*, vol. 3, Recortes de prensa sobre Carlos Vaz Ferreira (Anáforas. Universidad de la República de Uruguay. Facultad de Información y Comunicación), 42, https://anaforas.fic.edu.uy/jspui/handle/123456789/42906.

108. Sánchez, *Balance y liquidación del novecientos*, 115.

109. Cdo. T. U., "*Moral para intelectuales de Vaz Ferreira*," *La Razón* (September 9, 1909), in *Cuaderno de Recortes*, vol. 1, Recortes de prensa sobre Carlos Vaz Ferreira (Anáforas. Universidad de la República de Uruguay. Facultad de Información y Comunicación), 79, https://anaforas.fic.edu.uy/jspui/handle/123456789/42849.

110. According to Vaz Ferreira, "humanity is sick of rhythm: it cannot oscillate in a measured fashion between extremes." Vaz Ferreira, "Del doctor Carlos Vaz Ferreira," *Evolución* 1, no. 1 (1905): 49. It is also worth pointing out that Rodó does not appear in *Evolución* until 1907, when he is afforded but a passing reference.

111. Dussel, "Philosophy in 20th Century Latin America," in *Contemporary Philosophy: A New Survey*, vol. 8: Philosophy in Latin America, ed. Guttorm Fløistad (London: Kluwer Academic Publishers, 2003), 20; *Oxford English Dictionary Online*,

3rd edition (2015), s.v. "conceptualism," n.1.

112. El Estudiante X, "Notas y apuntes: el Dr. Vaz Ferreira y los estudiantes," *La Razón* (April 5, 1913), in *Cuaderno de Recortes*, vol. 2, Recortes de prensa sobre Carlos Vaz Ferreira (Anáforas. Universidad de la República de Uruguay. Facultad de Información y Comunicación), 11, https://anaforas.fic.edu.uy/jspui/handle/123456789/42864.

113. "Decanato de Preparatorios. Los doctores Vaz Ferreira y Maggiolo," *La Democracia* (March 22, 1906), in *Cuaderno de Recortes*, vol. 1, 52. See Ardao, *Espiritualismo y positivismo en el Uruguay* (México: Fondo de Cultura Económica, 1950), 256–60 for details on this episode.

114. In his travel diaries, Einstein refers to Vaz Ferreira as "Ras Fereida." Albert Einstein, *The Collected Papers of Albert Einstein*, vol. 14: *The Berlin Years: Writings and Correspondence, April 1923–May 1925*. The Digital Einstein Papers (Princeton University Press, 2014), 694. https://einsteinpapers.press.princeton.edu/vol14-doc/796.

115. "En honor del Dr. Vaz Ferreira: una iniciativa estudiantil," *El Día* (April 11, 1913), in *Cuaderno de Recortes*, vol. 2, 13.

116. Alberto Lasplaces, *Opiniones literarias: prosistas uruguayo contemporáneos* (Montevideo: Claudio García, 1919), 159–60.

117. For example, in recognition of his centrality in those endeavors, in 1939 the Federación Universitaria Argentina invited him to be a guest of honor at its celebration of the twenty-first anniversary of the 1918 university reform of Córdoba.

118. Emilio Frugoni and Justino Jiménez de Aréchaga, "Vaz Ferreira: el homenaje en su honor," *La Razón* (April 17, 1913), in *Cuaderno de Recortes*, vol. 2, 16: "Por interés nacional el Estado debe facilitar la acción educadora del maestro consagrado por la juventud como el eje de una fecunda renovación espiritual."

119. "Compatriotas en el extranjero," *La Mañana* (May 1, 1922), in *Cuaderno de Recortes*, vol. 3, 21; "La entrada en funciones del Maestro de Conferencias," *El Día* (August 8, 1913), in *Cuaderno de Recortes*, vol. 2, 93.

120. "La primera conferencia pedagógica: El doctor Vaz Ferreira en el Ateneo," *La Razón* (April 7, 1911, in *Cuaderno de Recortes*, vol. 2, 2.

121. José Pedro Segundo, "N. de la D.," *Evolución* 5, no. 1 (August 1910): 23.

122. Rodó, *Liberalismo*, 6.

123. Rodó, *Liberalismo*, 5.

124. For detailed treatments of these polemics, see Caetano, *Los uruguayos del Centenario*, 17–119.

125. "A las claras," *El Liberal* (February 20, 1909), in *Cuaderno de Recortes*, vol. 1, 66.

126. Frank Lenz, "Monteverde of Montevideo," *Association Men* 48, no. 12 (July 1923): 561–62.

127. The Pan American Union building in DC opened in 1910.

128. Homer Stuntz, "The South American Opportunity," *Men and Missions* 5, no. 1 (September 1913): 20.

129. Latin America was a primary concern for *The Outlook*, which

published opinion pieces about US intervention in the Philippines, Central America, and Mexico, profiles on Colombia, Venezuela, Ecuador, and Peru, and Roosevelt's chronicles from Brazil, Montevideo (where Roosevelt described José Batlle y Ordóñez's purported elaborate praise of his defense of the Monroe Doctrine), Argentina, the Andes, Chile, and Paraguay.

130. The First Congress was held in Santiago de Chile in 1909.

131. There were other evangelical conferences in Latin America in subsequent years, such as the Congress on Christian Work in South America that was held in Montevideo (1925).

132. Inman, "A Notable Pan-American Conference," *The Outlook* (March 29, 1916): 754.

133. Erasmo Braga, *Pan-Americanismo: aspecto religioso*, trans. Eduardo Monteverde (Nueva York: Sociedad para la Educación Misionera en los Estados Unidos y el Canadá, 1917), 127, 44.

134. Braga, *Pan-Americanismo*, 94-95.

135. Braga, *Pan-Americanismo*, 103.

136. Braga, *Pan-Americanismo*, 195.

137. The lone speaker from Latin America was Luis Berenguer, manager and son of the eponymous founder of the Cuban Telephone Company in Santiago de Cuba, who spoke about "Latin America."

138. In 1920, Braga was made general secretary of the Brazilian Committee on Cooperation (BCC), a branch of the Committee on Cooperation in Latin America (CCLA), whose

leaders were Robert E. Speer and Samuel Guy Inman.

139. Inman, "A Notable Pan-American Conference," 754.

140. Alberto Zum Felde, *Índice crítico de la literatura hispanoamericana: los ensayistas* (Mexico: Guarania, 1954), 110.

141. V. A. S., "Los maestros en su cátedra: Frente al doctor Carlos Vaz Ferreira," *El Día* (March 29, 1925), in *Cuaderno de Recortes*, vol. 3, 85.

142. Vaz Ferreira, *Moral para intelectuales*, ed. Manuel Claps and Sara Vaz Ferreira (Caracas: Ayacucho, 1979), 291.

143. Vaz Ferreira, *Moral para intelectuales*, 273–74.

144. Vaz Ferreira, *Moral para intelectuales*, 307.

145. Vaz Ferreira, *Moral para intelectuales*, 309. While he affirms that religions do permit an equitable degree of intellectual autonomy, such as Protestantism's free examination and Catholic modernism, Vaz Ferreira maintains that a faith uncomplicated by the influence of incompatible intellectual and moral ideas has sociocultural benefits. When, on the other hand, a primitive religiosity must be legitimated by the criteria valued by modern psychology and science, it can have negative ramifications.

146. Vaz Ferreira, *Lógica viva*, ed. Manuel Claps and Sara Vaz Ferreira (Caracas: Ayacucho: 1979), 81.

147. In line with the continually evolving nature of his pedagogy, in the

prologue Vaz Ferreira talks about the book that he is writing as if he were not writing that book: "I have a book in the pipeline that would be positively useful if I could someday write it, and if its realization could even come close to the ideal I conceive. It would be a study of the way in which people think, debate, get things right, or make mistakes—especially of how they get things wrong—but in fact: an analysis of the most common confusions, of the paralogisms most frequently put into practice, exactly as they are, not as they would be if psychological processes were superimposable to their verbal schemes. Not a Logic, then, but a Psycho-Logic. . . . Simply, a book (that would be, if you will, the second part of any treatise on common logic), with more examples, taken not only from science but from everyday life, from daily conversations; destined, not to demonstrate or to apply any systematic doctrine, but rather only for positively practical ends for any ordinary person, who, after having read that book, would be somewhat more capable than before of reasoning well, on the one hand, and more qualified, on the other, to avoid some errors and confusions that he would not have been able to avoid prior, or would have avoided with less ease." Vaz Ferreira, *Lógica viva*, 3.

148. Vaz Ferreira, *Lógica viva*, 25.

149. Rodó, *La vida nueva*. vol. 1: *El que vendrá. La nueva novela*

(Montevideo: Dornaleche y Reyes, 1897), 27.

150. Vaz Ferreira, *Lógica viva*, 65, 88.

151. Traditional metaphysics has been primarily concerned with providing explanations for phenomena it is unable to accurately explain, but still insists on veiling this incapacity. Vaz Ferreira argues that metaphysics is not precise, but legitimate: "it constitutes now and forever the most elevated form of activity of human thought, as long as it does not seek to have the geometrical and falsely precise aspect that it has sought to give to it . . ." According to Vaz Ferreira, metaphysics' elasticity is valid because it has other uses than precision. The moral contributions made by metaphysics are relevant, but not when it seeks to define them. Instead, the success of metaphysics depends on its ability to suggest, as well as offer hope and alternative possibilities to counter rigid positivistic frameworks. Following Bergson and James' anti-mechanicist ideas, Vaz Ferreira sees the utility of metaphysics in bringing humanity into closer contact with the inherent dynamism of life. Vaz Ferreira, *Lógica viva*, 85, 76; *Moral para intelectuales*, 311.

152. Vaz Ferreira, *Lógica viva*, 127–28.

153. Vaz Ferreira, *Lógica viva*, 91: "Pero hay otro buen sentido que viene después del razonamiento, o, mejor, junto con él. Cuando hemos visto y pesado por el raciocinio las razones en pro y las razones en contra que

hay en casi todos los casos; cuando hemos hecho toda la lógica (la buena lógica) posible, cuando las cuestiones se vuelven de grados, llega un momento en que una especie de instinto—lo que yo llamo el buen sentido hiperlógico—es el que nos resuelve las cuestiones en los casos concretos. Y sería bueno que la lógica no privara a los hombres de esta forma superior de buen sentido."

154. Oscar Martí, "Early Critics of Positivism," in *A Companion to Latin American Philosophy*, ed. Susana Nuccetelli, Ofelia Schutte and Otávio Bueno (Malden, MA: Blackwell, 2010), 73.

155. Vasconcelos, "La juventud intelectual mexicana y el actual momento histórico de nuestro país," in *Conferencias del Ateneo de la Juventud*, ed. Juan Hernández Luna (México: UNAM, 1962), 135–36. The importance of the Ateneo de la Juventud has been extensively documented by both its members and later critics. See, for example, Emmanuel Carballo, "El Ateneo de la Juventud y el triste papel de los escritores," in *Notas de un francotirador* (México: Instituto Politécnico Nacional/Sociedad General de Escritores de México, 1996): 139–43; Fernando Curiel, *Ateneo de la Juventud (A-Z)* (México: Universidad Nacional Autónoma de México, 2001); Pedro Ángel Palou, "The Ateneo de la Juventud: The Foundations of Mexican Intellectual Culture," in *A History of Mexican Literature*, ed.

Ignacio M. Sánchez Prado, Anna M. Nogar, and José Ramón Ruisánchez Serra (New York: Cambridge University Press, 2016): 233–45.

156. For details of the *ateneístas'* varied political views, see José Rojas Gardueñas, *El Ateneo de la Juventud y la Revolución* (México: Patronato del Instituto Nacional de Estudios Históricos de la Revolución Mexicana, 1979); Susana Quintanilla, *Nosotros: la juventud del Ateneo de México* (México: Tusquets, 2008); Guillermo Hurtado, "The Anti-Positivist Movement in Mexico," in *A Companion to Latin American Philosophy*, ed. Susana Nuccetelli, Ofelia Schutte, and Otávio Bueno (Malden, MA: Wiley-Blackwell, 2010): 82–94; Horacio Legrás, *Culture and Revolution: Violence, Memory, and the Making of Modern Mexico* (Austin: University of Texas Press, 2017).

157. Rodó would remain an important object of study for Mexican intellectuals in the decades after the Ateneo. See Castro Morales, "Un proyecto intelectual"; García Morales, "Un capítulo del 'arielismo': Rodó en México," 95–105.

158. Henríquez Ureña, "Nota de la edición mexicana," in *Ariel*, by José Enrique Rodó (Monterrey: Talleres Modernos de Lozano, 1908), 6.

159. Henríquez Ureña, "La obra de José Enrique Rodó," in *Conferencias del Ateneo de la Juventud*, ed. Antonio Caso, et al. (México: Lacaud, 1910), 69.

160. García Morales, *El Ateneo de México*, 170.

161. Rodó, *Motivos de Proteo* (Caracas: Ayacucho, 1976), 63.

162. Henríquez Ureña, "La obra de José Enrique Rodó," 69.

163. Antonio Caso, "La filosofía moral de Don Eugenio M. de Hostos," in *Conferencias del Ateneo de la Juventud*, eds. Antonio Caso, et al. (México: Lacaud, 1910), 27.

164. Krauze, *Redeemers*, 62.

165. Vasconcelos, *Discursos, 1920–1950* (México: Botas, 1950), 13.

166. William James, *The Varieties of Religious Experience* (New York: Longmans, Green, and Co., 1917), 53–77.

167. Caso, *La filosofía de la intuición* (México: Nosotros, 1914), 6–7.

168. Caso, *La filosofía de la intuición*, 7.

169. Caso, *La filosofía de la intuición*, 9.

170. Caso, *La filosofía de la intuición*, 9.

171. Caso, *La filosofía de la intuición*, 7: "Las intuiciones inmediatas son la base de todo conocimiento, las premisas de toda demostración. El método analítico y sintético de los lógicos no es capaz de producir la simultaneidad del conocimiento, la integración de las verdades científicas en la verdad universal concreta. Para lograr esto último, hay que volver a recurrir al único procedimiento que causa la simultaneidad en el conocimiento, a saber: la intuición. Hay que sumergir sus datos abstractos en la intuición."

172. Caso, *La filosofía de la intuición*, 5–10.

173. Caso, *La filosofía de la intuición*, 5.

174. Caso, *La filosofía de la intuición*, 6.

175. Caso, *La filosofía de la intuición*, 10.

176. I am analyzing the 1916 edition since it is the one that is most immediate in the *arielista* context and because, furthermore, the 1919 edition does not contain crucial updates that would problematize my reading of the essay's initial publication.

177. José Gaos, "El sistema de Caso," in *Obras completas*, vol. 3: *La existencia como economía, como desinterés y como caridad*, by Antonio Caso (México: UNAM, 1972), 12.

178. Caso, *La existencia como economía y como caridad: ensayo sobre la esencia del cristianismo* (México: Porrúa, 1916), 5.

179. Caso, *La existencia como economía*, 15–16.

180. Caso, *La existencia como economía*, 18.

181. Caso, *La existencia como economía*, 16.

182. Caso, *La existencia como economía*, 16.

183. Terry Eagleton, *The Ideology of the Aesthetic* (Cambridge, MA: Blackwell, 1990), 7.

184. Eagleton, *The Ideology of the Aesthetic*, 27.

185. Eagleton, *The Ideology of the Aesthetic*, 25.

186. Eagleton puts it another way: "The enheartening expression of this doctrine, politically speaking, would be: 'what appears as my subordination to others is in fact self-determination'; the more cynical view would run: 'my subordination to others is so effective that it appears to me in the mystified guise of governing myself,'" Eagleton, *The Ideology of the Aesthetic*, 25–27.

187. Eagleton, *The Ideology of the Aesthetic*, 28.

188. Caso, *La existencia como economía*, 18.

189. Caso, *La existencia como economía*, 21.

190. Caso, *La existencia como economía*, 20: "el orden sobrenatural [del amor] cae sobre el biológico y lo inunda en su ímpetu divino."

191. Marcuse, *Negations: Essays in Critical Theory* (London: MayFlyBooks, 2009), 80.

192. "The mind cannot escape reality without denying itself; the soul can, and is supposed to do so. [. . .] An individual full of soul is more compliant, acquiesces more humbly to fate, and is better at obeying authority." Marcuse, *Negations*, 85, 93.

193. Rodó, *Ariel*, 231.

194. Ernst Bloch, *The Principle of Hope*, vol. 1, trans. Neville Plaice, Stephen Plaice, and Paul Knight (Cambridge: MIT Press, 1996), 13.

CHAPTER 3

1. Pérez Petit, *Rodó*, 192: "es un evangelio para la juventud suramericana: su numen excelso la ha bautizado con un ósculo sereno, todo fragancia de nardos, todo diafanidad de luz. *Ariel* es la voz y conciencia de nuestra raza."

2. Rama, *La ciudad letrada*, 111.

3. José María Vargas Vila, *Ante los bárbaros: el yanki; he ahí el enemigo* (Barcelona: Ramón Palacio Viso, 1930), viii.

4. Vargas Vila, *Ante los bárbaros*, vii, x.

5. Vargas Vila, *Ante los bárbaros*, ix.

6. Miguel Ángel Carbonell, *El peligro de el águila* (La Habana: Seoane y Fernández, 1922), 169.

7. Carbonell, *El peligro de el águila*, 141: "Terrible iconoclasta, detesta mitos y creencias; sus labios no pronuncian nunca palabras de piedad, es un desgarrador de velos y un azote de ídolos. Aspira a emancipar las multitudes, pero no quiere formar parte de ellas. Ansía redimir, pero no le evanece el lauro

de la popularidad. Aborrece tanto a las muchedumbres analfabetas soportadoras de la tiranía, como a los viles centuriones que la ejercen. Detesta por igual aquella plebe y este pulpo."

8. Carbonell, *El peligro de el águila*, 134, 170: "evangélica doctrina domina y se impone. Al resplandor de su genio poderoso y original, desaparecen las sombras; todo es claridad en torno suyo"; "voz evangélica y apocalíptica es escuchada con veneración en todo el Continente, con la fe con que los creyentes atienden al sacerdote que levanta entre sus manos la sagrada hostia, y unge con el óleo de sus virtudes a los fieles de su iglesia."

9. Vargas Vila, *Ante los bárbaros*, 36.

10. Rodó, *Ariel*, 231.

11. Vargas Vila, *Ante los bárbaros*, 23.

12. Vargas Vila, *Ante los bárbaros*, 28.

13. Vargas Vila, *Ante los bárbaros*, 105.

14. Vargas Vila, *Ante los bárbaros*, 9.

15. Vargas Vila, *Ante los bárbaros*,

55–56: "se anunciaron como los hijos de Wáshington, y fueron los filibusteros de Walker; / cayeron sobre esos pueblos como el pie de paquidermo, y aplastaron su corazón; / así agoniza entre sus brazos la República Cubana, la República Dominicana, la República Nicaragüense y la República de Panamá; así murió ahogada en sangre la República Filipina; así estranguladas por la mano amiga de los republicanos del Norte; / en Cuba la protección, conquista disfrazada; en Manila, la batalla, conquista declarada; en Puerto Rico la posesión, conquista tolerada; en Santo Domingo la ocupación, conquista descarada; en Panamá la intervención, conquista desvergonzada; siempre y doquiera la Conquista; / y a este despojo vil lo llaman: la Victoria."

16. Ugarte, "Carta abierta al Presidente de los Estados Unidos," in *La nación latinoamericana*, ed. Norberto Galasso (Caracas: Ayacucho, 1978), 83.

17. Vargas Vila, *Ante los bárbaros*, 196–97.

18. Rodó, *Ariel*, 202; Vargas Vila, *Ante los bárbaros*, 197.

19. Vargas Vila, *Ante los bárbaros*, 157: "el odio al yanki, debe ser nuestra divisa, pues, que ese odio es nuestro deber; un deber imperativo."

20. Carlos A. Jáuregui, *Canibalia: canibalismo, calibanismo, antropofagia cultural y consumo en América Latina* (Madrid: Iberoamericana/Vervuert, 2008), 354.

21. Jáuregui, *Canibalia*, 348, 354.

22. Jáuregui, *Canibalia*, 348.

23. Jáuregui, *Canibalia*, 256.

24. Jáuregui, *Canibalia*, 355.

25. Vargas Vila, prologue to *Huerto agnóstico: cuadernos de un solitario* (Paris: Libería de la vuida de Ch. Bouret, 1912), 5n2.

26. Vargas Vila, "Prólogo," *Huerto agnóstico*, 4n1.

27. Vargas Vila, "Prólogo," *Huerto agnóstico*, 5n2: "¿por qué, he de sentir Remordimiento, de ver abrirse rojas de sangre las flores que yo siembro?: destruir es más glorioso que crear."

28. Vargas Vila, *Huerto agnóstico: cuadernos de un solitario* (Barcelona: Ramón Sopena, 1920), 4–6: "que el Ateísmo de mis libros, desnudo como un Titán, aterroriza las almas; [. . .] ¿que el agnosticismo de mis libros, siembra la desolación en los espíritus y, los hace inermes para toda forma de esfuerzo pecórico, es decir, de Sacrificio? [. . .] que [mis libros] cierran brutalmente los horizontes de la Esperanza; [. . .] que mis libros corroponen la Juventud. [. . .] que yo soy un sembrador de la Muerte, porque mis teorías sobre el Suicidio, fructificando en ciertos cerebros, los han hecho saltar al golpe de un revólver . . .;

que mis libros son hechos contra Dios;
contra la Religión;
contra la Patria;
contra la Sociedad;
contra la Familia
contra la Mujer . . .
contra todos mis Ídolos;
contra todas las esclavitudes;
contra todos los yugos . . .
. . .

tenéis razón;
quemad mis libros … "

29. Vargas Vila, *Huerto agnóstico*, 15.
30. Vargas Vila, *Huerto agnóstico*, 14, 102, 126, 130, 136.
31. Vargas Vila, *Huerto agnóstico*, 102–3: "ningún Hombre Superior, es un Constructor; / por su Instinto Sublime, es un Destructor."
32. Vargas Vila, "Prólogo," 7, 120.
33. Gerard Aching, *The Politics of Spanish American Modernismo: By Exquisite Design* (Cambridge, UK: Cambridge University Press, 1997), 27.
34. Aching, *The Politics of Spanish American Modernismo*, 36.
35. Aching, *The Politics of Spanish American Modernismo*, 40–41.
36. Rodó, *Ariel*, 160.
37. Rodó, *Ariel*, 161.
38. Pérez Petit, *Rodó*, 164–69.
39. Pérez Petit, *Rodó*, 154.
40. Rodó, *Ariel*, 154.
41. Pérez Petit, *Rodó*, 244.
42. Pérez Petit, *Rodó*, 42. In a similar vein, Mario Benedetti opines, "Solitude (and its variant: misogyny) was a constant in Rodó's life. His best friendships were epistolary ones, to the point that if one wished to find the man in a straightforward way, deliberately hidden behind the exquisiteness of style and intellectual rigor, there is no recourse but to delve into his correspondence, which is in my view the most revealing zone of everything we wrote." Benedetti, *Genio y figura de José Enrique Rodó*, 17.
43. Solitude is also an important topic in *Motivos de Proteo*, where Rodó describes it as a "diamond shield" and "reparative sleep" that can, in certain situations for a limited amounts of time, help the subject on its quest to "interior liberty." At the same time, if solitude is the lone mechanism upon which the subject relies, it is capable of producing erroneous perceptions. Rodó, *Motivos de Proteo*, 201–2.
44. Vargas Vila, *Huerto agnóstico*, 55.
45. Vargas Vila, *Huerto agnóstico*, 4n1.
46. Vargas Vila, "Prólogo," 10; Vargas Vila, *Huerto agnóstico*, 61.
47. Vargas Vila, *Huerto agnóstico*, 57.
48. Vargas Vila, *Huerto agnóstico*, 75.
49. Vargas Vila, *Huerto agnóstico*, 118.
50. Vargas Vila, *Huerto agnóstico*, 59, 77–78.
51. Vargas Vila, *Ante los bárbaros*, 52; Vargas Vila, *Huerto agnóstico*, 220.
52. José de la Luz León, "Reparos a un bello libro," *El Fígaro* 39, no. 26 (1922): 410.
53. Vitier, "A modo de prólogo," in *La higuera de Timón: consejos al pequeño Antonio*, by Fernando Lles y Berdayes (Matanzas: Imprenta Casas y Mercado, 1921), 5; Diego V. Tejera, "*La higuera de Timón*," *El Fígaro* 39, no. 15 (1922): 230.
54. Vitier, "A modo de prólogo," 5.
55. Vitier, "Más sobre *La higuera de Timón*," *El Fígaro* 40, no. 3 (1923): 3.
56. Vitier, "Más sobre *La higuera de Timón*," 3.
57. Vitier, "Más sobre *La higuera de Timón*," 3.
58. José J. Nodarse y Cabrera, "La filosofía social y política de Lles," *Revista Cubana* 27 (1950): 99, 101.

59. Greg Grandin, *Empire's Workshop: Latin America, the United States, and the Rise of the New Imperialism* (New York: Owl Books, 2007).

60. Fernando Ortiz used the term *cacocracia* in 1930 to define the Machado regime. Julio Le Reverend, "Fernando Ortiz y su obra cubana," in *Fernando Ortiz*, by Fernando Ortiz (La Habana: UNEAC, 1973), 34. Earlier, during the presidency of Mario García Menocal, José Antonio Ramos published *Manual del perfecto fulanista* (1916), a scathing critique of political corruption stemming from US intervention and complicit Cuban bourgeoisie actors and entities. See chapter 3 of Sergio Díaz-Briquets and Jorge Pérez-López, *Corruption in Cuba: Castro and Beyond* (Austin: University of Texas Press, 2006).

61. Julio Antonio Mella, "Cuba, un páis que jamás ha sido libre," in *Mella, documentos y artículos*, ed. Eduardo Castañeda, et al. (La Habana: Editorial de Ciencias Sociales, Instituto Cubano del Libro, 1975), 174–83.

62. José Manuel Poveda, *Proemios de Cenáculo* (La Habana: Ministerio de Educación, 1948), 77: "No somos independientes. No somos sino una factoría colonial, obligada a trabajar, y a dar su cosecha y su fruto compelida por el látigo. [. . .] [U]n soplo de desilusión ha disgregado todas las energías creadoras del alma nacional. Somos la sombra de un pueblo, el sueño de una democracia, el ansia de una libertad. No existimos."

63. Castellanos, "Rodó y su "Proteo" (La Habana: Comas y López, 1910), 9.

64. Raúl Argastabe, "A los pies de Ariel," *Letras* 10, no. 30 (1914): 363.

65. The poetry collections co-authored by Fernando and Francisco Lles in their early years are *Crepúsculos* (Matanzas: El Escritorio, 1909), *Sol de invierno* (Matanzas: Bertrán y Dulzaides, 1911), and *Limoneros en flor* (Matanzas: El Radium, 1921).

66. José Manuel Carbonell, "Fernando Lles," 92: "Su filiación mental parece estar en Rodó. Su estilo es armonioso y sencillo."

67. José Antonio Portuondo, *El contenido social de la literatura cubana* (México: Centro de Estudios Sociales, 1944), 59. Juan J. Remos y Rubio echoes this opinion, writing "José Enrique Rodó's influence has been felt strongly among Cuban essayists. Fernando Lles and Emilio Gaspar Rodríguez have been the ones that have received this influence most intensely." Juan J. Remos y Rubio, *Historia de la literatura cubana*, tomo 3: Modernismo (Havana: Cárdenas y Compañía, 1945), 457.

68. Remos y Rubio, *Proceso histórico de las letras cubanas* (Madrid: Ediciones Guadarrama, 1958), 282.

69. Raimundo Lazo, *Historia de la literatura cubana* (México: UNAM, 1974), 213. Enrique Ubieta, who classifies Lles's perspective as "rodoniana" (that is, in the vein of Rodó), is representative of such assessments. Enrique Ubieta, "El ensayo

y la crítica," in *Historia de la literatura cubana*, tomo 2, ed. Rinaldo Acosta, Ingry González Hernández, and Ana María Muñoz Bachs (La Habana: Letras Cubanas, 2003), 94.

70. Carlos Loveira y Chirino, *Un gran ensayista: Fernando Lles. Discurso de ingreso como miembro de número de la Sección de Literatura leído por [. . .] en la sesión solemne celebrada por la Academia Nacional de Artes y Letras, la noche del 30 de enero de 1926* (La Habana: El Siglo XX, 1926), 10–11: "A propósito de estos paralelos literarios, he leído que Fernando Lles, como casi todos los ensayistas de nuestra América, surgidos al calor de Rodó, ha inspirado su labor en los cánones del renombrado escritor uruguayo. El concepto es erróneo en mi opinión. Una lectura completa, serena, desapasionada, de los libros de nuestro compatriota, basta para no admitir esa identidad y desautorizar esa comparación. [. . .] Decir que Lles debe a Rodó su iniciación en el pensamiento y en el arte, no puede ser más que opinión formada por somera impresión, cuando no a libro medio abierto."

71. Loveira y Chirino, *Un gran ensayista*, 10.

72. González Echevarría, *The Voice of the Masters*, 20.

73. Fernando Lles y Berdayes, *La higuera de Timón: consejos al pequeño Antonio* (Matanzas: Imprenta Casas y Mercado, 1921), 7, 27.

74. Lles, *La higuera de Timón*, 33.

75. Lles, *La higuera de Timón*, 61: "un albañal monstruo, muchos gérmenes,

todo fétido, horrible como una pústula gigantesca [que] hervía como un pudridero."

76. Lles, *La higuera de Timón*, 38.

77. Lles, *La higuera de Timón*, 98: "el misántropo sabe que existe un gozo inmenso en el fondo del vaso que contiene las heces de nuestro dolor."

78. Rodó, *Ariel*, 166.

79. Lles, *La higuera de Timón*, 22–23.

80. Lles, *La higuera de Timón*, 20, 36.

81. Lles, *La higuera de Timón*, 15.

82. Lles, *La higuera de Timón*, 13: "una rama, frondosa y compasiva, del árbol secular de mi huerto, de la que puedes colgarte muy bonitamente, a sabiendas de que nunca más será turbado tu reposo."

83. To put this in Eagleton's terms: "The Schopenhauerian subject thus masters its own murder by suicide, outwits its predators through the premature self-abnegation of the aesthetic. The Schopenhauerian aesthetic is the death drive in action, though this death is secretly a kind of life . . .: the subject cannot be entirely negated as long as it still delights, even if what it takes pleasure in is the process of its own dissolution. The aesthetic condition thus presents an unsurmountable paradox, as Keats knew in contemplating the nightingale: there is no way in which one can savour one's own extinction. The more exultantly the aesthetic subject experiences its own nullity before the object the more, by that very token, the experience must have failed." Eagleton, *The Ideology of the Aesthetic*, 165.

84. Freud, *The Future of an Illusion*.

85. Lles, *La higuera de Timón*, 7. For uses and abuses of Martí's ideas and image, see Guerra, *The Myth of José Martí*); Rojas, *José Martí: la invención de Cuba* (Madrid: Colibrí, 2000); Rojas, *Tumbas sin sosiego: revolución, disidencia y exilio del intelectual cubano* (Barcelona: Anagrama, 2006); Enrique del Risco, *Elogio de la levedad: mitos nacionales cubanos y sus reescrituras literarias en el siglo XX* (Madrid: Colibrí, 2008); Antonio José Ponte, "Martí: historia de una bofetada," *Cuadernos Hispanoamericanos* 696 (June 2008): 21–32.

86. José Martí, "Nuestra América," in *José Martí: ensayos y crónicas*, ed. José Olivio Jiménez (Madrid: Anaya y Mario Muchnik, 1995), 118.

87. Flora Díaz Parrado, for instance, took to the pages of *Social* and called the aforementioned *ceiba* tree an "indisputable triumph over the fraternity of imperialism and dictatorships of our Continent." Although *Social* was, as Salvador Bueno points out, a "mirror for those nouveau riche, those fortunate *criollos* who floated in the golden crest from good sales of sugar," it took on more overt sociopolitical tones after Emilio Roig de Leuchsenring assumed the role of literary director in 1925. Flora Díaz Parrado, "La pobre ceiba," *Social* 13, no. 10 (1928): 25; Salvador Bueno, "El periodismo literario en Cuba. De *El Fígaro* a *Social*," *Crucero* 1, no. 2 (1960): 38.

88. Manuel González Prada, "Discurso en el Politeama," in *Manuel González Prada. ¡Los jóvenes a la obra! Textos esenciales*, ed. David Sobrevilla (Lima: Fondo Editorial del Congreso del Perú, 2009), 240.

89. Lles, *La higuera de Timón*, 77.

90. Lles, *La higuera de Timón*, 10, 64, 95: "lo que a queriendas y a sabiendas se falsea"; Pierre Bourdieu, "Men and Machines," in *Advances in Social Theory and Methodology: Toward an Integration of Micro- and Macro-Sociologies*, ed. Karin Knorr-Cetina and A. V. Cicourel (London: Routledge, 2015), 307.

91. Max Stirner, *The Ego and Its Own*, ed. David Leopold (Cambridge: Cambridge University Press, 1995), 133; Ralph Waldo Emerson, "Self-Reliance," in *Self-Reliance and Other Essays* (New York: Dover, 1993), 25.

92. Giorgio Agamben, *Homo Sacer: Sovereign Power and Bare Life*, tran. Daniel Heller-Roazen (Stanford, CA: Stanford University Press, 1998), 46.

93. Lles, *La higuera*, 104.

94. Lles, *La sombra de Heráclito* (La Habana, Imp. El Siglo XX, 1923); Lles, *La escudilla de Diógenes. Etopeya del cínico* (La Habana, Editorial Nuestra Novela, 1924).

95. Émile Durkheim, *Suicide: A Study in Sociology*, trans. John A. Spaulding and George Simpson (New York: Free Press, 1951).

96. Marx, *Marx on Suicide*, tran. Eric A. Plaut, Gabrielle Edgcomb, and Kevin Anderson (Evanston, IL: Northwestern University Press, 1999), 47.

97. See Daniel Nemser, *Infrastructures of Race: Concentration and Biopolitics in Colonial Mexico* (Austin: University of Texas Press, 2017), which illustrates how the logics and practices of *reconcentración* pre-date the Cuban War of Independence in colonial Mexico.

98. I am grateful to the Biblioteca Histórica Cubana y Americana Francisco González del Valle in Havana for their generosity in allowing me to consult this letter. The trial of Francisco's murderer, Juan Peñate, was well publicized in the Matanzas newspaper El Mundo in April 1921. While the facts surrounding this tragic event were murky, as numerous witnesses took the stand in the trial and offered inconsistent testimonies, it is possible that it was a completely random occurrence. Even Lles attributes the act to "obscure plans of the incomprehensible" (*oscuros designios de lo incomprensible*). Lles, "Carta a Emilio Roig de Leuchsenring," (April 3, 1921), Fondo Emilio Roig de Leuchsenring, La Biblioteca Histórica Cubana y Americana Francisco González del Valle, Havana, Cuba.

99. Numerous portions of *La higuera de Timón* first appeared in "La caridad en sus aspectos del Pasado y del Presente. Los insolidarios, los pródigos, los artistas y los convencionales," published in 1913 in *Conferencias*, accompanied by two texts by Filomeno Rodríguez and Justo G. Betancourt.

100. Louis Pérez, *To Die in Cuba: Suicide and Society* (Chapel Hill: University of North Carolina Press, 2005), 202.

101. Kirwin Shaffer, "The Radical Muse: Women and Anarchism in Early-Twentieth-Century Cuba," *Cuban Studies* 34 (January 2003): 134.

102. Rodó, *Ariel*, 146.

103. The following excerpt from Fernando Ortiz's *Entre cubanos: psicología tropical* demonstrates the commonality with which *arielista*-saturated remedies were proposed for the social ills of apathy and lack of ideals during the Cuban Republic: "in societies seeded in democracy like ours, where for various causes mental aristocracy is scarce and weak, culture will not be able to germinate without everyone, both the giants of thought and action, and the small and humble laborers, give ourselves to the regenerative task, devote ourselves to the work of plough the virginal homeland of our psychology, spread in every direction the ideas of modern life that will have to be a cultivation of hope if we water them not with the sterile sorrow of the desperate, but with fertilizing sweat of work; that doing things in this way will make the fields of the Cuban homeland green, the sweet lifeblood of culture will fill its cane fields and the future harvest of prosperity will be rich and good for all." Ortiz, *Entre cubanos*, 9-10. Similarly, in *La crisis de la altura cultura en Cuba* Jorge Mañach outlines the "national vices" responsible for Cuba's "cultural decadence," and sets his sights on forging "a true Patria in the most spiritual and fertile sense of the

rescued term." Jorge Mañach, *La crisis de la alta cultura en Cuba. Indagación del choteo* (Miami: Ediciones Universal, 1991), 38, 44.

104. It is also worth noting that Rodó's aura was difficult to sustain during the more militant 1920s. In 1928, for instance, an eighteen-year-old Cuban communist writer named José Antonio Foncueva (1910–1930) took to the pages of *Bohemia* and penned one of the most direct takedowns of Rodó in which he declared that *arielismo* was no longer the ideological standard for Latin American youth. According to Foncueva, "Rodó's *Ariel* is an incomplete and shapeless message, an overly idealistic mix of French romanticism and sterile Hispanic *quijotismo*. It lacks meaning in reality. [. . .] Rodó has passed. He's now a symbol of another time. [. . .] The best thing about his lesson is what he did not say." José Antonio Foncueva, "Ingenieros, Rodó y el pensamiento de la América nueva," *Bohemia* 20, no. 41 (1928): 19.

105. As José Russinyol points out, "[Lles] began to educate himself—an unparalleled autodidact—behind the counter of a small bodega in a tiny country town, without libraries, professors, schools, nor scholarships." José Russinyol, "Fernando Lles: el hombre y el medio," *Revista Cubana* 27 (1950): 105.

106. Rojas, "Insularidad y exilio de los intelectuales cubanos," *Estudios. Filosofía-Historia-Letras* 43 (Winter 1995-1996), 82; Luis Toledo Sande, *Tres narradores agonizantes: tanteos*

acerca de la obra de Miguel de Carrión, Jesús Castellanos y Carlos Loveira (La Habana: Editorial Letras Cubanas, 1980), 78.

107. Enrique Labrador Ruiz, "Escribe Enrique Labrador Ruiz: Lles, ese desconido," in *Escritos periodísticos de Enrique Labrador Ruiz*, ed. Adis Barrio Tosar (La Habana: Ediciones Extramuros, 2013), 40: "[d]esconocido de mala fe, olvidado por maldad, silenciado por conveniencia, embalsamado de nébula errabunda por inconcebible espíritu de compadreo, muerto y sepultado por las cuatro cabezas de avestruz que gobiernan a su modo esta desgraciada republiquilla de las letras."

108. Labrador Ruiz, "Escribe Enrique Labrador Ruiz," 40.

109. Vitier, *Apuntaciones literarias*, 166.

110. Rojas, "Insularidad y exilio de los intelectuales cubanos," 82–83.

111. Luis Rodríguez Rivero, "Noticia bibliográfica de Fernando Lles y Berdayes," *Revista Cubana* 27 (1950): 113–14.

112. Lles, *La higuera de Timón*, 34.

113. Žižek, *The Ticklish Subject: The Absent Centre of Political Ontology* (London: Verso, 2000), 153–54.

114. Bourdieu, *Practical Reason: On the Theory of Action* (Stanford: Stanford University Press, 1998), 77.

115. Lles, *La higuera de Timón*, 23. See Frantz Fanon, *The Wretched of the Earth*, tran. Richard Philcox (New York: Grove Press, 2004), 1–62.

116. Lles, *La higuera de Timón*, 11: "En el error te amamantaron: para el terror creciste . . ."

117. Plutarch, *Plutarch's Lives*, vol. 9, tran. Thomas North (London: J. M. Dent, 1899), 96-98.

118. In Sumidero (Limonar, Matanzas) some people marked the sixtieth anniversary of Berdayes's assassination (2017) with a tribute at the obelisk that marks the spot where his decapitated body was left. See "Acto en homenaje al 60 aniversario del asesinato de Antonio Berdayes Núñez," *Personalidades de la cultura limonareña* (November 6, 2017), http://lisgj79.cubava.cu/2017/11/06/acto-en-homenaje-al-60-aniversario-del-asesinato-de-antonio-berdayes-nunez.

119. Émile Armand, "Mini-Manual of the Anarchist Individualist," in *Anarchism: A Documentary History of Libertarian Ideas*, vol. 1, ed. Robert Graham (Montreal: Black Rose Books, 2005), 146.

120. According to Labrador Ruiz, Lles was also at work on a three volume *Historia Universal*, which to my knowledge was never published. Labrador Ruiz, "Escribe Enrique Labrador Ruiz," 40; José J. Nodarse y Cabrera, "La filosofía social y política de Lles," 93.

121. Jean Grave, *Moribund Society and Anarchy*, tran. Voltairine de Cleyre (San Francisco: A. Isaak, 1899), 76.

122. See Guerra, *Visions of Power*.

123. Fidel Castro, *La historia me absolverá* (Buenos Aires: Ediciones del Pensamiento Nacional, 1993), 107-108: "ser cubano implica un deber, no cumplirlo es crimen y es traición. Vivimos orgullosos de la historia de nuestra patria; [. . .] Se nos enseñó a venerar desde temprano el ejemplo glorioso de nuestros héroes y de nuestros mártires. [. . .] y que morir por la patria es vivir. Todo eso aprendimos y no lo olvidaremos . . ."

124. Lles, *La higuera de Timón*, 20.

CHAPTER 4

1. Carlos Fuentes, prologue to *Ariel*, by Jose Enriqué Rodó, trans. Margaret Sayers Peden (Austin: University of Texas Press, 1988), 28. Two important exceptions are the numerous activities of the Sociedad Rodoniana in Uruguay—from concerts to an international conference and a wide array of events throughout the country, and, second, the publication of an ambitious and lucid book about Rodó's life and work, Gustavo San Román, *A Companion to José Enrique Rodó* (Woodbridge, UK: Tamesis, 2018). The edited volumes published to commemorate the centenary of *Ariel* include, Ottmar Ette and Titus Heydenreich, *José Enrique Rodó y su tiempo: cien años de Ariel* (Frankfurt: Vervuert, 2000); San Román, *This America We Dream Of: Rodó and Ariel One Hundred Years On* (London: Institute of Latin American Studies, 2001); Leopoldo Zea and Hernán Taboada, *Arielismo y globalización* (México: Fondo de Cultura Económica, 2002).

2. Rodó, *Ariel*, 181. This is made clear by the fact that variations of the word *superior* (such as superiority) are mentioned almost fifty times in *Ariel*.

3. Prospero says in *Ariel*: "The powerful federation is effecting a kind of moral conquest among us. Admiration for its greatness and power is making impressive inroads in the minds of our leaders and, perhaps even more, in the impressionable minds of the masses, who are awed by its incontrovertible victories. And it is a very short trip from admiring it, to imitating it." Rodó, *Ariel*, 196.

4. For a chronology and analysis of Darío and Groussac's uses of the Caliban metaphor, see Jáuregui, *Canibalia*, 327–47.

5. Rodríguez Monegal, "Sobre el anti-imperialismo de Rodó," *Revista Iberoamericana* 80, no. 38 (July-September 1972): 495.

6. See, for example, David Dent, *Historical Dictionary of U.S.–Latin American Relations* (Westport, CT; London: Greenwood, 2005), 318; Peter Smith, *Talons of the Eagle: Dynamics of U.S.–Latin American Relations* (New York and Oxford: Oxford University Press, 2000), 111.

7. Gordon Brotherston, Introduction to *Ariel*, by José Enrique Rodó (Cambridge: Cambridge University Press, 1967), 9. See pages 9–17 for a discussion of Rodó's resistance to reductionist interpretations of the Ariel/Caliban dichotomy.

8. Cited in Gómez-Gil, *Mensaje y vigencia de José Enrique Rodó*, 56.

9. Enrique Anderson-Imbert, *Spanish-American Literature: A History*,

trans. John V. Falconieri (Detroit, MI: Wayne State University Press, 1963), 316.

10. Rodó, *Ariel*, 202.

11. Rodó, *Ariel*, 202.

12. José de la Riva Agüero, *Carácter de la literatura del Perú independiente* (Lima: Librería Francesa Científica Galland, 1905), 263: "Si la sinceridad de Rodó no se trasparentara en cada una de sus páginas, era de sospechar que "Ariel" oculta una intención secreta, una sangrienta burla [. . .] Proponer la Grecia antigua como modelo para una raza contaminada con el híbrido mestizaje con indios y negros; hablarle de recreo y de juego libre de la fantasía a una raza que si sucumbe será por una espantosa frivolidad; celebrar el ocio clásico ante una raza que se muere de pereza!"

13. See Miller, *In the Shadow*, 115–16 for an overview of Rodó's influence on Mella.

14. José Carlos Mariátegui, "La revolución socialista latinoamericana," in *El marxismo en América Latina*, by Michael Löwy (Santiago de Chile: LOM, 2007), 119: "Es ridículo hablar todavía del contraste entre una América sajona materialista y una América Latina idealista, entre una Roma rubia y una Grecia pálida. Todos éstos son tópicos irrremisiblemente desacreditados. El mito de Rodó no obra ya—no ha obrado nunca—útil y fundamentalmente sobre las almas. Descartemos, inexorablemente, todas esas caricaturas de ideologías y lugares y hagamos las cuentas, seria y francamente con la realidad."

15. Juan Zorrilla de San Martín, "Ariel y Calibán americanos," in *Detalles de historia* (Montevideo: Imprenta Nacional Colorada, 1930), 213–33.

16. Luis Humberto Delgado, *El suplicio de Ariel* (Lima: American Express, 1935), 22.

17. Aníbal Ponce, *Humanismo burgués y humaniso proletario* (México: América, 1938). See Jáuregui, *Canibalia*, 371–73 for more information about Ponce's engagement with *arielismo*.

18. Luis Alberto Sánchez, *Balance y liquidación del novecientos: ¿Tuvimos maestros en nuestra América?*, 106. The anti-*arielista* critiques outlined in *Balance y liquidación* are anticipated in an article Sánchez wrote in 1933 called "El Anti-Rodó."

19. Sánchez, *¿Existe América Latina?* (México: Fondo de Cultura Económica, 1945), 108.

20. Real de Azúa, *Historia visible e historia esotérica*, 129.

21. Fernando Díez de Medina, *Sariri: una réplica al "Ariel" de Rodó* (La Paz: A. Tejerina, 1954), 11–13: "los sudamericanos de hoy, crecidos en la dramática perplejidad de dos guerras mundiales [. . .] en el umbral tal vez de una tercera se preguntan: ¿El arielismo es una utopía idealista o un instrumento de edificación colectiva? ¿Conservan vigencia las ideas del maestro, en el mundo actual sembrado de pasión y confusión? La democracia idealizada que predicó el pensador ¿coincide con el tumulto y el retraso de nuestra América mestiza? [. . .] la síntesis simbólica de Calibán y Ariel peca de simplista [. . .;] el 'arielismo' es un producto demasiado literario [. . .]. El idealismo estético, didactizante, de Rodó no es para nosotros lo que fue para nuestros padres [. . . y] carece de significación social. [. . . S]e necesitan herramientas mejor templadas que el finísimo estilete de 'Ariel', para construir la dura América presente. [. . . L]a palabra rodoniana no sirve en estos años convulsos."

22. Jáuregui, *Canibalia*, 377.

23. John F. Kennedy, "Address at a White House Reception for Members of Congress and for the Diplomatic Corps of the Latin American Republics, March 13, 1961," in *Public Papers of the Presidents of the United States. John F. Kennedy: Containing the Public Messages, Speeches, and Statements of the President, January 20 to December 31, 1961* (Washington, DC: United States Government Printing Office, 1962), 174–75.

24. Ernesto Che Guevara, "On Growth and Imperialism," in *Venceremos! The Speeches and Writings of Ernest Che Guevara*, ed. John Gerassi (New York: Macmillan, 1968), 153.

25. A joint "Cuban Resolution" was approved on October 3, 1962, which begins by referencing the Monroe Doctrine, and cites the Foreign Ministers of the OAS meeting at Punta del Este (January 1962), who declared, "The present government of Cuba has identified itself with the principles of Marxist-Leninist ideology, has established a political, economic, and social system based

on that doctrine, and accepts military assistance from extracontinental Communist powers, including even the threat of military intervention in America on the part of the Soviet Union." "Cuban Resolution," in *Legislation on Foreign Relations* (Washington, DC: US Government Printing Office, 1975): 1035–36. This was later followed by a "Resolution on Communist Subversion in the Western Hemisphere," which was approved by the US House of Representatives, Sept. 20, 1965.

26. Although Ramos targets Rodó as an example of Latin American intellectuals who assimilate foreign ways of thinking, he explicitly excludes some *arielistas*—such as Ugarte, Vasconcelos, Ingenieros, and Blanco-Fombona—from this critique, although, as I have illustrated in earlier parts of this book, this is not the case.

27. Jorge Abelardo Ramos, *Historia de la nación latinoamericana* (Buenos Aires: A. Peña Lillo, 1968), 317.

28. "The aestheticizing speaker from the motionless Uruguay worries about the undertaking spirit of the practical North Americans. He does not explicitly condemn the Yankee's outrageous acts, but rather his pragmatic style." Ramos, *Historia de la nación latinoamericana*, 317.

29. Ramos, *Historia de la nación latinoamericana*, 319.

30. Ramos, *Historia de la nación latinoamericana*, 317.

31. Aimé Césaire, *Une tempête* (Paris: Éditions du Seuil, 1969).

32. Roberto Fernández Retamar, *Caliban and Other Essays*, tran. Edward Baker (Minneapolis: University of Minnesota Press, 1989), 14.

33. According to Rangel, "Of course, U.S. imperialism in Latin America is no myth. It is only a consequence, and not a cause of U.S. power and our weakness. Even the most unjust theft, no matter how reprehensible, is no excuse to look for a rational explanation for the strength of the thief and the fragility of his victim." Carlos Rangel, *Del buen salvaje al buen revolucionario: mitos y realidades en América Latina* (Caracas: Monte Avila, 1976), 42.

34. Rangel, *Del buen salvaje al buen revolucionario*, 94.

35. Rangel, *Del buen salvaje al buen revolucionario*, 94.

36. Rangel, *Del buen salvaje al buen revolucionario*, 94.

37. Rangel, *Del buen salvaje al buen revolucionario*, 97.

38. According to Ardao, "At this point we arrive at what is the key to the vault of the anti-*Ariel* myth in all its versions: the mistaken believe that for Rodó Latin America is Ariel or the residence of Ariel or is represented or symbolized by Ariel; with the addition, at the same time, that Ariel itself, for Rodó, represents or symbolizes the act of dreaming or fantasizing. All of this contrasts with the United States, which is certainly symbolized in his work by Caliban, since it is in effect, in his judgment, "the embodiment of the utilitarian verb." Ardao, *Nuestra*

América Latina (Montevideo: Ediciones de la Banda Oriental, 1968), 133.

39. Hugo Torrano, *Rodó: acción y libertad: restauración de su imagen* (Montevideo: Bareiro y Ramos, 1973).

40. San Román, "Influencia y actualidad del pensamiento de José Enrique Rodó," in *José Enrique Rodó: concurso internacional de ensayo*, 11–12 (Montevideo: Biblioteca Nacional, 2013).

41. Benedetti writes, "Today it is easy to linger on Rodó's deficiencies, on his myopia, on his failed proclamations, on his wrong predictions, on the ample volutes (today out of fashion) of his style, so often devoid of warmth. Today it is simple to point out which paths he should have followed, in which fork in the road he got wrong. Benedetti, *Genio y figura de José Enrique Rodó*, 116.

42. Vitier, *Del ensayo americano* (México: Fondo de Cultura Económica, 1945), 117.

43. Castro Morales, introduction to *Ariel*, 127.

44. Fernández Retamar, *Caliban*, 14. In the words of Julio Antonio Mella, "Haya de la Torre is the epitome (*arquetipo*) of Latin American youth, he is Rodó's dream come to life, he is Ariel." Mella, *Documentos y artículos*, 76. For a review of the *arielista* influence Haya de la Torre, see Claudio Vélez, *The New World of the Gothic Fox: Culture and Economy in English and Spanish America* (Berkeley: University of California Press, 1994), 7–8.

45. See San Román, "La recepción de Rodó en Cuba," *Revista de la Biblioteca Nacional* 3.1, no. 3 (2009): 83-85 for details on how Rodó's work has been appreciated from leftist angles in contemporary Cuba, particularly in Jorge E. González Rodríguez's *Rodó: prolegómenos de un siglo para la ética y la política* (2003).

46. Arnoldo Mora, *El arielismo: de Rodó a García Monge* (San José, Costa Rica: EUNED, 2008), 49-50: "La realidad geopolítica imperante en esta primera década del siglo XX devuelve a su plena actualidad, si bien en una nueva versión que se adecua al contexto imperante hoy día, las ideas y el credo arielista. El arielismo es algo más que una página gloriosa de la historia ideológica y cultural de Nuestra América. Hoy posee nuevo vigor y más actualidad que nunca."

47. Juan Martín Posadas, "Ubicación internacional," *El País* (March 3, 2008), www.elpais.com.uy/08/03/09/predit_334505.asp.

48. For details regarding Brazil's role in Rodó's Americanist writings, see Robert Patrick Newcomb, *Nossa and Nuestra América: Inter-American Dialogues* (West Lafayette, IN: Purdue University Press, 2012), 57–86.

49. Navarro, La hora americana," 265.

50. These include Gabriel Boric, Karol Cariola, Giorgio Jackson, and Camila Vallejo.

51. Matías Marambio de la Fuente, "Neoarielismo, educación, y estado actual de las movilizaciones," *La*

Chispa (July 7, 2011), http://www.la-chispa.cl/2011/07/07/609/: "Medio en serio y medio en broma, una de las consignas con las que salimos a marchas algunxs compañerxs fue 'Neoarielistas indignadxs.' La pregunta era: ¿qué es el neoarielismo? Y, más aún, ¿qué tiene que ver con el movimiento estudiantil? Son preguntas estrechamente ligadas. Si entendemos, como yo entiendo, al neoarielismo como crítica latino-americanista . . . de la hegemonía del saber utilitario, a la vez que como afirmación del valor fundamental de la educación/experiencia estética, entonces es posible vislumbrar algunas conexiones. No hay un vínculo natural entre neoarielismo y movimiento estudiantil, como tampoco lo hubo entre arielismo y reforma universitaria. Lo que sí hay, son posibilidades."

52. Grínor Rojo, *Las armas de las letras: ensayos neoarielistas* (Santiago de Chile: LOM, 2008), 9–10.

53. Rojo, *Las armas de las letras*, 16, 51.

54. Rojo, *Las armas de las letras*, 172.

55. Javier Sanjinés, "The Nation: An Imagined Community?" *Cultural Studies* 21, no. 2–3 (2007): 303.

56. Sanjinés, "The Nation," 304.

57. John Beverley, *Latinamericanism after 9/11* (Durham, NC: Duke University Press, 2011), 92-93. Charles Hatfield argues that Beverley's proposal for a new Latin Americanism ends up being a retrenchment into the same identity paradigms that he seeks to dispel. Hatfield, *The Limits of Identity*, 101–5.

58. For a discussion on Cuban and Dominican writers in New York City issuing correctives to Rodó's take on the United States in *Ariel*, see McDaniel, "Rodó en Nueva York," in *Lecturas contemporáneas de José Enrique Rodó*, ed. José Ramiro Podetti (Montevideo: Sociedad Rodoniana, 2018): 349–59.

59. Barrera Enderle, *La reinvención de Ariel*, 13.

60. Barrera Enderle, *La reinvención de Ariel*, 68: "un sujeto que puede pensar y actuar, y volver concretas las diversas circunstancias que lo envuelven, sin dejarse tentar por el canto de las sirenas del poder. Ariel pide a la juventud que se instruya; Calibán le pide que actúe y haga audible su propia voz. El neoarielismo sería una forma de combinar ambas propuestas para tratar de crear nuevos espacios para el diálogo y la crítica."

61. "Diego Canessa autor de "Ariel digital"; para atravesar este momento de discontinuidad sistémica, es muy importante religarse a nuestro patrimonio cultural intangible," *La Onda Digital* 928 (2019), www.laondadigital.uy/archivos/38253: "Lo que busca el mensaje es traer nuestro patrimonio cultural intangible al siglo XXI y decirles a los 20 millones de estudiantes latino-americanos actuales; éste es tu patrimonio cultural, sin este patrimonio cultural no podés atravesar este momento de discontinuidad sistémica que está viviendo el planeta. Porque no tenés referencias

éticas, geográficas ni conceptuales. Es de una importancia mayúscula, por lo menos, 'ordenarles la cancha' diciéndoles a los jóvenes ésta fue el inicio de la conciencia histórica latinoamericana."

BIBLIOGRAPHY

"A las claras." *El Liberal* (February 20, 1909). *Cuaderno de Recortes*, vol. 1. Recortes de prensa sobre Carlos Vaz Ferreira. Anáforas. Universidad de la República de Uruguay. Facultad de Información y Comunicación: 66. https://anaforas.fic.edu.uy/jspui/handle/123456789/42849.

Aching, Gerard. *The Politics of Spanish American Modernismo: By Exquisite Design*. Cambridge, UK: Cambridge University Press, 1997.

"Acto en homenaje al 60 aniversario del asesinato de Antonio Berdayes Núñez." *Personalidades de la cultura limonareña* (November 6, 2017). http://lisgj79.cubava.cu/2017/11/06/acto-en-homenaje-al-60-aniversario-del-asesinato-de-antonio-berdayes-nunez/.

Adorno, Theodor W. "The Essay as Form." *Notes to Literature*, vol. 1. Translated by Sherry Weber Nicholsen, 3–23. New York: Columbia University Press, 1991.

Agamben, Giorgio. *Homo Sacer: Sovereign Power and Bare Life*. Translated by Daniel Heller-Roazen. Stanford, CA: Stanford University Press, 1998.

_____. *Potentialities: Collected Essays in Philosophy*. Translated by Daniel Heller-Roazen. Stanford, CA: Stanford University Press, 1999.

Aguilar Rivera, José Antonio. "La dialéctica de la redención." *Nexos en línea*. February 1, 2012. www.nexos.com.mx/?p=14683.

Aguirre, Gisela. *José Ingenieros*. Buenos Aires: Planeta, 1999.

Aillón Soria, Esther. "La política cultural de Francia en la génesis y difusión del concepto *l'Amérique latine*, 1860–1930." In *Construcción de las identidades latinoamericanas: ensayos de historia intelectual (siglos XIX y XX)*, edited by Aimer Granados and Carlos Marichal, 71–105. México: Colegio de México, 2004.

Aínsa, Fernando. "El centenario de *Ariel*: una lectura para 2000." In

Arielismo y globalización, edited by Leopoldo Zea and Hernán Taboada, 89–106. México: Fondo de Cultura Económica, 2002.

Alas, Leopoldo [Clarín]. "Reseña sobre *Ariel.*" *Revista Literaria, Los Lunes de El Imparcial* (April 23, 1900): 4.

Alfaro Gómez, Héctor Guillermo. "Arielismo." In *Diccionario de Filosofía Latinoamericana*, edited by Horacio Cerutti-Guldberg, Mario Magallón Anaya, Isaías Palacios Contreras, María del Rayo Ramírez Fierro, and Sandra Escutia Díaz, 44–46. Toluca: Universidad Nacional Autónoma de México, 2000.

Allen, Theodore. *The Invention of the White Race*, vol. 1. London: Verso, 1994.

Alonso, Carlos. "The *criollista* novel." In *The Cambridge History of Latin American Literature*, vol. 2, edited by Roberto González Echevarría and Enrique Pupo-Walker, 195-212. Cambridge, UK: Cambridge University Press, 1996.

———. *The Spanish American Regional Novel: Modernity and Autochthony*. New York: Cambridge University Press, 1990.

Alonso, Diego. *José Enrique Rodó: una retórica para la democracia*. Montevideo: Trilce, 2009.

Altamirano, Carlos. *Historia de los intelectuales en América Latina: los avatares de la "ciudad letrada" en el siglo XX*. Buenos Aires: Katz Editores, 2008.

Anderson-Imbert, Enrique. *Spanish-American Literature: A History*.

Translated by John V. Falconieri. Detroit, MI: Wayne State University Press, 1963.

Andrews, George Reid. *Afro-Latin America, 1800–2000*. Oxford: Oxford University Press, 2004.

Antuña, José G. "José E. Rodó." *Homenaje a José Enrique Rodó. Ariel: Revista del Centro Estudiantil Ariel* 1, no. 8–9 (February-May 1920): 139–44.

Ardao, Arturo. *Espiritualismo y positivismo en el Uruguay*. México: Fondo de Cultura Económica, 1950.

———. *Introducción a Vaz Ferreira*. Montevideo: Barreiro y Ramos, 1961.

———. *Nuestra América Latina*. Montevideo: Ediciones de la Banda Oriental, 1968.

Argastabe, Raúl. "A los pies de Ariel." *Letras* 10, no. 30 (1914): 363.

Armand, Émile. "Mini-Manual of the Anarchist Individualist." In *Anarchism: A Documentary History of Libertarian Ideas*, vol. 1, edited by Robert Graham, 145–49. Montreal: Black Rose Books, 2005.

Ashcroft, Bill, Gareth Griffiths, and Helen Tiffin. *The Empire Writes Back: Theory and Practice in Post-Colonial Literatures*. London: Routledge, 2002.

Badiou, Alain. *The Century*. Translated by Alberto Toscano. Cambridge, UK: Polity Press, 2007.

———. *The True Life*. Translated by Susan Spitzer. Cambridge, UK: Polity Press, 2017.

Baigini, Hugo E. "Redes estudiantiles en el Cono Sur (1900–1925)."

Revista Universum 17 (2002): 279–96.

Barbagelata, Hugo. *Una centuria literaria: poetas y prosistas uruguayos, 1800–1900*. París: Biblioteca Latino-Americana, 1924.

Barrera Enderle, Víctor. *La reinvención de Ariel. Reflexiones neo-arielistas sobre posmodernidad y humanismo crítico en América Latina*. Monterrey: Conarte, 2013.

Barreto, Amílcar Antonio. "Enlightened Tolerance or Cultural Capitulation? Contesting Notions of American Identity." In *Colonial Crucible: Empire in the Making of the Modern American State*, edited by Alfred McCoy and Francisco Scarano, 145–50. Madison: University of Wisconsin Press, 2009.

Barrios, Miguel Ángel. *El latinoamericanismo en el pensamiento político de Manuel Ugarte*. Buenos Aires: Biblos, 2007.

Baujín, José Antonio. *Del donoso y grande escrutinio del cervantismo en Cuba*. La Habana: Letras Cubanas, 2005.

Benedetti, Mario. *Genio y figura de José Enrique Rodó*. Buenos Aires: Editorial Universitaria de Buenos Aires, 1966.

Benjamin, Walter. *Early Writings (1910–1917)*. Translated by Howard Eiland. Cambridge, MA: Harvard University Press, 2011.

Bello, Andrés. *La eterna juventud de Andrés Bello*, edited by Alfonso Calderón. Santiago de Chile: Ministerio de Educación Pública, 1984.
_____. "Modo de estudiar la historia." In *Obras completas*, vol. 19,

243–52. Caracas: Ministerio de Educación, 1957.

Beorlegui, Carlos. *Historia del pensamiento filosófico latinoamericano: una búsqueda incesante de la identidad*. Bilbao: Universidad de Deusto, 2004.

Berger, Peter L. *The Sacred Canopy: Elements of a Sociological Theory of Religion*. Garden City, NY: Doubleday, 1967.

Beverley, John. *Latinamericanism after 9/11*. Durham: Duke University Press, 2011.

Birkenmaier, Anke. *The Specter of Races: Latin American Anthropology and Literature between the Wars*. Charlottesville: University of Virginia Press, 2016.

Blanco-Fombona, Rufino. "Carta abierta." In *Ensayos históricos*, 209–20. Caracas: Ayacucho, 1981.
_____. *El conquistador español del siglo XVI*. In *Ensayos históricos*, 3–152. Caracas: Ayacucho, 1981.
_____. "La España materna." In *La lámpara de Aladino: notículas*, 11–230. Madrid: Renacimiento, 1915.

Bloch, Ernst. *The Principle of Hope*, vol. 1. Translated by Neville Plaice, Stephen Plaice, and Paul Knight. Cambridge: MIT Press, 1996.

Bonilla-Silva, Eduardo. *Racism without Racists: Color-Blind Racism and the Persistence of Racial Inequality in America*. Lanham, MD: Rowman & Littlefield, 2014.

Borge, Jason. *Latin American Writers and the Rise of Hollywood Cinema*. New York: Routledge, 2008.

Borrero Echeverría, Esteban. *Alrededor del Quijote*. La Habana: Moderna Poesía, 1905.

Bosteels, Bruno. "'Así habló Próspero': La eficacia de la ideología en el modernismo hispanoamericano." *Torre de Papel* 7, no. 3 (1997): 43–108.

Bourdieu, Pierre. "Men and Machines." *Advances in Social Theory and Methodology: Toward an Integration of Micro- and Macro-Sociologies*, edited by Karin Knorr-Cetina and A. V. Cicourel, 304–17. London: Routledge, 2015.

———. *Practical Reason: On the Theory of Action*. Stanford, CA: Stanford University Press, 1998.

Braga, Erasmo. *Pan-Americanismo: aspecto religioso*. Translated by Eduardo Monteverde. Nueva York: Sociedad para la Educación Misionera en los Estados Unidos y el Canadá, 1917.

Brotherston, Gordon. Introduction to *Ariel*, by José Enrique Rodó, 1–19. Cambridge: Cambridge University Press, 1967.

Brown, Wendy. *Regulating Aversion: Tolerance in the Age of Identity and Empire*. Princeton, NJ: Princeton University Press, 2008.

Buck-Morss, Susan. *Hegel, Haiti, and Universal History*. Pittsburgh, PA: University of Pittsburgh Press, 2009.

Bueno, Salvador. "El periodismo literario en Cuba. De *El Fígaro* a *Social*." *Crucero* 1, no. 2 (1960): 17–22, 38.

Buero, Juan Antonio. "Sesión de Enseñaza Secundaria." *Evolución*.

Relación oficial del Primer Congreso Internacional de Estudiantes Americanos, 3, no. 21–24 (March–June 1908): 208–18.

Bunge, Carlos Octavio. *Nuestra América: ensayo de psicología social*. Buenos Aires: Casa Vaccaro, 1918.

Buscaglia-Salgado, José F. "Race and the Constitutive Inequality of the Modern/Colonial Condition." In *Critical Terms in Caribbean and Latin American Thought*, edited by Yolanda Martínez-San Miguel, Ben Sifuentes-Jáuregui, and Marisa Belausteguigoitia, 109–24. New York: Palgrave Macmillan 2016.

Byrne, Bonifacio. "Mi bandera." In *Lira y espada*, 174–75. La Habana: El Fígaro, 1901.

Caetano, Gerardo, ed. *Los uruguayos del del Centenario: nación, ciudadanía, religión y educación (1910–1930)*. Montevideo: Ediciones Santillana, 2000.

Camacho, Jorge. *Miedo negro, poder blanco en la Cuba colonial*. Madrid: Iberoamericana, 2015.

Carballo, Emmanuel. "El Ateneo de la Juventud y el triste papel de los escritores." In *Notas de un francotirador*, 139–43. México: Instituto Politécnico Nacional/ Sociedad General de Escritores de México, 1996).

Carbonell, José Manuel. "Fernando Lles." In *La prosa en Cuba*, tomo 1, 92–106. La Habana: Montalvo y Cardenas, 1928.

Carbonell, Miguel Ángel. *El peligro de la águila*. La Habana: Seoane y Fernández, 1922.

_____. *Hombres de nuestra América.*
La Habana: La Prueba, 1915.

Carbonell, Néstor. "Mario Muñoz
Bustamante." In *Prosas oratorias,*
7–37. La Habana: Editorial Guáimaro, 1926.

"Carlos Vaz Ferreira." *Claridad* 196
(December 14, 1929). *Cuaderno de
Recortes,* vol. 5. Recortes de prensa
sobre Carlos Vaz Ferreira. Anáforas. Universidad de la República
de Uruguay. Facultad de Información y Comunicación. 119.
https://anaforas.fic.edu.uy/jspui/
handle/123456789/43145.

Carlyle, Thomas. *Heroes and Hero
Worship.* London: Chapman and
Hall, 1869.

Carrión, Benjamín. *Los creadores de la
nueva América.* Madrid: Sociedad
General Española de Librería, 1928.

Caso, Antonio. *La existencia como
economía y como caridad: ensayo
sobre la escencia del cristianismo.*
México: Porrúa, 1916.

_____. *La filosofía de la intuición.*
México: Nosotros, 1914.

_____. "La filosofía moral de Don
Eugenio M. de Hostos." In *Conferencias del Ateneo de la Juventud,* edited by Antonio Caso et al.,
11–31. México: Lacaud, 1910.

Castellanos, Jesús. "Los dos peligros
de América: a propósito de dos
libros nuevos." In *Los optimistas,* 213–27. La Habana: Avisador
Comercial, 1914.

_____. "Rodó y su "Proteo." La
Habana: Comas y López, 1910.

Castro, Fidel. *La historia me absolverá.*
Buenos Aires: Ediciones del
Pensamiento Nacional, 1993.

Castro Fernández, Silvio. *La masacre
de los Independientes de Color en
1912.* La Habana: Ciencias Sociales,
2002.

Castro-Gómez, Santiago. "(Post)
Coloniality for Dummies: Latin
American Perspectives on
Modernity, Coloniality, and the
Geopolitics of Knowledge." In
*Coloniality at Large: Latin Amer-
ica and the Postcolonial Debate,*
edited by Mabel Moraña, Enrique
Dussel, and Carlos Jáuregui, 259–
85. Durham, NC: Duke University
Press, 2008.

Castro Morales, Belén. Introduction
to *Ariel,* by José Enrique Rodó,
9–128. Madrid: Cátedra, 2000.

_____. "José Enrique Rodó en tres
ensayistas mexicanos: Carlos Fuentes, Carlos Monsiváis y
Enrique Krauze." *Latinoamérica*
66, no. 1 (2018): 145–69.

_____. "Un proyecto intelectual en la
encrucijada de la modernidad." In
Ariel, by José Enrique Rodó, 125–
61. Madrid: Anaya y Mario Muchnik, 1995.

_____. "Utopía y naufragio del
intelectual arielista: representaciones espaciales en José Enrique
Rodó." In *José Enrique Rodó y su
tiempo: cien años de Ariel,* edited
by Ottmar Ette and Titus Heydenreich, 95–104. Madrid:
Iberoamericana/Vervuert, 2000.

Cdo. T. U. "*Moral para intelectuales*
de Vaz Ferreira." *La Razón* (September 9, 1909). *Cuaderno de
Recortes,* vol. 1. Recortes de prensa
sobre Carlos Vaz Ferreira. Anáforas. Universidad de la República

de Uruguay. Facultad de Información y Comunicación: 79. https://anaforas.fic.edu.uy/jspui/handle/123456789/42849.

Césaire, Aimé. *Une tempête*. Paris: Éditions du Seuil, 1969.

"Compatriotas en el extranjero." *La Mañana* (May 1, 1922). *Cuaderno de Recortes*, vol. 3. Recortes de prensa sobre Carlos Vaz Ferreira. Anáforas. Universidad de la República de Uruguay. Facultad de Información y Comunicación: 21. https://anaforas.fic.edu.uy/jspui/handle/123456789/42906.

Contreras, Francisco. "El problema de América Latina." *El Fígaro* 11, no. 5 (1926): 14, 100.

Costa Pinto, António. *Latin American Dictatorships in the Era of Fascism: The Corporatist Wave*. New York: Routledge, 2020.

"Cuban Resolution." *Legislation on Foreign Relations*. Washington, DC: US Government Printing Office, 1975: 1035–36.

Curiel, Fernando. *Ateneo de la Juventud (A-Z)*. México: Universidad Nacional Autónoma de México, 2001.

Daut, Marlene. *Tropics of Haiti: Race and the Literary History of the Haitian Revolution in the Atlantic World, 1789–1865*. Liverpool: Liverpool University Press, 2015.

"Decanato de Preparatorios: Los doctores Vaz Ferreira y Maggiolo." *La Democracia* (March 22, 1906). *Cuaderno de Recortes*, vol. 1. Recortes de prensa sobre Carlos Vaz Ferreira. Anáforas.

Universidad de la República de Uruguay. Facultad de Información y Comunicación: 52. https://anaforas.fic.edu.uy/jspui/handle/123456789/42849.

Degiovanni, Fernando. *Los textos de la patria: nacionalismo, políticas culturales y canon en Argentina*. Rosario: Beatriz Viterbo, 2007.

———. *Vernacular Latin Americanisms: War, the Market, and the Making of a Discipline*. Pittsburgh, PA: University of Pittsburgh Press, 2018.

de la Luz León, José. "Reparos a un bello libro." *El Fígaro* 39, no. 26 (1922): 410–11.

de la Riva Agüero, José. *Carácter de la literatura del Perú independiente*. Lima: Librería Francesa Científica Galland, 1905.

Delgado, Luis Humberto. *El suplicio de Ariel*. Lima: American Express, 1935.

del Risco, Enrique. *Elogio de la levedad: mitos nacionales cubanos y sus reescrituras literarias en el siglo XX*. Madrid: Colibrí, 2008.

Dent, David. *Historical Dictionary of US-Latin American Relations*. London: Greenwood, 2005.

Devés Valdés, Eduardo. *El pensamiento latinoamericano en el siglo XX, tomo 1: Del Ariel de Rodó a la CEPAL (1900–1950)*. Buenos Aires: Biblios, 2000.

Díaz-Briquets, Sergio, and Jorge Pérez-López. *Corruption in Cuba: Castro and Beyond*. Austin: University of Texas Press, 2006.

Díaz Parrado, Flora. "La pobre ceiba." *Social* 13, no. 10 (1928): 25.

"Diego Canessa autor de "Ariel digital"; para atravesar este momento de discontinuidad sistémica, es muy importante religarse a nuestro patrimonio cultural intangible." *La Onda Digital* 928 (2019). www. laondadigital.uy/archivos/38253.

Díez de Medina, Fernando. *Sariri: una réplica al "Ariel" de Rodó*. La Paz: A. Tejerina, 1954.

Dubois, Laurent. *Haiti: The Aftershocks of History*. New York: Picador, 2013.

Dudley, Edgar S. "Report of Civil Affairs Considered in Office of the Judge-Advocate of the Department, Calendar Year 1900." In *Annual Reports of the War Department for the Fiscal Year Ended June 30, 1900.* Part 11: Report of the Military Governor of Cuba on Civil Affairs, vol. 1, part 3. Washington: Government Printing Office, 1901: 425–31.

Durkheim, Émile. *Suicide: A Study in Sociology*. Translated by John A. Spaulding and George Simpson. Glencoe, IL: Free Press, 1951.

Dussel, Enrique. *1492: el encubrimiento del otro: hacia el origen del "mito de la modernidad": Conferencias de Frankfurt, Octubre de 1992*. Bogotá: Ediciones Antropos, 1992.

———. "Philosophy in Twentieth Century Latin America." In *Contemporary Philosophy: A New Survey*, vol. 8: Philosophy in Latin America, edited by Guttorm Fløistad, 15–59. London: Kluwer Academic Publishers, 2003.

Eagleton, Terry. *The Ideology of the Aesthetic*. Cambridge, MA: Blackwell, 1990.

Earle, Peter, and Robert Mead. *Historia del ensayo hispanoamericano*. México: Ediciones de Andrea, 1973.

Einstein, Albert. *The Collected Papers of Albert Einstein*, vol. 14: The Berlin Years: Writings and Correspondence, April 1923–May 1925. The Digital Einstein Papers. Princeton University Press, 2014. https://einsteinpapers.press. princeton.edu/vol14-doc/796.

"El gran día de la Repúbica Oriental del Uruguay." *América Central* (August 26, 1916). *Cuaderno de Recortes*, vol. 3. Recortes de prensa sobre Carlos Vaz Ferreira. Anáforas. Universidad de la República de Uruguay. Facultad de Información y Comunicación: 42. https://anaforas.fic.edu.uy/jspui/ handle/123456789/42906.

"El idioma de Cervantes nunca fue una lengua de imposición, sino de encuentro." *ABC.es*. April 24, 2001. www.abc.es/cultura/abci-idioma-cervantes-nunca-lengua-imposicion-sino-encuentro-200104240300-26646_noticia. html.

Emerson, Ralph Waldo. "Self-Reliance." In *Self-Reliance and Other Essays*, 19–38. New York: Dover, 1993.

"En honor del Dr. Vaz Ferreira: una iniciativa estudiantil." *El Día* (April 11, 1913). *Cuaderno de Recortes*, vol. 2. Recortes de prensa sobre Carlos Vaz Ferreira. Anáforas. Universidad de la República de Uruguay. Facultad de Información y Comunicación: 13. https://anaforas.fic.edu.uy/jspui/handle/123456789/42864.

Escobar, Fernando. "Quienes deben emigrar a Cuba." *Cuba en Europa* 6, no. 128 (1915): 1–2.

Estudiante X, El. "Notas y apuntes: el Dr. Vaz Ferreira y los estudiantes." *La Razón* (April 5, 1913). *Cuaderno de Recortes*, vol. 2. Recortes de prensa sobre Carlos Vaz Ferreira. Anáforas. Universidad de la República de Uruguay. Facultad de Información y Comunicación: 11. https://anaforas.fic.edu.uy/jspui/handle/123456789/42864.

Ette, Ottmar and Titus Heydenreich, ed. *José Enrique Rodó y su tiempo: cien años de Ariel.* Frankfurt: Vervuert, 2000.

Fanon, Frantz. *The Wretched of the Earth.* Translated by Richard Philcox. New York: Grove Press, 2004.

Farmer, Paul. *AIDS and Accusation: Haiti and the Geography of Blame.* Berkeley: University of California Press, 2006.

Fernández, Frank. *Cuban Anarchism: The History of a Movement.* Translated by Charles Bufe. Tucson, AZ: See Sharp Press, 2001.

Fernández Retamar, Roberto. *Caliban and Other Essays.* Translated by Edward Baker. Minneapolis: University of Minnesota Press, 1989.

Ferrer, Ada. *Freedom's Mirror: Cuba and Haiti in the Age of Revolution.* New York: Cambridge University Press, 2014.

Fischer, Sibylle. *Modernity Disavowed: Haiti and the Cultures of Slavery in the Age of Revolution.* Durham, NC: Duke University Press, 2004.

Foncueva, José Antonio. "Ingenieros, Rodó y el pensamiento de la América nueva." *Bohemia* 20, no. 41 (1928): 19.

Foucault, Michel. *The Archaeology of Knowledge.* Translated by A. M. Sheridan Smith. New York: Pantheon, 1972.

———. "The Subject and Power." *Critical Inquiry* 8, no. 4 (Summer 1982): 777–95.

Franco, Jean. *An Introduction to Spanish-American Literature.* Cambridge, UK: Cambridge University Press, 1994.

Frankenberg, Ruth. Introduction to *Displacing Whiteness: Essays in Social and Cultural Criticism,* edited by Ruth Frankenberg, 1–33. Durham, NC: Duke University Press, 1997.

Freud, Sigmund. "Remembering, Repeating, and Working-Through." In *Beyond the Pleasure Principle and Other Writings.* Translated by John Reddick, 31–42. New York: Penguin, 2003.

———. *The Future of an Illusion.* Translated by James Strachey. New York: W. W. Norton and Company, 1975.

Frugoni, Emilio and Justino Jiménez de Aréchaga. "Vaz Ferreira: el homenaje en su honor." *La Razón* (April 17, 1913). *Cuaderno de Recortes*, vol. 2. Recortes de prensa sobre Carlos Vaz Ferreira. Anáforas. Universidad de la

República de Uruguay. Facultad de Información y Comunicación: 16. https://anaforas.fic.edu.uy/jspui/handle/123456789/42864.

Fuentes, Carlos. Prologue to *Ariel*, by Jose Enriqué Rodó. Translated by Margaret Sayers Peden, 13-28. Austin: University of Texas Press, 1988.

Funes, Patricia. "Literatura y nación en tiempos del Centenario. Argentina y Uruguay (1910–1930)." In *Los uruguayos del del Centenario: nación, ciudadanía, religión y educación (1910–1930)*, edited by Gerardo Caetano, 245–75. Montevideo: Ediciones Santillana, 2000.

Gallardo, Helio. *500 años. Fenomenología del mestizo: violencia y resistencia*. San José de Costa Rica: Departamento Ecuménico de Investigaciones, 1993.

Gallinal, Gustavo. *El Uruguay hacia la dictadura*. Montevideo: Editorial Nueva América, 1938.

Gaos, José. "El sistema de Caso." In *Obras completas*, vol. 3: *La existencia como economía, como desinterés y como caridad*, by Antonio Caso, 7–26. México: UNAM, 1972.

García Calderón, Francisco. "Apreciación de Francisco García Calderón." In *Los ídolos del foro: ensayo sobre las supersticiones políticas*, by Carlos Arturo Torres, 7–15. Madrid: Editorial América. 1916.

_____. *De litteris (crítica)*. Lima: Librería e Imprenta Gil, 1904.

_____. *Latin America: Its Rise and Progress*. Translated by Bernard Miall. New York: Scribner's, 1913.

García Godoy, Federico. "*Los conquistadores* por Emilio Gaspar Rodríguez." In *Obras casi completas*, tomo 3: *Notas críticas*, edited by Andrés Blanco Díaz, 455–56. Santo Domingo: Centenario, 2017.

García Morales, Alfonso. *El Ateneo de México (1969–1914)*, Sevilla: Escuela de Estudios Hispano-Americanos, 1992.

_____. *Literatura y pensamiento hispánico de fin de siglo: Clarín y Rodó*. Sevilla: Universidad de Sevilla, 1992.

_____. "Un capítulo del 'arielismo': Rodó en México." In *La crítica literaria española frente a la literatura latinoamericana*, edited by Leonor Fleming and María Teresa Bosque Latra, 95–105. México: UNAM, 1993.

García-Peña, Lorgia. *The Borders of Dominicanidad: Race, Nation, and Archives of Contradiction*. Durham, NC: Duke University Press, 2016.

Gay Calbó, Enrique. "Bibliografía: Emilio Gaspar Rodríguez." *Cuba Contemporánea* 15, no. 43 (March 1927): 266–73.

Giaudrone, Carla. "El gaucho en el ámbito iconográfico del Centenario uruguayo (1925–1930)." *Revista Hispánica Moderna* 61, no. 2 (December 2008): 149–65.

Gil Lázaro, Alicia. "Las señas de identidad de un escritor 'ausente': América Latina y Perú en el pensamiento de Francisco García Calderón." In *Construcción de las identidades latinoamericanas: ensayos de historia intelectual (siglos XIX y XX)*, edited by Aimer

Granados and Carlos Marichal, 129–57. México: Colegio de México, 2004.

Gómez-Gil, Orlando. *Historia crítica de la literatura hispanoamericana: desde los orígenes hasta el momento actual*. New York: Holt, Rinehart and Winston, 1968.

_____. *Mensaje y vigencia de José Enrique Rodó*. Miami: Ediciones Universal, 1992.

González, Aníbal. "Modernist Prose." In *The Cambridge History of Latin American Literature*, vol. 2, edited by Roberto González Echevarría and Enrique Pupo-Walker, 69–113. Cambridge, UK: Cambridge University Press, 1996.

González Echevarría, Roberto. *The Voice of the Masters: Writing and Authority in Modern Latin American Literature*. Austin: University of Texas Press, 1985.

González-Espitia, Juan Carlos. *On the Dark Side of the Archive: Nation and Literature in Spanish America at the Turn of the Century*. Lewisburg, PA: Bucknell University Press, 2010.

González Prada, Manuel. "Discurso en el Politeama." In *Manuel González Prada. ¡Los jóvenes a la obra! Textos esenciales*, edited by David Sobrevilla, 237–42. Lima: Fondo Editorial del Congreso del Perú, 2009.

González Rodríguez, Jorge E. *Rodó: prolegómenos de un siglo para la ética y la política*. La Habana: Centro Félix Varela, 2003.

González y Contreras, Gilberto. "Un notable ensayista cubano." *América* 3, no. 1 (July 1939): 14–18.

Granados, Aimer and Carlos Marichal, ed. *Construcción de las identidades latinoamericanas: ensayos de historia intelectual (siglos XIX y XX)*. México: Colegio de México, 2004.

Grandin, Greg. *Empire's Workshop: Latin America, the United States, and the Rise of the New Imperialism*. New York: Owl Books, 2007.

Grave, Jean. *Moribund Society and Anarchy*. Translated by Voltairine de Cleyre. San Francisco: A. Isaak, 1899.

Grosfoguel, Ramón. "Developmentalism, Modernity, and Dependency Theory in Latin America." In *Coloniality at Large: Latin America and the Postcolonial Debate*, edited by Mabel Moraña, Enrique Dussel, and Carlos Jáuregui, 307–34. Durham, NC: Duke University Press, 2008.

Guerra, Lillian. *The Myth of José Martí: Conflicting Nationalisms in Early Twentieth-Century Cuba*. Chapel Hill: University of North Carolina Press, 2006.

_____. *Visions of Power in Cuba: Revolution, Redemption, and Resistance, 1959–1971*. Chapel Hill: University of North Carolina Press, 2012.

Guevara, Ernesto Che. "On Growth and Imperialism." In *Venceremos! The Speeches and Writings of Ernesto Che Guevara*, edited by John Gerassi, 153–181. New York: Macmillan, 1968.

Guglielmo, Jennifer. Introduction to *Are Italians White? How Race is Made in America*, edited by Jennier Guglielmo and Salvatore Salerno, 17–28. New York: Routledge, 2003.

Habermas, Jürgen. *Postmetaphysical Thinking: Philosophical Essays*. Translated by William Mark Hohengarten. Cambridge: MIT Press, 1992.

Haddox, John. "Latin American Personalist: Antonio Caso." *The Personalist Forum* 8, no. 1 (Spring 1992): 109–18.

Hale, Charles. "Political Ideas and Ideologies in Latin America, 1870–1930." In *Ideas and Ideologies in Twentieth Century Latin America*, edited by Leslie Betrell, 133–206. Cambridge, UK: Cambridge University Press, 1996.

Halperín Donghi, Tulio. "¿Para qué la inmigración? Ideología y política inmigratoria y aceleración del proceso modernizador: el caso argentino (1810–1914)." *Jahrbuch für Geschichte Lateinamerikas. Anuario de Historia de America Latina* 13, no. 1 (December 1976): 437–89.

Hardt, Michael and Antonio Negri. *Empire*. Cambridge: Harvard University Press, 2000.

Hatfield, Charles. *The Limits of Identity: Politics and Poetics in Latin America*. Austin: University of Texas Press, 2015.

Henríquez Ureña, Pedro. *Historia cultural y literaria de la América Hispánica*. Madrid: Verbum, 2012.

_____. "La obra de José Enrique Rodó." In *Conferencias del Ateneo de la Juventud*, edited by Antonio Caso et al., 63–83. México: Lacaud, 1910.

_____. "Nota de la edición mexicana." In *Ariel*, by José Enrique Rodó, 5–6. Monterrey: Talleres Modernos de Lozano, 1908.

Hill, Ruth. "Ariana Crosses the Atlantic: An Archaeology of Aryanism in the 19th-Century River Plate." *Hispanic Issues On Line* 12 (2013): 92–110.

_____. "Entre lo transatlántico y lo hemisférico: Los proyectos raciales de Andrés Bello." *Revista Iberoamericana* 75, no. 228 (July–September 2009): 719–35.

_____. "Primeval Whiteness: White Supremacists, (Latin) American History, and the Trans-American Challenge to Critical Race Studies," in *Teaching and Studying the Americas: Cultural Influences from Colonialism to the Present*, edited by Michael Emerson, Caroline Levander, and Anthony Pinn. New York: Palgrave Macmillan, 2010. 109–38.

Hooker, Juliet. *Theorizing Race in the Americas: Douglass, Sarmiento, Du Bois, and Vasconcelos*. New York: Oxford University Press, 2017.

Hurtado, Guillermo. "The Anti-Positivist Movement in Mexico." In *A Companion to Latin American Philosophy*, edited by Susana Nuccetelli, Ofelia Schutte, and Otávio Bueno, 82–94. Malden, MA: Wiley-Blackwell, 2010.

Ingenieros, José. *El hombre mediocre.* Buenos Aires: L. J. Rosso, 1917.
_____. *Hacia una moral sin dogmas: lecciones sobre Emerson y el eticismo.* Buenos Aires: L. J. Rosso, 1917.
_____. "La justicia de Bertoldo." In *Crónicas de viaje (1905–1906),* 49–59. Buenos Aires: L. J. Rosso, 1919.
_____. "Las razas inferiores." In *Crónicas de viaje (1905–1906),* 161–72. Buenos Aires: L. J. Rosso, 1919.
_____. *Sociología argentina.* Buenos Aires: L. J. Rosso, 1918.
Inman, Samuel Guy. "A Notable Pan-American Conference." *The Outlook* (March 29, 1916): 750–55.
_____. *Problems in Pan Americanism.* New York: George H. Doran Company, 1921.
Jacob, Raúl. *El Uruguay de Terra, 1931–1938: una crónica del terrismo.* Montevideo: Ediciones de la Banda Oriental, 1983.
Jacobson, Matthew Frye. *Whiteness of a Different Color: European Immigrants and the Alchemy of Race.* Cambridge, MA: Harvard University Press, 1999.
James, William. *The Varieties of Religious Experience.* New York: Longmans, Green, and Co., 1917.
Jaramillo Uribe, Jaime. *El pensamiento colombiano en el siglo XIX.* Bogotá: Editorial Temis, 1964.
Jáuregui, Carlos A. *Canibalia: canibalismo, calibanismo, antropofagia cultural y consumo en América Latina.* Madrid: Iberoamericana/Vervuert, 2008.

Kanellos, Nicolás, ed. *Herencia: The Anthology of Hispanic Literature of the United States.* Oxford: Oxford University Press, 2002.
Keiger, John F. V. *Raymond Poincaré.* Cambridge, UK: Cambridge University Press, 1997.
Kennedy, John F. "Address at a White House Reception for Members of Congress and for the Diplomatic Corps of the Latin American Republics, March 13, 1961." In *Public Papers of the Presidents of the United States. John F. Kennedy: Containing the Public Messages, Speeches, and Statements of the President, January 20 to December 31, 1961,* 170–75. Washington, DC: United States Government Printing Office, 1962.
Krauze, Enrique. "Mirándolos a ellos. Actitudes mexicanas frente a Estados Unidos." *Letras libres* 9, no. 102 (June 2007): 38–46.
_____. *Redeemers: Ideas and Power in Latin America.* Translated by Hank Heifetz and Natasha Wimmer. New York: Harper Collins, 2011.
"La entrada en funciones del Maestro de Conferencias." *El Día* (August 8, 1913). *Cuaderno de Recortes,* vol. 2. Recortes de prensa sobre Carlos Vaz Ferreira. Anáforas. Universidad de la República de Uruguay. Facultad de Información y Comunicación: 93. https://anaforas.fic.edu.uy/jspui/handle/123456789/42864.
"La primera conferencia pedagógica: El doctor Vaz Ferreira en el Ateneo."

La Razón (April 7, 1911). *Cuaderno de Recortes*, vol. 2. Recortes de prensa sobre Carlos Vaz Ferreira. Anáforas. Universidad de la República de Uruguay. Facultad de Información y Comunicación: 2. https://anaforas.fic.edu.uy/jspui/handle/123456789/42864.

Labrador Méndez, Germán. "Dynamiting *Don Quijote*: Literature, Colonial Memory and the Crisis of the National Subject in the Monumental Poetics of the Cervantine Tercentenary (Spain 1915-1921)." *Journal of Iberian and Latin American Studies* 19, no. 3 (December 2013): 185–209.

Labrador Ruiz, Enrique. "Escribe Enrique Labrador Ruiz: Lles, ese desconido." In *Escritos periodísticos de Enrique Labrador Ruiz*, edited by Adis Barrio Tosar, 39–41. La Habana: Ediciones Extramuros, 2013.

Lamar Schweyer, Alberto. "Emilio Gaspar Rodríguez." *El Fígaro* 39, no. 3 (1922): 44.

————. "José Ingenieros y su aporte al pensamiento americano." *Social* 10, no. 12 (December 1925): 13, 76.

————. "Latinoamericanismo." *El Fígaro* 40, no. 10–11 (1923): 143.

Lasplaces, Alberto. *Opiniones literarias: prosistas uruguayo contemporáneos*. Montevideo: Claudio García, 1919.

Lazo, Raimundo. *Historia de la literatura cubana*. México: UNAM, 1974.

Le Reverend, Julio. "Fernando Ortiz y su obra cubana." In *Fernando Ortiz*, by Fernando Ortiz, 7–51. La Habana: UNEAC, 1973.

Legrás, Horacio. *Culture and Revolution: Violence, Memory, and the Making of Modern Mexico*. Austin: University of Texas Press, 2017.

Lenz, Frank. "Monteverde of Montevideo." *Association Men* 48, no. 12 (July 1923): 561–62.

Lewandowski, Joseph. "Rethinking Power and Subjectivity after Foucault." *symplokē* 3, no. 2 (July 1995): 221–43.

Leyva Pagán, Georgina. *Historia de una gesta libertadora, 1952–1958*. La Habana: Editorial de Ciencias Sociales, 2009.

Lizaso, Félix. *Ensayistas contemporáneos, 1900–1920*. La Habana, Editorial Trópico, 1938.

Lles y Berdayes, Fernando. "Carta a Emilio Roig de Leuchsenring" (April 3, 1921). Fondo Emilio Roig de Leuchsenring, La Biblioteca Histórica Cubana y Americana Francisco González del Valle, Havana, Cuba.

————. *La escudilla de Diógenes. Etopeya del cínico*. La Habana, Editorial Nuestra Novela, 1924.

————. *La higuera de Timón: consejos al pequeño Antonio*. Matanzas: Imprenta Casas y Mercado, 1921.

————. *La sombra de Heráclito*. La Habana, Imp. El Siglo XX, 1923.

Loeza, Alejandro. "Del idealismo al carnaval: el *Quijote* en Cuba." In *Comentarios a Cervantes: actas selectas del VIII Congreso Internacional de la Asociación de Cervantistas*, edited by Emilio

Martínez Mata and María Fernández Ferreiro, 702–13. Asturias: Fundación María Cristina Masaveu Peterson, 2014.

López, Alfred J. Introduction to *Postcolonial Whiteness*, edited by Alfred J. López, 1–30. Albany: SUNY Press, 2005.

Loveira y Chirino, Carlos. *Un gran ensayista: Fernando Lles. Discurso de ingreso como miembro de número de la Sección de Literatura leído por [. . .] en la sesión solemne celebrada por la Academia Nacional de Artes y Letras, la noche del 30 de enero de 1926*. La Habana: El Siglo XX, 1926.

Lukács, Georg. "On the Nature and Form of the Essay." In *Soul and Form*. Translated by Anna Bostock, 1–18. London: Merlin Press, 1974.

Maciel, Carlos Néstor. *La italianización de la Argentina: tras la huella de nuestros antepasados*. Buenos Aires: J. Menéndez e hijo, 1924.

Mackinder, Halford. "The Geographic Pivot of History." *The Geographic Journal* 4, no. 23 (April 1904): 421–37.

Maeterlinck, Maurice. *The Measure of the Hours*. Translated by Alexander Teixeira de Mattos. New York: Dodd, Mead and Company, 1913.

Maldonado-Torres, Nelson. "Secularism and Religion in the Modern/Colonial World-System: From Secular Postcoloniality to Postsecular Transmodernity." In *Coloniality at Large: Latin America and the Postcolonial Debate*, edited by Mabel Moraña, Enrique Dussel, and Carlos Jáuregui, 360–84. Durham, NC: Duke University Press, 2008.

Mañach, Jorge. *La crisis de la alta cultura en Cuba. Indagación del choteo*. Miami: Ediciones Universal, 1991.

Marambio de la Fuente, Matías. "Neoarielismo, educación, y estado actual de las movilizaciones." *La Chispa* (July 7, 2011). www.lachispa.cl/2011/07/07/609/.

Marchetti, Gina. *Romance and the "Yellow Peril": Race, Sex, and Discursive Strategies in Hollywood Fiction*. Berkeley: University of California Press, 1993.

Marcuse, Herbert. *Negations: Essays in Critical Theory*. Translated by Jeremy J. Shapiro. London: MayFlyBooks, 2009.

_____. *One-Dimensional Man: Studies in the Ideology of Advanced Industrial Society*. Boston: Beacon Press, 1964.

Mariátegui, José Carlos. "La revolución socialista latinoamericana." In *El marxismo en América Latina*, edited by Michael Löwy, 119–20. Santiago de Chile: LOM, 2007.

Márquez Sterling, Manuel. *Alrededor de nuestra psicología*. Habana: Avisador Comercial, 1906.

_____. *Psicología profana*. Habana: Avisador Comercial, 1905.

Martel, James. *The Misinterpellated Subject*. Durham, NC: Duke University Press, 2017.

Martí, José. "Nuestra América." In *José Martí: ensayos y crónicas*, edited by José Olivio Jiménez,

117–26. Madrid: Anaya y Mario Muchnik, 1995.

Martí, Oscar. "Early Critics of Positivism." In *A Companion to Latin American Philosophy*, edited by Susana Nuccetelli, Ofelia Schutte and Otávio Bueno, 68–81. Malden, MA: Blackwell, 2010.

Marx, Karl. *Marx on Suicide*. Translated by Eric A. Plaut, Gabrielle Edgcomb, and Kevin Anderson. Evanston, IL: Northwestern University Press, 1999.

Marx, Karl and Friedrich Engels, *The German Ideology* including *Theses on Feuerbach* and *Introduction to the Critique of Political Economy*. Amherst, NY: Prometheus Books, 1998.

McDaniel, Shawn. "La *Revista de Cayo Hueso* (1897) como arbitraje del anticolonialismo en Cuba: intervenciones crítico-literarias entre Nueva York, la Florida y Perú." *La Habana Elegante* 56 (Fall–Winter 2014). www.habanaelegante.com/Fall_Winter_2014/Invitation_McDaniel.html.

———. "Rodó en Nueva York." In *Lecturas contemporáneas de José Enrique Rodó*, edited by José Ramiro Podetti, 349–59. Montevideo: Sociedad Rodoniana, 2018.

McGuinness, Aims. "Searching for 'Latin America': Race and Sovereignty in the Americas in the 1850s." In *Race and Nation in Modern Latin America*, edited by Nancy P. Appelbaum, Anne S. Macpherson, and Alejandra

Rossemblat, 87–107. Chapel Hill: University of North Carolina Press, 2003.

McPherson, Alan. "Anti-Americanism in Latin America." In *Anti-Americanism: History, Causes, and Themes*, edited by Brendon O'Connor, 77–102. Oxford: Greenwood World Publishing, 2007.

Mella, Julio Antonio. "Cuba, un páis que jamás ha sido libre," in *Mella, documentos y artículos*, edited by Eduardo Castañeda, et al., 174–83. La Habana: Editorial de Ciencias Sociales, Instituto Cubano del Libro, 1975.

Methol Ferré, Alberto. *Las corrientes religiosas*. Montevideo: *Nuestra Tierra* 35 (1969).

Meyer, G. J. *A World Undone: The Story of the Great War, 1914–1918*. New York: Bantam Dell, 2006.

Mezzera, Rodolfo. "Discurso del doctor Rodolfo Mezzera, Ministro de Instrucción Pública." *Homenaje a José Enrique Rodó. Ariel: Revista del Centro Estudiantil Ariel* 1, no. 8–9 (February–May 1920): 171–76.

Mignolo, Walter. "La colonialidad a lo largo y a lo ancho: el hemisferio occidental en el horizonte colonial de la modernidad." In *La colonialidad del saber: eurocentrismo y ciencias sociales: perspectivas latinoamericanas*, edited by Edgardo Lander, 55–86. Buenos Aires: Consejo Latinoamericano de Ciencias Sociales, 2000.

———. *The Darker Side of the Renaissance: Literacy, Territoriality, and Colonization*. Ann Arbor:

University of Michigan Press, 1995.

———. *The Idea of Latin America*. Malden, MA: Blackwell, 2005.

———. *Local Histories/Global Designs: Coloniality, Subaltern Knowledges, and Border Thinking*. Princeton, NJ: Princeton University Press, 2000.

Mill, John Stuart. *A System of Logic, Ratiocinative and Inductive, Being a Connected View of the Principles of Evidence, and the Methods of Scientific Investigation*, vol. 2. London: Longmans, Green, and Co., 1865.

Miller, Marilyn. *Rise and Fall of the Cosmic Race: The Cult of Mestizaje in Latin America*. Austin: University of Texas Press, 2004.

Miller, Nicola. *In the Shadow of the State: Intellectuals and the Quest for National Identity in Twentieth-Century Spanish America*. London: Verso, 1999.

———. *Reinventing Modernity: Intellectuals Imagine the Future, 1900-1930*. New York: Palgrave Macmillan, 2008.

Molloy, Sylvia. "Postcolonial Latin America and the Magic Realist Imperative: A Report to an Academy." In *Nation, Language, and the Ethics of Translation*, edited by Sandra Bermann and Michael Wood, 370–79. Princeton, NJ: Princeton University Press, 2005.

———. "The Politics of Posing." In *Hispanisms and Homosexualities*, edited by Sylvia Molloy and Robert McKee Irwin, 141–60.

Durham. NC: Duke University Press, 1998.

Montero, Oscar. "Hellenism and Homophobia in José Enrique Rodó." *Revista de Estudios Hispánicos* 31, no. 1 (1997): 25–39.

———. "Modernismo and Homophobia: Darío and Rodó." In *Sex and Sexuality in Latin America*, edited by Daniel Balderston and Donna J. Guy, 101–17. New York: New York University Press, 1997.

Montero Yávar, Gonzalo. "Democratic *Arielismo*, Utopian Imaginaries and the Transnational Cultural Practices in the Chilean Group 'Los Diez' (1914–1924)." *Confluencia: Revista de Hispánica de Cultura y Literatura* 31, no. 2 (Spring 2016): 138–52.

Mora, Arnoldo. *El arielismo: de Rodó a García Monge*. San José, Costa Rica: EUNED, 2008.

Moraña, Mabel, Enrique Dussel, and Carlos A. Jáuregui, ed. *Coloniality at Large: Latin America and the Postcolonial Debate*. Durham, NC: Duke University Press, 2008.

———. Introduction to *Coloniality at Large: Latin America and the Postcolonial Debate*, edited by Mabel Moraña, Enrique Dussel, and Carlos Jáuregui, 1–20. Durham, NC: Duke University Press, 2008.

Moreiro, Juan. "Los pensadores de fin de siglo. El periodismo y la crítica." In *Manual de la literatura hispanoamericana*, tomo 3, edited by Felipe B. Pedraza Jiménez, 535–604. Pamplona: Cénlit Ediciones, 2008.

Moya, Paula M. L. *The Social Imperative: Race, Close Reading, and Contemporary Literary Criticism.* Stanford, CA: Stanford University Press, 2015.

Musser, Charles. *Edison Motion Pictures, 1890–1900: An Annotated Filmography.* Germona, Italy: Giornate del Cinema Muto, 1997.

Navarro, Mina Alejandra. "La hora americana." *OSAL* 13, no. 31 (April 2012): 259–67.

Nemser, Daniel. *Infrastructures of Race: Concentration and Biopolitics in Colonial Mexico.* Austin: University of Texas Press, 2017.

Newcomb, Robert Patrick. *Nossa and Nuestra América: Inter-American Dialogues.* West Lafayette, IN: Purdue University Press, 2012.

Nietzsche, Friedrich. *Human, All Too Human. A Book for Free Spirits.* Translated by R. J. Hollingdale. Cambridge, UK: Cambridge University Press, 2005.

_____. *The Gay Science.* Translated by Walter Kaufman. New York: Vintage, 1974.

Nodarse y Cabrera, José J. "La filosofía social y política de Lles." *Revista Cubana* 27 (1950): 89–101.

Ochoa Antich, Nancy. "El pensamiento de Rodó y su influencia en Ecuador." In *Lecturas contemporáneas de José Enrique Rodó,* edited by José Ramiro Podetti, 313–25. Montevideo: Sociedad Rodoniana, 2018.

Omi, Michael, and Howard Winant. *Racial Formation in the United States: From the 1960s to the 1990s.* New York: Routledge, 1994.

Opiniones sobre la obra de Emilio Gaspar Rodríguez. La Habana: Montalvo y Cardenas, 1928.

Oribe, Emilio. *Rodó: estudio crítico y antología.* Buenos Aires: Losada, 1971.

Ortega, Francisco. "Postcolonialism and Latin American writing, 1492–1850." In *The Cambridge History of Postcolonial Literature,* vol. 1, edited by Ato Quayson, 288–308. Cambridge, UK: Cambridge University Press, 2011.

Ortiz, Fernando. *Entre cubanos . . . (psicología tropical).* Paris: Paul Ollendorf, 1913.

_____. *José Antonio Saco y sus ideas cubanas.* La Habana: El Universo, 1929.

_____. "La inmigración desde el punto de vista criminológico." In *Archivos de psiquiatría y criminología aplicadas a las ciencias afines,* vol. 6, edited by José Ingenieros, 332–40. Buenos Aires: Talleres Gráficos de la Penitenciaría Nacional, 1907.

_____. *La reconquista de América: reflexiones sobre el panhispanismo.* París: Paul Ollendorf, 1911.

Oviedo, José Miguel. *Breve historia del ensayo hispanoamericano.* Madrid: Alianza, 1990.

_____. *Historia de la literatura hispanoamericana,* vol. 2. Madrid: Alianza, 2001.

_____. "The Modern Essay in Spanish America." In *The Cambridge History of Latin American Literature,* vol. 2, edited by Roberto González Echevarría and Enrique

Pupo-Walker, 365–424. Cambridge, UK: Cambridge University Press, 1996.

Pakkasvirta, Jussi. *Un continente, una nación?: intelectuales latinoamericanos, comunidad política y las revistas culturales en Costa Rica y el Perú (1919–1930)*. San José: Universidad de Costa Rica, 2005.

Palmer, Steven, José Antonio Piqueras, and Amparo Sánchez Cobos. Introduction to *State of Ambiguity: Civic Life and Culture in Cuba's First Republic*, edited by Steven Palmer, José Antonio Piqueras, and Amparo Sánchez Cobos, 1–21. Durham, NC: Duke University Press, 2014.

Palou, Pedro Ángel. "The Ateneo de la Juventud: The Foundations of Mexican Intellectual Culture," in *A History of Mexican Literature*, edited by Ignacio M. Sánchez Prado, Anna M. Nogar, José Ramón Ruisánchez Serra, 233–45. New York: Cambridge University Press, 2016.

Pensado, Jaime. "Student Activism: Utopian Dreams." *ReVista: Harvard Review of Latin America* (Fall 2012). https://archive.revista. drclas.harvard.edu/pages/book/ universities-fall-2012.

Pérez, Louis A. *On Becoming Cuban: Identity, Nationality, and Culture*. Chapel Hill: University of North Carolina Press, 1999.

———. *To Die in Cuba: Suicide and Society*. Chapel Hill: University of North Carolina Press, 2005.

Pérez Antón, Romeo. "Arielismo ¿impulso o freno para América

Latina?" *Prisma* 17 (December 2001): 33–42.

Pérez Petit, Víctor. *Rodó: su vida, su obra*. Montevideo: Latina, 1918.

Platt, Orville H. "The Pacification of Cuba." *The Independent* 53 (June 27, 1901): 1464–68.

Plutarch. *Plutarch's Lives*, vol. 9. Translated by Thomas North. London: J. M. Dent, 1899.

Poincaré, Raymond. Preface to *Latin America: Its Rise and Progress*, by Francisco García Calderón. Translated by Bernard Miall, 9–14. New York: Scribner's, 1913.

Ponce, Aníbal. *Humanismo burgués y humaniso proletario*. México: América, 1938.

Ponte, Antonio José. "Martí: historia de una bofetada." *Cuadernos Hispanoamericanos* 696 (June 2008): 21–32.

Portier, Philippe. "Religion and Democracy in the Thought of Jürgen Habermas." *Society* 48, no. 5 (September-October 2011): 426–32.

Portuondo, José Antonio. *El contenido social de la literatura cubana*. México: El Colegio de México, Centro de Estudios Sociales, 1944.

Posada Carbó, Eduardo. "Las guerras civiles del siglo XIX en la América Hispánica." In *Memoria de un país en guerra: los Mil Días: 1899-1902*, edited by Gonzalo Sánchez and Mario Aguilera, 59–73. Bogotá: Planeta Colombiana, 2001.

Posadas, Juan Martín. "Ubicación internacional." *El País*. March 3, 2008. www.elpais.co m.uy/08/03/09/predit_334505.asp.

Poveda, José Manuel. *Proemios de Cenáculo*. La Habana: Ministerio de Educación, 1948.

Price, Rachel. *The Object of the Atlantic: Concrete Aesthetics in Cuba, Brazil, and Spain, 1868-1968*. Evanston, IL: Northwestern University Press, 2014.

Quijano, Aníbal. "Colonialidad y modernidad/racionalidad." In *Los conquistados: 1492 y la población indígena de las Américas*, edited by Robin Blackburn and Heraclio Bonilla, 437–47. Bogotá: Tercer Mundo, 1992.

Quintanilla, Susana. *"Nosotros": la juventud del Ateneo de México*. México: Tusquets, 2008.

Quiroga, José. *Cuban Palimpsests*. Minneapolis: University of Minnesota Press, 2005.

Rama, Ángel. *La ciudad letrada*. Hanover, NH: Edicions del Norte, 1984.

Ramírez, Juan Vicente. "Discurso del señor Juan Vicente Ramírez, Presidente de la Delegación de estudianos paraguayos." *Homenaje a José Enrique Rodó. Ariel: Revista del Centro Estudiantil Ariel* 1, no. 8–9 (February-May 1920): 211–18.

Ramos, Jorge Abelardo. *Historia de la nación latinoamericana*. Buenos Aires: A. Peña Lillo, 1968.

Ramos, Julio. *Divergent Modernities: Culture and Politics in Nineteenth-Century Latin America*. Translated by John D. Blanco. Durham, NC: Duke University Press, 2001.

Ramos Mejía, José María. *Las multitudes argentinas*. Buenos Aires: Félix LaJouane, 1899.

Rangel, Carlos. *Del buen salvaje al buen revolucionario: mitos y realidades en América Latina*. Caracas: Monte Avila, 1976.

Real de Azúa, Carlos. *Historia visible e historia esotérica: personajes y claves del debate latino-americano*. Montevideo: Arca, 1975.

_____. *Medio siglo de Ariel: su significación y trascendencia literario-filosófica*. Montevideo: Academia Nacional de Letras, 2001.

Remos y Rubio, Juan J. *Historia de la literatura cubana*, tomo 3. La Habana: Cárdenas y Compañía, 1945.

_____. *Proceso histórico de las letras cubanas*. Madrid: Ediciones Guadarrama, 1958.

Ripley, William Z. *The Races of Europe: A Sociological Study*. New York: D. Appleton, 1915.

Robbins, Dylon Lamar. "War, Modernity, and Motion in the Edison Films of 1898." *Journal of Latin American Cultural Studies* 26, no. 3 (July 2017): 351–75.

Rodó, José Enrique. *Ariel*. Madrid: Cátedra, 2000.

_____. "El centenario de Chile." In *El mirador de Próspero*, vol. 1, 164–71. Madrid: Editorial América, 1915.

_____. "La filosofía del Quijote y el descubrimiento de América." In *El camino de Paros (meditaciones y andanzas)*, 27–31. Valencia: Cervantes, 1918.

_____. *La vida nueva*, vol.1, *El que vendrá. La nueva novela*. Montevideo: Dornaleche y Reyes, 1897.

_____. *Liberalismo y jacobinismo.* Montevideo: Librería y papelería "La Anticuaria" de A. Ossi, 1906.

_____. *Motivos de Proteo.* Caracas: Ayacucho, 1976.

_____. "Rumbos nuevos." In *El mirador de Próspero,* 31–61. Valencia: Editorial Cervantes, 1919.

Rodríguez, Emilio Gaspar. *Los conquistadores: héroes y sofistas.* Nuremberg: J. Rosenfeld, 1919.

Rodríguez Monegal, Emir. "América/utopía: García Calderón, el discípulo favorito de Rodó." *Cuadernos Hispanoamericanos* 417 (March 1985): 166–72.

_____. "Sobre el anti-imperialismo de Rodó." *Revista Iberoamericana* 80, no. 38 (July–September 1972): 495–501.

Rodríguez Rivero, Luis. "Noticia bibliográfica de Fernando Lles y Berdayes." *Revista Cubana* 27 (1950): 111–22.

Röhl, John. *Young Wilhelm: The Kaiser's Early Life, 1859–1888.* Cambridge: Cambridge University Press, 1993.

Roig, Arturo. *Teoría y crítica del pensamiento latinoamericano.* México: Fondo de Cultura Económica, 1981.

Roig de Leuchsenring, Emilio. "Mario Muñoz Bustamante." *Social* 6, no. 2 (February 1921): 37, 66.

Rojas, Rafael. "El lenguaje de la juventud: En diálogo con *Ariel* de José Enrique Rodó." *Nueva Sociedad* 238 (March–April 2012): 28–40.

_____. *Essays in Cuban Intellectual History.* New York: Palgrave Macmillan, 2008.

_____. "Insularidad y exilio de los intelectuales cubanos." *Estudios. Filosofía-Historia-Letras* 43 (invierno 1995-1996): 69–83.

_____. *José Martí: la invención de Cuba.* Madrid: Colibrí, 2000.

_____. *Tumbas sin sosiego: revolución, disidencia y exilio del intelectual cubano.* Barcelona: Anagrama, 2006.

Rojas Garcidueñas, José. *El Ateneo de la Juventud y la Revolución.* México: Patronato del Instituto Nacional de Estudios Históricos de la Revolución Mexicana, 1979.

Rojo, Grínor. *Las armas de las letras: ensayos neoarielistas.* Santiago de Chile: LOM, 2008.

Romero, Francisco. *Sobre la filosofía en América.* Buenos Aires: Raigal, 1952.

Roy, Joaquín. "José Enrique Rodó." In *Encyclopedia of the Essay,* edited by Tracy Chevalier, 1499–1503. Chicago and London: Fitzroy Deaborn Publishers, 1997.

Rusich, Luciano. *El inmigrante italiano en la novela argentina del 80.* Madrid: Playor, 1974.

Russinyol, José. "Fernando Lles: el hombre y el medio." *Revista Cubana* 27 (1950): 102–10.

Salazar Cáceres, Carlos Gabriel. *Carlos Arturo Torres Peña: vida, época, pensamiento.* Boyacá, Colombia: Editorial Talleres Gráficos Ltda., 1997.

Saldaña-Portillo, María Josefina. *Indian Given: Racial Geographies across Mexico and the*

United States. Durham, NC: Duke University Press, 2016.

Salessi, Jorge. *Médicos, maleantes y maricas: higiene, criminología y homosexualidad en la construcción de la nación argentina (Buenos Aires, 1871–1914)*. Buenos Aires: Beatriz Viterbo, 1995.

Salles, Arleen. "Rodó, Race, and Morality." In *Forging People: Race, Ethnicity, and Nationality in Hispanic American and Latino/a Thought*, edited by Jorge J. E. Gracia, 181–202. Notre Dame, IN: University of Notre Dame Press, 2011.

Sánchez, Luis Alberto. *Balance y liquidación del novecientos: ¿Tuvimos maestros en nuestra América?* Lima: Universidad Nacional Mayor de San Marcos, 1968.

———. *¿Existe América Latina?* México: Fondo de Cultura Económica, 1945.

Sánchez Cobos, Amparo. *Sembrando ideales: anarquistas españoles en Cuba, 1902–1925*. Sevilla: Consejo Superior de Investigaciones cientificas, 2008.

Sanjinés, Javier. "The Nation: An Imagined Community?" *Cultural Studies* 21, no. 2–3 (2007): 295–308.

San Román, Gustavo. *A Companion to José Enrique Rodó*. Woodbridge: Tamesis, 2018.

———. "Influencia y actualidad del pensamiento de José Enrique Rodó." In *José Enrique Rodó: concurso internacional de ensayo*, 9–68. Montevideo: Biblioteca Nacional, 2013.

———. "La recepción de Rodó en Cuba." *Revista de la Biblioteca Nacional* 3.1, no. 3 (2009): 71–86.

———, ed. *This America We Dream Of: Rodó and Ariel One Hundred Years On*. London: Institute of Latin American Studies, 2001.

Sartorius, David. *Ever Faithful: Race, Loyalty, and the Ends of Empire in Spanish Cuba*. Durham, NC: Duke University Press, 2013.

Segundo, José Pedro. "N. de la D." *Evolución* 5, no. 1 (August 1910): 23.

Shaffer, Kirwin. "The Radical Muse: Women and Anarchism in Early-Twentieth-Century Cuba." *Cuban Studies* 34, no. 1 (January 2003): 130–53.

Sierra Mejía, Rubén. *Carlos Arturo Torres*. Bogotá: Editorial Nomos, 1989.

Siskind, Mariano. *Cosmopolitan Desires: Global Modernity and World Literature in Latin America*. Evanston, IL: Northwestern University Press, 2014.

Sixto Solá, José. "El pesimismo cubano." *Cuba Contemporánea* 1, no. 4 (December 1913): 273–303.

Smith, Peter. *Talons of the Eagle: Dynamics of US-Latin American Relations*. New York and Oxford: Oxford University Press, 2000.

Sorensen, Diana. *A Turbulent Decade Remembered: Scenes from the Latin American Sixties*. Stanford, CA: Stanford University Press, 2007.

Stabb, Martin. *América Latina en busca de una identidad: modelos del ensayo ideológico hispanoamericano, 1890–1960*. Translated by Mario Giacchino. Caracas: Monte Ávila Editores, 1969.

Stirner, Max. *The Ego and Its Own.* Edited by David Leopold. Cambridge, UK: Cambridge University Press, 1995.

Stuntz, Homer. "The South American Opportunity." *Men and Missions* 5, no. 1 (September 1913): 19–20.

Suárez, Josefina and Pío E. Serrano. "El *Quijote* en Cuba. Introducción." In *El Quijote en América.* Instituto Cervantes. Centro Virtual Cervantes. https://cvc.cervantes.es/literatura/quijote_america/cuba/introduccion.htm.

Tejera, Diego V. "*La higuera de Timón.*" *El Fígaro* 39, no. 15 (1922): 230.

Toledo Sande, Luis. *Tres narradores agonizantes: tanteos acerca de la obra de Miguel de Carrión, Jesús Castellanos y Carlos Loveira.* La Habana: Editorial Letras Cubanas, 1980.

Torrano, Hugo. *Rodó: acción y libertad: restauración de su imagen.* Montevideo: Bareiro y Ramos, 1973.

Torres, Carlos Arturo. *Los ídolos del foro: ensayo sobre las supersticiones políticas.* Madrid: Editorial América, 1916.

Torres, Arlene, and Norman E. Whitten Jr. Introduction to *Blackness in Latin America and the Caribbean,* vol. 2, edited by Arlene Torres and Norman E. Whitten Jr., 3–33. Bloomington: Indiana University Press, 1998.

Twinam, Ann. *Purchasing Whiteness: Pardos, Mulattos, and the Quest for Social Mobility in the Spanish Indies.* Stanford, CA: Stanford University Press, 2015.

Ubieta, Enrique. "El ensayo y la crítica." In *Historia de la litertura cubana,* tomo 2, edited by Rinaldo Acosta, Ingry González Hernández, and Ana María Muñoz Bachs, 63–108. La Habana: Letras Cubanas, 2003.

Ugarte, Manuel. "Carta abierta al Presidente de los Estados Unidos." In *La nación latinoamericana,* edited by Norberto Galasso, 79–84. Caracas: Ayacucho, 1978.

———. *El epistolario de Manuel Ugarte, 1896-1951,* edited by Graciela Swiderski. Buenos Aires: El Archivo, 1999.

———. *El porvenir de la América Latina.* Valencia: Prometeo, 1920.

———. *Enfermedades sociales.* Barcelona: Casa Editorial Sopena, 1907.

———. "La juventud sud-americana." In *Crónicas del bulevar,* 69–86. París: Garnier, 1903.

———. *Las ideas del siglo.* Buenos Aires: Editorial Partido Socialista de la Argentina, 1904.

———. *Mi campaña hispanoamericana.* Barcelona: Cervantes, 1922.

van Aken, Mark. "The Radicalization of the Uruguayan Student Movement." *The Americas* 33, no. 1 (July 1976): 109–29.

Vanguardia 15, no. 996 (1909): 2.

Varela Petito, Gonzalo. "*Ariel* en su centenario." In *Arielismo y globalización,* edited by Leopoldo Zea and Hernán Taboada, 61–87. México: Fondo de Cultura Económica, 2002.

Vargas Vila, José María. *Ante los bár-baros: el yanki; he ahí el enemigo.* Barcelona: Ramón Palacio Viso, 1930.

_____. *Huerto agnóstico: cuadernos de un solitario.* Barcelona: Ramón Sopena, 1920.

_____. Prologue to *Huerto agnóstico: cuadernos de un solitario*, by José María Vargas Vila, 7–14. París: Libería de la vuida de Ch. Bouret, 1912.

V. A. S., "Los maestros en su cáte-dra: Frente al doctor Carlos Vaz Ferreira." *El Día* (March 29, 1925). *Cuaderno de Recortes*, vol. 3. Recortes de prensa sobre Carlos Vaz Ferreira. Anáforas. Universidad de la República de Uruguay. Facultad de Infor-mación y Comunicación: 84–85. https://anaforas.fic.edu.uy/jspui/handle/123456789/42906.

Vasconcelos, José. "Cuba, guía de la estirpe." *El Fígaro* 42, no. 13–15 (1925): 13, 80.

_____. *Discursos, 1920–1950.* México: Botas, 1950.

_____. "La juventud intelectual mexicana y el actual momento histórico de nuestro país." In *Con-ferencias del Ateneo de la Juventud*, edited by Juan Hernández Luna, 135–38. México: UNAM, 1962.

_____. *La raza cósmica.* México: Porrúa, 2003.

Vaz Ferreira, Carlos. "Del doctor Car-los Vaz Ferreira." *Evolución* 1, no. 1 (1905): 49–50.

_____. *Fermentario.* Montevideo: Tipografía Atlántida, 1938.

_____. *Moral para intelectuales.* *Lógica viva*, edited by Manuel Claps and Sara Vaz Ferreira. Cara-cas: Ayacucho: 1979.

Vélez, Claudio. *The New World of the Gothic Fox: Culture and Economy in English and Spanish America.* Berkeley: University of California Press, 1994.

Vellon Peter. *A Great Conspiracy against Our Race: Italian Immi-grant Newspapers and the Con-struction of Whiteness in the Early Twentieth Century.* New York: New York University Press, 2014.

_____. "Between White Men and Negroes." In *Anti-Italianism: Essays on a Prejudice*, edited by William J. Connell and Fred Gar-daphé, 23–32. New York: Palgrave Macmillan, 2010.

Verdesio, Gustavo. "Un fantasma recorre el Uruguay: la reemergen-cia charrúa en un 'país sin indios,'" *Cuadernos de literatura* 18, no. 36 (July–December 2014): 86–107.

Vitier, Medardo. "A modo de prólogo." In *La higuera de Timón: consejos al pequeño Antonio*, by Fernando Lles y Berdayes, 3–5. Matanzas: Imprenta Casas y Mercado, 1921.

_____. *Apuntaciones literarias.* La Habana, Editorial Minerva, 1935.

_____. *Del ensayo americano.* México: Fondo de Cultura Económica, 1945.

_____. "Más sobre *La higuera de Timón.*" *El Fígaro* 40, no. 3 (1923): 3.

Wuthnow, Robert. *Rediscovering the Sacred: Perspectives on Religion in Contemporary Society.* Grand

Rapids, MI: William B. Eerdmans, 1992.

Zea, Leopoldo, and Hernán Taboada, ed. *Arielismo y globalización.* México: Fondo de Cultura Económica, 2002.

Žižek, Slavoj. *First as Tragedy, Then as Farce.* London and New York: Verso, 2009.

_____. *"Homo Sacer* as the Object of the Discourse of the University." *Lacan.com.* September 25, 2003. https://www.lacan.com/hsacer.htm.

_____. "On Ecology." In *Examined Life*, directed by Astra Taylor. Montreal: Zeitgeist Films, 2009. DVD.

_____. *The Ticklish Subject: The Absent Centre of Political Ontology.* London: Verso, 2000.

Zorrilla de San Martín, Juan. "Ariel y Calibán americanos." In *Detalles de historia*, 195–224. Montevideo: Imprenta Nacional Colorada, 1930.

Zum Felde, Alberto. *Índice crítico de la literatura hispanoamericana: los ensayistas.* México: Guarania, 1954.

INDEX

CPSIA information can be obtained
at www.ICGtesting.com
Printed in the USA
LVHW090322131121
703236LV00015B/1282